# proficiency

# Gold

## exam maximiser

Richard Mann

with Jacky Newbrook and Judith Wilson

Longman

# Contents

# Introduction to the *Exam Maximiser*

## What is the *Proficiency Gold Exam Maximiser*?

The *Proficiency Gold Exam Maximiser* is specially designed to maximise students' chances of success in the Cambridge Certificate of Proficiency in English examination.

## The *Exam Maximiser* offers:

- *further practice* of all the important grammar and skills that you study in the *Proficiency Gold Coursebook*, plus the opportunity to revise and extend your vocabulary work.
- *the facts* about the papers and questions in the Proficiency exam. The *Exam overview* on pages 6 and 7 gives you information on each of the five papers.
- *step-by-step guidance* with the strategies and techniques you need to get a good grade in the exam. There are also *Exam Tips!* to help you to improve your performance and avoid common pitfalls.
- *exercises in exam format* so that you can practise using the strategies, and familiarise yourself with the demands of the exam task.
- *Study Tips* to guide you to more analytical and productive approaches to recording and using vocabulary.
- *practical advice* about how and when to use new language most effectively.
- *writing skills training*, including sample answers, to lead you to thoughtful planning, improving and editing of summaries and compositions.
- *a complete Practice exam* which shows you exactly what you need to do in the Proficiency exam.

## Who is the *Proficiency Gold Exam Maximiser* for and in what situations can it be used?

The *Exam Maximiser* is extremely flexible and can be used by students in a variety of ways. Here are some typical situations.

**1**

You are doing a Proficiency course with other students, probably over an academic year. You are all planning to take the exam at the same time.

You are using the *Proficiency Gold Coursebook* in class. You may sometimes do related exercises, or even a whole unit of the *Exam Maximiser* in class. Your teacher may set exercises from it to do as homework, to revise and extend your classwork. You could use the entire *Exam Maximiser* as part of your course, or you and your teacher may use it to focus on your particular revision needs, depending on the time available.

**2**

You have already done a longer Proficiency course, and are now doing a short intensive course before taking the exam.

You have already worked through the *Proficiency Gold Coursebook*, or perhaps another Proficiency level coursebook, and so you will be using the *Exam Maximiser* in class. The exam-format tasks and strategies in the *Exam Maximiser* will help you to improve your performance and confidence, while the Practice exam will show you everything you need to do in the Proficiency exam.

**3**

You have a very short period in which to prepare for the Proficiency exam.

Your level of English is already nearing Proficiency exam standard. What you now need is an understanding of the demands of the exam and the skills and strategies necessary to pass. The *Exam Maximiser* has been designed to help you to activate what you know, and to build the exam awareness and the confidence you need in order to approach the Proficiency exam successfully.

**4**

> You are retaking the Proficiency exam, as you were unfortunately not successful in your first attempt.

You may be having to retake Proficiency because you were not sufficiently familiar with the exam requirements, or the best way to approach each task. You probably have a clear idea of the areas you need to focus on. You will not need to follow a coursebook, but can use the *Exam Maximiser* to develop your exam techniques, and build up your confidence.

**5**

> You are preparing for the exam on your own.

- Perhaps you are in a class where the teacher is using the *Proficiency Gold Coursebook* as a general high level English course. This means there may be few or no other students in your class who feel ready to take the exam. Your teacher may already be using the *Exam Maximiser* to consolidate and extend your classwork. However, you can also use it on your own to prepare for the exam. The tips and strategies, together with the Practice exam, will guide you through all you need to know to approach the exam with confidence.
- You are not attending a Proficiency class, but wish to prepare for and take the exam independently. The *Exam Maximiser* by itself can give you the exam training and practice you need.

# For the student: how to use this book

To be successful in the Proficiency exam you need to:
- revise and extend the grammar and vocabulary you already know
- organise your learning in an effective way
- understand what the exam is testing and how best to tackle each task
- practise as much as you can to get used to the exam format.

This book helps you to do all of these things through appropriate support, information and advice.

## Graded support

The texts and tasks in the *Exam Maximiser* reflect the level and complexity of the exam right from the start of the book. Graded tasks in the early units focus on specific

aspects of the language or skill that is being tested, so as to build your confidence.

## Information and advice

- **About the exam** boxes give you information about the nature and timing of each paper in the Proficiency exam. Use them to make sure you are well aware of what you need to do.
- **Exam Strategy** boxes extend your exam skills, and are followed by tasks which practise the strategies outlined and assess their effectiveness for you. Use them to improve your approach to exam tasks.
- **Exam checklists** give you the opportunity to analyse any errors you make in exam tasks. Use them to gain an accurate awareness of your strengths and weaknesses.
- **Exam Tip!** boxes give you advice on how to handle the timing and stress of the Proficiency exam. Use them to help you be organised and effective in the exam room, so that you can avoid common pitfalls.
- **Watch Out!** boxes focus on the problem areas and typical student mistakes for each grammar point, while the exercises which follow them are designed to test these common pitfalls in particular. Use these boxes to test yourself and highlight where you need to revise.
- **Study Tip** boxes give you advice on how to organise and revise your notes. Use them to help you reproduce the vocabulary you have learnt accurately, in speaking and writing.

## The revision unit

Unit 14 of the *Exam Maximiser* is a revision unit, packed with exam format tasks which revise language from the whole course. It contains Exam Strategy advice and exam checklists which you can use while revising your course, or to give yourself extra guidance at any point as you are working through the *Exam Maximiser*.

## The Practice exam

The complete Practice exam gives you an opportunity to find out how it really feels to take the Proficiency exam.

## The Learning Key

The *Exam Maximiser* has a Key, which provides the answers to all exercises, but also explains why many answers are right or wrong. The explanations will help you increase what you can learn from the exercises throughout the *Exam Maximiser*. There are also full tapescripts for all listening material.

# Exam overview

| Paper | Content | Test focus |
|---|---|---|
| **Paper 1**<br>Reading<br><br>(1 hour) | **Section A**<br>25 separate sentences, each with a vocabulary item deleted, and four multiple-choice options. | Questions test your ability to work with vocabulary at the level of **phrases**, not just individual words. You need to:<br>• identify grammatical patterns, collocations and fixed expressions associated with certain words<br>• recognise the differences between words with similar forms or meanings<br>• use phrasal verbs correctly. |
| | **Section B**<br>Three reading texts, two non-fiction, and one literary, totalling 1500–1800 words. A total of 15 questions, each with four multiple-choice options. The length of each text and number of questions on each one can vary. | Questions test your ability to identify:<br>• the main points of the writer's argument and the details which support them<br>• the tone of the text<br>• what is **implied**<br>• issues of style and register.<br>In literary texts, there may be questions which focus on the interaction between characters. |
| **Paper 2**<br>Writing<br><br>(2 hours) | Two tasks, from a choice of five. These include narratives, descriptions, discursive compositions, or a task-directed composition, which could be a report, an article, or a letter. If you read the optional literary texts, you can answer one option on them here. All compositions should be about 350 words, except for the task-directed pieces, which require about 300 words. | Questions test your ability to:<br>• write accurate, well-organised compositions<br>• demonstrate a wide range of appropriate vocabulary and structures<br>• show sensitivity to issues of style, layout and register<br>• plan your work carefully<br>• show an awareness of **why** the composition is being written, and **who** for, which is particularly important for the task-directed questions. |
| **Paper 3**<br>Use of English<br><br>(2 hours) | **Section A**<br>A short titled cloze passage, containing twenty gaps, each to be filled with one suitable word. | Questions test your ability to understand:<br>• the text as a whole<br>• grammatical structures such as complex tenses, determiners and articles<br>• some vocabulary items such as collocations and fixed phrases. |
| | Eight separate transformation sentences to be rewritten, using a 'lead in' phrase which is provided. | Questions test your ability to produce a wide range of grammatical structures, such as complex tenses, conditionals, passives and common fixed expressions. |
| | Six separate gapped sentences, to be completed with a word or short phrase. | Questions require you to produce vocabulary items such as phrasal verbs and idioms, and a range of expressions, fitting their structure to the context given. |

| Paper | Content | Test focus |
|---|---|---|
| | Eight 'key word' transformations, each of which has a separate sentence to be rewritten, using a provided word. | Questions test your ability to paraphrase or to say the same thing using a variety of expressions and structures, including idioms and phrasal verbs, and your ability to manipulate the forms of words to fit the context. |
| | **Section B**<br>A titled text of 550–650 words, with 11–14 comprehension questions, each to be answered with a few words or a short sentence. | Questions test your ability to:<br>• understand the main points of the writer's argument, the details which support these, and the opinions implied by the style or use of language in the text<br>• appreciate the tone or implied opinion of the writer<br>• comment on the use of language in the text.<br>You may need to deduce vocabulary from context, and to paraphrase certain expressions used by the writer. |
| | A summary task, which requires a written passage of approximately 60–90 words. | The questions test your ability to:<br>• identify relevant parts of the writer's argument<br>• paraphrase these coherently and concisely in your own words<br>• answer the questions fully within a specified word limit. |
| **Paper 4**<br>Listening<br><br>(approx. 40 minutes) | Three or four recordings, including monologues and conversations, with 25–30 questions in total. There is a variety of tasks, which may include multiple-choice, sentence completion, note-taking, and matching opinions with speakers. Each recording is played twice. | Questions test your ability to:<br>• identify the main facts and ideas expressed by the speakers, and the details which support these<br>• listen intensively for short words or phrases<br>• identify where the information you need is in the recording to complete paraphrased sentences<br>• identify the feelings implied by speakers, through use of intonation and choice of language. |
| **Paper 5**<br>Speaking<br><br>(approx. 15 minutes)<br>Longer interviews, with 2 or 3 candidates are also possible.<br><br>There is normally another examiner in the room who will not participate in the conversation. | A conversation in three separate parts between the examiner and one or more candidates. | Questions test your ability to speak accurately and naturally, with appropriate pronunciation, fluency, range of vocabulary and full interaction with the interviewer and any other candidates. |
| | Comparison of three photographs, establishing the theme of the interview. | This part aims to give you an opportunity to speculate and justify your opinions, and to talk at length on a single topic. A knowledge of specialised vocabulary is not expected when comparing the pictures. |
| | Commentary on one or more short passages related to the main theme. These could include letters, announcements, articles, advertisements, regulations, etc., or language which would originally have been spoken. | This part requires you to identify and discuss the possible source of the passage(s), without worrying about particular words or expressions it/they contain(s). You should be able to relate it/them to the general theme of the interview, giving reasons for your opinions. |
| | A communication activity based on the same theme, which could involve making a selection, solving a problem, discussion on a theme or making choices. | This part of the interview focuses on discussing a topic or problem in a particular situation, which will be outlined by the examiner. Questions test your ability to converse co-operatively and naturally, negotiating, persuading, justifying and collaborating, as the task requires. |

# 1 A friend in need

## Vocabulary: what's in a word?

> ### Study Tip
>
> A good knowledge of vocabulary is essential for all papers of the Proficiency exam. To understand a word fully, you need to be aware of meaning, grammar, register (level of formality), collocations and related words (derivatives like verb, noun and adjective forms). A good monolingual (English–English) dictionary will supply this information.

**1** Study the following extract from the *Longman Dictionary of Contemporary English*. You will see that the words *exam, examine* and *examination* can be used in several different ways, and have a variety of collocations.

**ex·am** *n* [C] **1** a spoken or written test of knowledge, especially an important one: *How did you do in your exams?* | *an oral exam* | **pass/fail an exam** (=succeed / not succeed) *Did you pass the exam?* | **chemistry/French etc exam** (=an exam in a particular subject) | **take/sit an exam** *He failed his English exam and had to take it again.* **2** *AmE* a set of medical tests: *an eye exa.* **3** *AmE* the paper on which the questions for an exam are written: *Do not open your exams until I tell you.*

**ex·am·i·na·tion** *n* **1** [C] *formal* a spoken or written test of knowledge: *The examination results will be announced in September.* **2** [C,U] the process of looking at something carefully in order to see what it is like: *a detailed examination of population statistics* | **be under examination** *The proposals are still under examination.* | **on closer examina·tion** *On closer examination the vases were seen to be cracked in several places.* **3** a set of medical tests **4** [C,U] the process of asking questions to get specific information, especially in a court of law – see also CROSS-EXAMINATION

**ex·am·ine** *v* [T] **1** to look at something carefully in order to make a decision, find something, check something etc: *After examining the evidence, I can find no truth in these claims.* | **examine sth for** *The police will have to examine the weapon for fingerprints.* **2** if a doctor examines you, they look at your body to check that you are healthy **3** *formal* to ask someone questions to test their knowledge of a subject: **examine sb on** *You will be examined on American history.* **4** *technical* to officially ask someone questions in a law court.

## 2

**1** Use the dictionary extract to help you complete the following texts with an appropriate word or short phrase.

1 What an awful ............ that was! I made so many mistakes – I bet I haven't ............ it! Anyway, I suppose I can ............ it again next semester. By the way, I didn't realise that we were going to be ............ American history this afternoon. That'll probably be another disaster!

2 We ............ the weapon ............ fingerprints and found that they matched those of the suspect. After ............ examination of the other evidence, we are now convinced that we have found the man responsible for the crime.

3 At present, the proposal for the new shopping centre is ............ examination. The decision whether or not to proceed with the scheme will be made at a meeting later this month.

4 Mr Rawlings, would you please continue with the ............-examination of the witness?

**2** Now match each text to the context in which it was said or written. Choose from the list a)–d) below. Think about how formal each text is, and look at the example sentences in the dictionary extract to help you.

a) Official notice outside the offices of a Town Hall. .......

b) Student talking to another student. .......

c) Police officer talking to reporters. .......

d) Judge talking to a barrister in court. .......

**3** Are the following statements true (T) or false (F)? Use the dictionary extract and the texts in Exercise 2 to help you.

1 The word *examination* is always a countable noun.

2 The word *exam* can replace the word *examination* in any sentence.

3 The word *examination* is more formal than the word *exam*.

4 The preposition *for* is always used after the verb *examine*.

5 A successful student would say, '*I've succeeded in all my exams!*'

6 The word *examination* is used in a fixed phrase with the preposition *under*.

**4**  The following paragraph contains ten vocabulary errors. They are underlined to help you. Correct them in your notebook by looking up the words in a good monolingual dictionary. Check:

- spelling
- grammatical patterns
- common collocations
- dependent prepositions
- fixed phrases.

The (1) big majority of students who (2) make well in the Cambridge Proficiency Examination have learnt to use a good monolingual dictionary effectively. Such dictionaries provide (3) informations, not just about the (4) meanings for words but about their (5) pronounciation and grammar as well. A student who learns how to use a dictionary effectively will be able to work independently for much of the time, and will gain considerable (6) insight to the workings of the English language. He or she will be able to (7) confirm to the meanings of words in a text where contextual clues are insufficient, pronounce words accurately by studying the (8) phonological transcriptions, and use words accurately both when speaking and writing.

Make sure you make (9) the room for at least one good monolingual dictionary on your bookshelf – and then make sure you use it (10) at a regular basis!

**Study Tip**

For the Proficiency exam, you will need to learn new words, but also to understand familiar words in more depth. Organise your vocabulary learning right from the start.

1  You could try recording words in the following ways:
- by topic
- by grammatical pattern
- by similar meaning or form
- by collocation.

2  Record not just the word itself, but information about the meaning, usage, pronunciation and grammar.

3  Make a note of mistakes you commonly make, along with their corrections, of course!

**5**

1  Look at how a student recorded the word *information* in her notebook. Notice how her example sentences focus on grammatical patterns and errors she makes.

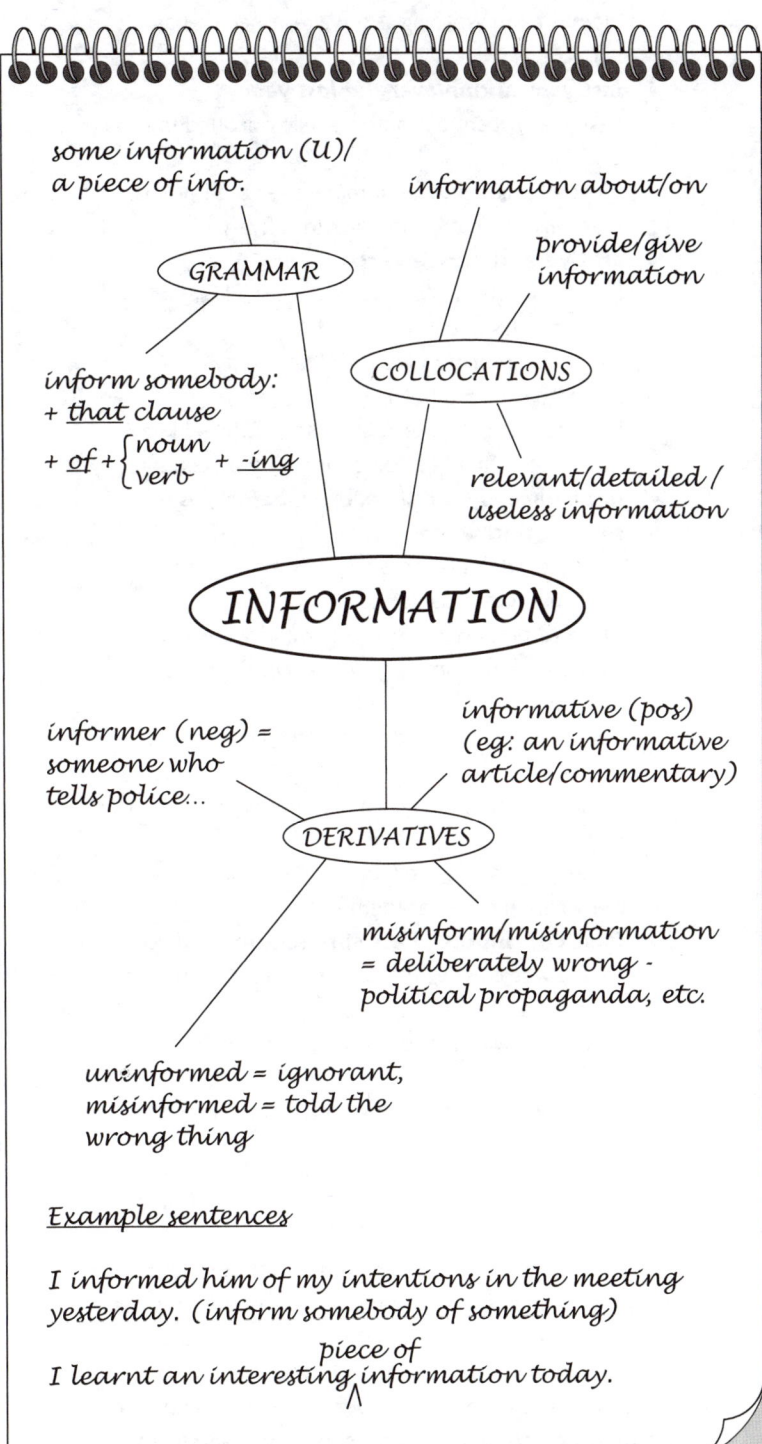

some information (U)/ a piece of info.

information about/on

GRAMMAR

inform somebody:
+ *that* clause
+ *of* + { noun / verb } + *-ing*

COLLOCATIONS

provide/give information

relevant/detailed / useless information

INFORMATION

informer (neg) = someone who tells police...

informative (pos) (eg: an informative article/commentary)

DERIVATIVES

misinform/misinformation = deliberately wrong - political propaganda, etc.

uninformed = ignorant, misinformed = told the wrong thing

*Example sentences*

I informed him of my intentions in the meeting yesterday. (inform somebody of something)

I learnt an interesting ^piece of^ information today.

2  Now make your own vocabulary record for the word *knowledge* and its derivatives (*know, knowledgeable*, etc.). Record the information from the dictionary which you consider useful – don't simply copy the dictionary entry into your notebook!

# Grammar: past tenses and Present perfect

> ### Watch Out! *problem areas*
>
> - **since**
>   He has been working as a waiter since he ~~has~~ left college.
> - ***last year* and *in/over the last year***
>   Last year I *spent* a month travelling around the USA. ✔
>   More progress *has been made* over the last year than *was made* over the previous five years. ✔
> - **stative and active verbs**
>   I've known her for over a year now. I first ~~knew~~ *met* her last August.
>   I've been ill for two weeks. I ~~was~~ *became* ill when I came back from holiday.
>   I've known about the mistake for a while. I ~~knew~~ *discovered* it while going through the accounts.
> - ***until, once, by the time, after, before, as soon as* and *when***
>   My boss *didn't allow* me to go home until *I'd finished* what I was doing. ✔
>   Once *I'd prepared* my speech, I *had* a break. ✔
>   By the time the fire brigade *arrived*, the house ~~had~~ burnt to the ground.
>   Before he read the letter he ~~had taken~~ *took* a deep breath.
>   As soon as she ~~had~~ heard the news she burst into tears.
>   Fortunately someone ~~had been~~ *was* waiting for me when I arrived at the hotel.
> - **Past continuous, Past simple and *used to***
>   As she *was crossing* the road she heard someone call her name. ✔
>   When she was a child she ~~was living~~ *lived* in Africa for five years.
>   When he was in the army he ~~was smoking~~ *used to smoke* heavily.

**1** In your notebook, combine the following sentences. Use the word in **bold** to link the sentences and put the verbs in brackets in an appropriate tense. Think about where the linking word should go in your new sentence. You may need to change the order of the information, or use passives or continuous tenses for your sentence to make sense and be grammatically correct. There may be more than one correct answer.

**EXAMPLE:**
He (do) the washing-up. He (collapse) in a chair in front of the TV. **after**
*After he had done the washing-up, he collapsed in a chair in front of the TV.*

1 The mistake (discover) yesterday. She (deny) all knowledge of it. **when**
2 I finally (win) the lottery. I (play) it for thirty years. **by the time**
3 She (overcome) her initial reservations. She actually (enjoy) the concert. **once**
4 He (cover) in splashes of paint at lunchtime. He (decorate) the kitchen all morning. **because**
5 He (think) briefly about the question. He (reply). **before**
6 There (be) absolute certainty of its location. The police (call) to the scene of the accident. **as soon as**
7 His latest novel (publish) last week. Tens of thousands of pounds (spend) on promoting it. **by the time**
8 She (check) all the safety catches on the windows. She (not go) to bed. **until**

**2** There are ten mistakes with tenses in the following short text. Find and underline the mistakes, then correct them in your notebook.

When I had been a little girl, my brother and I were going every New Year to stay with grandma and grandpa in their mysterious old cottage by the sea. Under its foundations were tunnels which had been used by smugglers and pirates in the past and, like many other houses in the village, it had been rumoured to be haunted. Grandma was convinced that she used to see the ghost of a pirate on several occasions in her bedroom, and she would like to frighten us by telling us stories about her experiences.

I will always remember what happened on one particular evening, a couple of days before New Year's Eve. It was snowing heavily all day and as a result the house was bitterly cold and rather gloomy. All of us had been sitting around the fire in the living room listening to one of grandma's favourite stories, when suddenly there was a tremendous crash from upstairs. All our thoughts turned to the ghost she had been telling us about and we looked at each other in horror. When we galloped up the stairs, however, we discovered that the branch of a tree was snapped in the wind and smashed one of the bedroom windows. I will always remember the expression on grandma's face. 'I was never so scared in all my life!' was all she could whimper.

**3**  **Use of English:** guided sentence transformations

1  Finish each of the following sentences in such a way that it is as similar as possible in meaning to the sentence printed before it. In the Proficiency exam, only the beginning of the sentence is provided, but in this exercise you have been given the beginning and the ending of each sentence to help you.

EXAMPLE:

Jenny is happier since she broke up with David.
Now that Jenny *has broken up with David she is* happier.

1  I've yet to see a lovelier city than Vienna.
Vienna is ........................................ ever visited.

2  I was amazed at how well they got on together.
I had ............................................ well together.

3  Anna's fear of the dark dates from when she was a little girl.
Ever ........................................ the dark.

4  The last time I spoke to Alex was ages ago.
It's ................................................ Alex.

5  The robber got away before the arrival of the police.
By the ........................................ escaped.

6  The terms of the contract have been under negotiation for over a week now.
They ............................................ now.

7  The installation of computers means that the staff don't have to file everything by hand any more.
The staff used ...................................... installed.

8  The level of atmospheric pollution has risen sharply this year.
There ........................................ this year.

9  It was only at the age of eighteen that Heather learned to swim.
Heather did ........................................ eighteen.

10  He lost his job over six months ago.
He has ...................................... months.

2  When you have checked your answers to Exercise 3.1, analyse any errors you made. Most transformations require you to change more than one thing to make a new sentence, and it is very common in this part of the exam for students to get their answers 'half right'. Did you forget to:

- change a tense?
- add a suitable preposition?
- change the part of speech of a word?

## Vocabulary: multiple-choice

**Paper1, Section A**

### About the exam

In **Paper 1, Section A**, you have to answer twenty-five multiple-choice vocabulary questions. A word or phrase is missing in each sentence, and you have to choose one option from four alternatives to complete it. This task tests your knowledge of:

- collocations and fixed expressions
- words with similar meanings or forms
- words with special grammatical patterns
- connectors and adverbial phrases
- phrasal verbs.

### Exam Strategy

Read the choices carefully and eliminate any words which you are sure are **not** correct. If you don't know the correct answer, have a guess! You should never leave a question unanswered.

Choose the word or phrase, **A, B, C** or **D** which best completes each of the following sentences. All the missing words in this exercise are adjective + noun or verb + adverb collocations.

1  The accident had a(n) ............ effect on her.
   A extensive   B profound   C wide   D total

2  It was his ............ belief that he could win.
   A utter   B single   C firm   D total

3  I have a(n) ............ admiration for work.
   A great   B high   C complete   D entire

4  I've been taking a(n) ............ interest in your progress.
   A endless   B extensive   C keen   D sharp

5  I would like to thank everybody for their ............ support.
   A undimming   B complete   C unfailing   D deep

6  I feel very ............ that this plan won't work.
   A hardly   B strongly   C greatly   D profoundly

7  Where's my handbag? I ............ remember leaving it here.
   A surely   B fully   C distinctly   D totally

8  William's refusal to accept the gift ............ offended her.
   A deeply   B utterly   C absolutely   D enormously

9  I've been ............ advised not to say anything.
   A strongly   B greatly   C seriously   D significantly

10  I don't think he ............ intended to be rude to her.
   A totally   B firmly   C genuinely   D utterly

# Vocabulary: phrasal verbs: *keep*

### 1

1   Read the dictionary entry for the phrasal verb *keep on*, from the *Longman Dictionary of Contemporary English*, and then study the sentences below.

**keep on** *phr v* **1 keep on doing sth** to continue doing something: *I've told him to stop but he keeps on scratching it!* **2 [T keep sb on]** to continue to employ someone: *If you're good they might keep you on after Christmas.* **3 [I]** *informal* to talk continuously in an annoying way: **[+ at/about]** *Do you have to keep on about your medical problems the whole time?*

1   John is getting on my nerves – he *keeps on* talking. ✓
2   I just saw Tracy crying – she says the company's in trouble, and the boss has told her that they can't *keep on* her. ✗
3   I wish you wouldn't *keep on* about the new car you've just bought. ✓

2   Is sentence 2 wrong because:

a)  it has a direct object?
b)  the word order is wrong?
c)  an extra preposition is needed?

### 2

In your notebook, replace the parts of the following sentences in *italics*, using phrasal verbs with *keep*. Use a monolingual dictionary to help you.

1   If you want to do well in politics, you need to *stay friendly with* people who have power and influence.
2   *Don't get involved in* this matter, Richard. It's nothing to do with you.
3   I've had enough of working with you, because you never *obey* the rules of our agreements.
4   She *prevented them from going to sleep* by telling them one story after another.
5   When you leave school or university it is quite difficult to *continue with* friendships, even those which have been particularly intimate.
6   You haven't told me everything, have you? I'm sure there is something you are *not telling me*.

### 3

The words in the box below are all used in expressions with *keep*. There are mistakes in the wording of the expressions in the following sentences. Find them and rewrite the sentences correctly in your notebook.

| eye | company | straight face | track | head |
|-----|---------|---------------|-------|------|

1   When you get married and start having children it is difficult to keep a track from all your friends and what they are doing.
2   The last thing we should do in this situation is panic. We must keep on our heads.
3   I feel very lonely tonight. Could you come over and keep company to me?
4   Can you to keep eyes on the baby for me while I'm out of the room.
5   Mr Roberts is funny when he gets angry. If he shouts, it's difficult to keep the straight face.

# Use of English: guided cloze

### Paper 3, Section A, Question 1

### About the exam

In **Paper 3, Section A Question 1**, you have to complete twenty numbered blanks in a passage. You can only write one word in each gap. This task tests your knowledge of:

*   word combinations (collocations, fixed phrases, phrasal verbs)
*   structural items (auxiliary verbs, prepositions, pronouns, articles, etc.)
*   conjunctions and connectors (*despite*, *but*, etc.)
*   vocabulary items.

**1** Read this extract from an article about gossip and the notes below, which a student made while doing the cloze task. He underlined the key words in the extract which helped him to find the missing words.

Gossip is enjoyable. Almost every human being in the world has <u>at some time or</u> (1) .......... indulged in some form of gossip, <u>irrespective</u> (2) .......... social background or education. Even famous <u>novelists and poets</u> have (3) .......... known <u>to be</u> notorious (4) .......... . Yet gossip has a bad name and most people <u>feel</u> slightly uneasy or guilty (5) .......... it afterwards.

1 *fixed phrase = at some time or <u>other</u>*
2 *'irrespective' = adjective + dependent preposition = <u>of</u>*
3 *famous novelists and poets are not the active subjects of this verb, and there's an infinitive 'to be' after it - must be a passive verb. The auxiliary = <u>been</u>*
4 *topic of the paragraph = gossip - no article, so need a plural noun following the adjective 'notorious'. Noun for people who gossip = <u>gossips</u>*
5 *need a preposition after the verb 'feel' = <u>about</u>*

### Exam Strategy

Follow these steps whenever you do a cloze task.
- Read the whole passage first.
- Put in words you are sure about.
- Decide the form of other missing words (e.g. noun/verb etc.).
- Look for clues in the sentences **before** and **after** each gap.
- Never leave any gaps.

**2** Read the following passage and find three things which made life pleasant for people living in the Stone Age.

**3** Read the passage again and fill each of the gaps with **one** suitable word. In this task, key words which will help you fill the gaps are underlined. There are also some hints to help you below the text, although in the exam you won't be given any help. Always read through the text when you have completed the gaps, to make sure it makes sense.

# Life in the Stone Age

It is a common misconception that (1) .......... in the Stone Age <u>lived</u> on the edge of starvation, in small groups, wandering around <u>from</u> (2) .......... <u>to place</u>. <u>On the</u> (3) .........., recent studies of archaeological sites have in fact shown that (4) .......... was probably <u>a</u> (5) .......... <u>deal</u> easier than it was for later farming communities. After the Ice Age the weather was warmer than it is today and (6) .......... was plentiful. (7) .......... <u>were</u> large numbers of <u>animals</u> to hunt, <u>fish</u> could easily be caught in rivers and the sea, and a huge variety of <u>plants and berries</u> (8) .......... in the forests.

During the Stone Age or Mesolithic Period, (9) .......... it is <u>known</u> to archaeologists, men and women led an active <u>social</u> and <u>spiritual</u> (10) ....... . Large encampments, where (11) .......... to 200 people may have lived, have been found in several parts of Europe, <u>in</u> (12) .......... <u>to</u> the remains of communal tombs and temples. Making stone tools <u>was</u> probably (13) .......... <u>as</u> a communal activity, in which even children (14) .......... <u>to</u> take part, learning from adults how to make the implements they would later use for weapons or to crush food (15) .......... <u>as</u> berries. Nor were women <u>thought</u> (16) .......... <u>as</u> inferior in these societies. It is very likely that they (17) .......... an important <u>role</u> in the life of the tribe. It was only later, with the arrival of farming, that they began to (18) .......... their <u>status</u>. Although life was more settled for the early farmers, the (19) .......... <u>of life</u> was not as good as it had been for (20) .......... hunter-gatherer ancestors.

**HINTS**

3 *This phrase introduces information which contradicts what came before.*
4 *What is the previous sentence about?*
6 *Look at the next sentence.*
9 *conjunction followed by a clause*
11 *fixed expression – in this context it means 'a maximum of 200'*
13 *a verb in passive form, which is used with 'as'*
16 *Which particle is normally used with 'think' – always used with 'as'? This means the same as 13.*
18 *Think about the meaning of the previous sentence. This sentence expresses a contrast with the positive status of women before farming.*
20 *This word refers back to 'farmers'.*

# Writing: paragraph organisation

**About the exam**

In **Paper 2**, you have to produce two pieces of writing in two hours. You will be marked not only on your grammar and vocabulary, but on your paragraph organisation as well. Good paragraphs normally have a topic sentence, which is supported by relevant, well-organised details.

**1**  The function of the topic sentence is to state or summarise the main idea of the paragraph. It is often, but not always, the first sentence. Read the following three paragraphs, and the three alternative topic sentences for each. Decide which alternative is:

- too general (covers areas broader than those in the paragraph)
- too specific (only refers to some of the areas covered in the paragraph)
- correct (summarises or introduces the main points appropriately).

Write the letter of the correct sentence in the space provided.

**1**  Mark had not enjoyed his childhood ............................ . He was only five when his parents were forced to leave the country and had to send him away to boarding school. This was difficult enough, but two years later his father went bankrupt and Mark was sent to live with his grandparents. Then, at the age of sixteen, he had a serious riding accident and had to spend six months in hospital.

a) It had been an unhappy time for him on the whole.
b) The routines of school life had been particularly unpleasant for him.
c) It had been spoilt by a number of unfortunate incidents.

**2**  ................................. For one thing, I had to work much longer hours. I often worked from six in the morning until eight at night. Another thing which was different was my social life. In England I had had a very active social life, whereas in Africa I found that there was little for me to do after work. Compared to my previous existence, I suppose my life in Africa was much healthier but it was not so much fun.

a) It took me a long time to get used to living abroad.
b) My job in Africa was a new experience for me.
c) Many things changed when I left England to go and live in Africa.

**3**  ................................. She hated the way they always found the warmest place in the house. She also disliked them because of the unnerving way they stared at you. It was almost as if they possessed an uncanny ability to penetrate the innermost secrets of your soul. Most of all, however, she hated cats because of the wailing noise they made at night. She had lost count of the number of times she had been woken up at night by the screeching of a cat in her backyard.

a) Dora had an almost pathological dislike of cats.
b) In Dora's view all cats were intensely selfish animals.
c) Dora was happy to live alone, without a cat.

**2**  Now write topic sentences for paragraphs 4 and 5. First, read the whole paragraph, and the questions which follow. These will help you focus on the most important information to include in your topic sentences.

**4**  .............................................................. ...................................... At the very least it should make sure that they all receive a pension and do not have to spend the last few years of their lives in poverty. It could also give them special bus and train passes, enabling them to travel cheaply on public transport, and could offer discounts on many other things. Finally, the state could even provide housing and hospital facilities for those old people who have no relatives to look after them.

- Who or what do *it* and *they* refer to in the first sentence?
- What, in general, would the effects of the proposed changes be?

**5**  .............................................................. ...................................... For example, there is a swimming pool designed for people who are confined to a wheelchair, and there is also a gym where those who are disabled in some way can work out safely and under the guidance of one of the sports centre's qualified assistants. Facilities for disabled people exist for a range of other sports and activities and everyone is given a huge amount of encouragement and help. I was extremely impressed by what I saw on my visit to the centre last week.

- Where are the pool and the gym?
- Who in particular is the paragraph concerned with?

**3** It's important that all the details you include in a paragraph are **relevant** and support the main idea of the paragraph (expressed in the topic sentence). Read the following paragraph and cross out the sentences and clauses which you consider irrelevant. The topic sentence is shown underlined to help you.

*When I was twelve, my sister went to university and we saw even less of her. <u>Whenever we did see her, however, we realised that she was no longer the same person.</u> Change is a part of life. Many things change in our lives, sometimes for the better but sometimes for the worse. Not only had she started to wear long, flowing dresses and lots of colourful make-up, but her hair was also quite different. Whereas previously she had always insisted on keeping it cut short, it was now startlingly long and rather unkempt. I've always longed to grow my hair myself, but my parents don't approve of long hair. Her attitude towards me had similarly undergone an enormous change. She now wanted to spend time with me, even though I was busy studying for my school exams and it was important for me to do well. She seemed to enjoy telling me all the gossip that was doing the rounds, about her life at university and her plans for the future, and she also helped me greatly with various problems I was facing at school, and there were plenty of those, I can tell you! Within a matter of weeks she had become my closest friend and confidante.*

**4**

1 The details supporting a topic sentence should always be organised clearly. In the following box there are four common ways of organising details. Indicate which one was used in each of the five paragraphs in Exercises 1 and 2.

para. 1 ...   para. 2 ...   para. 3 ...
para. 4 ...   para. 5 ...

---

## Methods of organising paragraphs

**A** **Comparison/contrast:** the writer provides details which show similarities and/or differences.

**B** **Examples:** the writer uses a list of examples or an illustration in support of the main idea.

**C** **Emphasis:** the writer organises the details in order of their importance, normally with the most significant detail last.

**D** **Chronological order:** the writer presents details in the order in which they happened.

---

2 Underline any connectors or phrases in the five paragraphs which helped you decide.

**5** Choose two of the topics below and write a paragraph of 120–150 words for each one.

Organise the details, linking them with appropriate connectors. For each question, a suitable method of paragraph organisation from the list **A–D** above has been suggested to help you.

1 Describe how you first met a close friend. Put the details of your paragraph in chronological order. **(D)**
2 Explain how two people you know are similar or different. Provide details which show these similarities and differences clearly. **(A)**
3 Explain what makes a good friendship. Put the details in order of emphasis. **(C)**
4 Describe how parents or teachers could reach a better understanding of young people. Provide examples or an anecdote to explain your meaning clearly or put the details in order of emphasis. **(B or D)**

---

### Study Tip

Whenever you have to produce a piece of writing, you should plan the sequence of your paragraphs carefully, making sure one leads on naturally to the next.

For each paragraph you should:
1 write a clear **topic sentence**, which expresses the main idea of the paragraph
2 support the topic sentence with **relevant details**
3 make sure your details are **well-organised**
4 use **linking words** to connect the details of the paragraph.

# 2 Learning for life

## Vocabulary review: multiple-choice

**Paper 1, Section A**

Choose the word or phrase, **A**, **B**, **C** or **D**, which best completes each sentence. In this exercise, all the missing words are **collocations** or **fixed expressions**.

1  The facilities at many schools today are still ............. inadequate.
   **A** sadly  **B** woefully  **C** regrettably  **D** grimly
2  After leaving school, he tried to ............. a living as a door-to-door salesman.
   **A** gain  **B** win  **C** obtain  **D** earn
3  She would make an excellent lawyer – she's conscientious and has a ............. mind.
   **A** well-trained  **B** well-intentioned
   **C** well-built  **D** well-informed
4  It's no use getting angry with your students. You'll have to ............. their respect first if you want them to co-operate.
   **A** possess  **B** promote  **C** win  **D** achieve
5  Dr Evans has ............. a valuable contribution to the life of the school.
   **A** done  **B** made  **C** caused  **D** created
6  We've got some time to ............. before the meeting begins, so let's go for a stroll in the park.
   **A** kill  **B** destroy  **C** pass  **D** spend
7  The ............. implications of the decision they made could be extremely serious.
   **A** long-gone  **B** long-term  **C** long-range
   **D** long-time
8  She's a thoughtful teacher, who really ............. into her own when dealing with children who have learning difficulties.
   **A** gets  **B** runs  **C** brings  **D** comes
9  Some sociologists believe that the ............. family is rapidly becoming a thing of the past.
   **A** basic  **B** closed  **C** nuclear  **D** immediate
10 I'm amazed they are thinking of getting divorced – they seemed to have such a(n) ............. relationship.
   **A** firm  **B** hard  **C** unshakable  **D** stable

## Grammar: conditional forms, *wish/if only*

> **Watch Out!** *problem areas*
>
> • *unless*
>   We'll go for a picnic tomorrow, unless it rains. (= *if it doesn't rain*) ✔
>   I'll be quite relieved ~~unless she comes~~ ‸*if she doesn't come*.
>   They would never have sold the car ~~unless we had~~ ‸*if we hadn't* agreed to a higher price.
>
> • *wish*
>   Past: They wish they ‸*had* had the chance to go abroad last year. (= *but they didn't*)
>   Present: I wish I ~~would be~~ ‸*were* in a different class. (= *but I'm not*)
>   I wish I ~~would~~ ‸*could* speak French. (= *but I can't*)
>   Irritating habit: I wish he ~~won't~~ ‸*wouldn't* interrupt me when I'm talking to someone. (= *but he does it regularly*)
>   Future: I wish I ~~am/would be~~ ‸*was* going on holiday this year. (= *but I'm not*)

**1  Use of English:** guided sentence transformations
Finish each of the following sentences in such a way that it is as similar as possible in meaning to the sentence printed before it. In this exercise the words you need to transform are in italics to help you.

1  I *couldn't* write *very well* in the exam, because I *was extremely* nervous.
   If ..................................................................
2  We'll have to cancel the school outing, *unless* the weather *gets better*.
   If there ............................................................
3  *It's a pity they are refusing to* reconsider their plans.
   I wish ...............................................................
4  *Having* to revise every night *made me really* bad tempered throughout my exams.
   If ...................................................................
5  *It's so annoying* that my car *never starts* on cold mornings.
   I wish ...............................................................

6   Thanks to *all the* money we *received, we were able to* build a new library.
    If ..............................................................................

7   *I'll continue* with my plans *unless I hear from you.*
    If you .........................................................................

8   One of the reasons that *I couldn't go* to the lecture was that I *had too* much work to do.
    I might ........................................................................

**2**   When you have checked the answers to Exercise 1, analyse any errors you made. Did you miss:

- changes to modal verbs in different tenses? (e.g. *can, must*)
- the adverb *so?*
- *will/would* to express irritation?

# Use of English: gapped sentences

> *Paper 3, Section A, Question 3*

### About the exam

For **Paper 3, Question 3**, you have to complete six gapped sentences with an appropriate word or phrase. You should use between one and five words to fill each gap. Some gapped sentences test fixed phrases, collocations or phrasal verbs, while others focus on structures. Both types normally demand that you remember **two things or more** (e.g. supplying a verb and its dependent preposition, or the right noun and the adjective it collocates with).

### Exam Strategy

- Always read the **whole sentence** first, thinking about the **meaning** only. Watch out especially for negatives, which change the meaning completely.
- When you think you know what the gapped word(s) should mean, try to decide what structure would fit.
- Now think about **grammar**. Look closely at the words before and after the gap. Look for dependent prepositions, verb forms or adverbs which might give you a clue about the forms of the missing words.

**1**   Read this example carefully before attempting the exercise below.

EXAMPLE:
I'd prefer it if you ............. much noise when I'm working!

The structure *I'd prefer* and the word *noise* after the gap suggest that the general meaning is that the speaker wants you to be less noisy. The verb which collocates with *noise* is *make*. We need a past tense form because the preference is for something hypothetical, as well as a negative: *didn't make*. Before the word *much*, we also need the adverb *so*.

ANSWER:
I'd prefer it if you *didn't make so* much noise when I'm working!

**2**   Fill each of the gaps with a suitable word or phrase. In this exercise, you are given the number of words which are missing to help you. (Contractions like *won't* are counted here as two words.)

1   I think I would enjoy the course more if ............. ............. ............. more feedback by the tutors.
2   I'm sure you won't have any problems, as ............. ............. ............. ............. careful what you do.
3   It's high ............. ............. ............. responsibility for his own problems.
4   Hadn't you ............. ............. ............. phone? It's already rung five or six times.
5   It looks as ............. ............. ............. ............. well in his exams next summer.
6   I'd rather ............. ............. ............. at me – I'm not deaf, you know.
7   Gerald doesn't want you to organise the party, because he'd ............. ............. the arrangements himself.
8   Why are you always interfering? It's time ............. ............. out of my affairs!

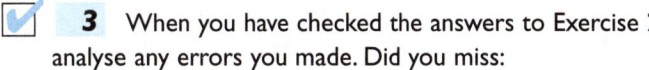

**3**   When you have checked the answers to Exercise 2, analyse any errors you made. Did you miss:

- important words which were not immediately around the gap?
- a phrasal verb or fixed expression?
- a place where the passive voice was needed?
- a necessary change of verb form?

# Listening: sentence completion

## About the exam

In **Paper 4** you may have to listen to a talk and fill in gaps or complete 'prompt' sentences. These sentences rephrase some of the main points of the recording, in the same order as you hear them. You will hear the recording twice.

## Exam Strategy

- Before you listen, look at the gaps and try to predict the type of information missing, e.g. an action, a person, a place, etc.
- While you listen, try to match the meaning of each prompt sentence to a specific part of the recording. Always try to listen for information concerning the current 'prompt' sentence **and the next one**, so you don't miss the information for one sentence and become 'lost'.
- Find and write down the answers the second time you listen. Write only one word or a short phrase in each gap. What you write should be grammatically correct within the context of the sentence.

**1** You will hear four extracts from a radio talk about a famous nineteenth century scholar and explorer called Richard Burton. Each extract is similar to one of the following prompt sentences, but not the same.

 1 The first time you listen, match each of the extracts to one of the following sentences. Write the letter of the extract in the space provided. Ignore the gaps in the sentences for the moment.

1 As Burton was very good at ............., his achievements were both numerous and varied. (extract ......)
2 Although the ............. he made to mankind cannot be compared to those of Darwin or Einstein, he was still a very remarkable man. (extract ......)
3 Not using any 'special method', Burton could not make his foreign language learning particularly ............. . (extract ......)
4 In foreign language learning, Burton owed his amazing ............. to the fact that he was so highly motivated. (extract ......)

 2 Now listen again to the four extracts and complete each of the sentences with a word or short phrase.

3 How are the sentences different from the extracts you heard? Which prompt sentence(s):

- rephrase(s) the extract using language of a different register (degree of formality)? Sentence(s) ......
- include(s) different forms of the same words (e.g. nouns instead of verbs)? Sentence(s) ......
- use(s) a different word order from the extract on the tape? Sentence(s) ......

 **2** Now listen to the whole radio talk and complete the following sentences with a word or short phrase. Listen to the recording twice.

Burton's [____ 1 ____] of sixteen volumes of the *Arabian Nights* is well known.

As an explorer, he searched for the [____ 2 ____] and made other journeys in northern Africa and the Near East.

His most impressive achievement was that he spoke [____ 3 ____] as well as numerous dialects.

It seems there [____ 4 ____] extraordinary in his learning methods.

When he set out on a new learning project he was very [____ 5 ____] and extremely [____ 6 ____] – nothing could distract him.

He had tremendous energy and determination, and would spend [____ 7 ____] studying a new language.

Burton spent most of his childhood [____ 8 ____]

As a child he had to learn foreign languages so that he could [____ 9 ____] of his own age.

On reaching [____ 10 ____], he had mastered impressive language skills and had a high degree of learning experience.

# Vocabulary: descriptive verbs

**1**   The following verbs are all descriptive or 'vivid'. Put them in the appropriate categories below, using a dictionary to help you if necessary.

| | | | | | |
|---|---|---|---|---|---|
| shriek | whine | frown | snatch | glare | stagger |
| yell | peer | stroll | moan | grasp | glance |
| amble | grip | stride | gaze | hug | groan |
| | stare | mutter | clutch | trudge | |

Make four lists in your notebook.

- ways of speaking
- ways of walking
- ways of looking
- ways of taking or holding

**2**   Complete each of the following sentences with an appropriate verb from the box above, in the correct form.

1   One of the boys came up to me, shoved me to the ground and ............. my bag from me.
2   'How dare you interrupt me!' he ............. at the top of his voice.
3   Absolutely shattered, he ............. homewards across the muddy field.
4   From the way she was ............. at me, I realised that I must have upset her.
5   We ............. into the darkness of the room, straining to see what was inside.
6   The old man often sat huddled in a corner ............. to himself.
7   One man, who was badly hurt, ............. down the road in search of help.
8   He ............. into her eyes and asked her to marry him.

## Study Tip

Group words with similar meanings in sets, and make contrastive records.

1   make example sentences, showing the different contexts in which each word would be most appropriate.
2   Put your words on a scale (e.g. quietest to loudest).
3   Make a table (e.g. for the ways of looking, which express a particular emotion/would be rude in certain situations, etc.).

Include grammatical information. For example, all of the verbs above have noun forms with the same spelling.

# Use of English: writing a summary

**Paper 3, Section B**

## About the exam

In **Paper 3, Section B** you have to read a passage of about 600 words, answer a number of comprehension questions, and then write a paragraph in answer to a specific question, summarising points from one or more parts of the passage.

## Exam Strategy

- Read the summary question, decide what information you need to answer it, and underline the parts of the passage which contain that information. Normally you need about four or five points to answer the question.
- Make brief notes, following the order of the passage.
- Check your notes against the summary task **before** you start writing. Make sure you have answered the task in full and without irrelevance.
- Rewrite your notes in a paragraph, **using your own words** as far as you can.
- Edit your summary to the correct length.

**1**

1   Read the following summary task.

> In a paragraph of 30–40 words, summarise what students should do to become effective learners.

2   Now read the title of the passage on page 20, to predict what it is about. Then read the passage all the way through to make sure you understand it.

3   Look at the parts underlined in the passage and the notes made by a student preparing to answer the summary task below it. Why has the student selected this information and omitted the rest (i.e. the parts not underlined)?

......................................................................................
......................................................................................

## Study habits to maximise your potential

It is of the utmost importance for students to be meticulously organised in the way they occupy their time. They should avoid squandering their hours on trivia, while not devoting enough time to (*1*) tasks
5  which are of prime importance to their studies.

One aspect of time management (*2*) is the making of lists. Students should acquire the habit of making detailed lists of the things they need to do and indicating, where possible, when they need to be
10  done by. Such a list might include, for example, the written assignments which have been set for a particular week or certain books and journals which have been recommended by tutors.

While on the subject of books and journals, it is worth
15  mentioning that effective learning inevitably means (*3*) effective reading. Reading is a skill which needs to be developed. Many students are very ineffective readers and this is ultimately reflected in their poor performance in exams.

20  (*4*) Note-taking is another area where students may need help. If students are not in the habit of keeping organised notes which cover all points, most of what they read or hear in lectures will be forgotten or not clearly understood later.

25  All of which brings us to the question of exams. (*5*) Success in exams can only be achieved if their preparation is approached in a systematic way. It is so important for students to start this well in advance of exams – so many students have failed exams or
30  done badly because they have not spent enough time going over their notes beforehand.

---

*Students should:*
*1 spend their time only on important things*
*2 make lists of things they need to do by certain times*
*3 develop effective reading habits*
*4 keep organised notes which cover all points*
*5 leave enough time for studying when preparing for exams.*

---

**2** Read the following summary, which the student wrote using his notes. Ignore the numbers and underlining for the moment. Notice he has:

- replaced the word *should* with other words and phrases to avoid monotony
- used participle clauses (*making*, *preparing*) and connectors (*also*, *finally*) to link the points.

**What does the student still need to do?**

.......................................................................................

*It is (1) extremely important for students to (2) spend their time only on things which are important, making lists of (3) things they need to do by certain times. They should also develop effective reading habits and keep notes (4) which are organised and cover all points. Finally, when (5) preparing for exams, it is essential for students to leave themselves enough time for this preparation. (62 words)*

**3** The first draft this student wrote is still too long. Knowing a wide range of vocabulary can give you the word-power to edit the summary further. Replace the underlined phrases with the single words in the box below making any other necessary changes. There are two words you won't need.

| revising | vital | evaluate | thorough |
|---|---|---|---|
| prioritise | deadlines | specific | |

The summary should now be the correct length.

**4** Now you're going to go through a similar process of reading, making notes, writing and editing a summary, based on another passage.

1  Read the title of the passage on page 21, which gives you an idea of what it is about. Before you read the passage, think of some ways in which computer games might have educational benefits for children. Make a list of at least three in your notebook.

**2**   Now read the passage to see if you agree with the experts. Ignore the numbers and underlining for the moment.

# Computer games in education

Computer games have come a long way since *Pong*, a high tech version of table tennis, became the first to hit the screen in 1972. The vast majority of children now regularly play games ranging from *3D Mario* to *Mortal Kombat*. One study has suggested that one teenager in fifteen devotes thirty hours a week to them, though the majority are moderate consumers. What does it do to young minds?

For years concern has been expressed by parents and teachers about the effect of computer games on the moral and mental make-up of the next generation. Some have warned that a relentless diet of whiz-bang 'shoot-'em-ups' fosters antisocial behaviour, even playground violence. Others believe that the age of the zombie is upon us.

But expert opinion is shifting radically. Psychologists in America and Britain now suggest that while computer games hold some dangers for children, (*1*) they also provide opportunities their parents never enjoyed to amplify powers of concentration and memory. Researchers have also highlighted (*2*) the positive response of children to the way computer games reward success, thereby spurring them on to look for greater challenges – a boon if the same attitude is applied to school work. A leading academic at the University of Washington has even claimed that (*3*) children think differently when they play computer games, learning to deal with problems in parallel rather than in sequence. In effect, children are being trained to tackle problems in a fashion which is not only more rapid but also more effective. In the long-term, (*4*) the facility that game players develop with computer graphics could help many a future career. It could, for example, be of particular benefit to children who go on to become engineers or scientists.

(*5*) Games are also now being developed for pre-school children to encourage reading and writing skills. At Lanterns, a private nursery in east London, computer games make up part of the syllabus. Each week its sixteen pupils – the youngest aged two – are treated to a whirlwind tour of cyberspace. Every day the pupils attend a special class, such as dance or drama, and on Tuesdays they have a computer workshop where they spend an hour playing games. All the children love it. There is not a technophobe among them.

**5**   Read this summary question and underline the words in the question that tell you what information you need to include in your answer.

> In a paragraph of 70–90 words summarise the educational benefits of computer games, according to the writer.

**6**   Now look back at the passage opposite, and use the numbers and the underlined sections to help you to complete the notes below.

1   *increase children's powers of ........................*
2   *potentially have a positive effect on children's ........................ by encouraging ........................ look for greater challenges when they complete tasks*
3   *game players think ........................ and learn to deal with problems more ........................*
4   *familiarity with ........................ could be useful for ........................*
5   *can help ........................ to learn ........................*

**7**   Using the notes from Exercise 6, write the first draft of your summary in your notebook. Since you are writing about people's opinions, you will probably need to use modal verbs (e.g. *may*) and expressions such as *it is believed that* or *games are thought to*. Points 3 and 4 could be combined in one sentence.

**8**   Check and edit your summary. Have you included all the information you need? Is it the right length or do you need to shorten it? Use this checklist to help you.

> ### Methods of editing summaries
> - Make sure each sentence makes a new point.
> - Remove examples which support your points.
> - Remove adjectives and adverbs.
> - Look for repetition and remove it.
> - Replace particular phrases with single words.
> - Replace full clauses with participle clauses.

**9**   Read through the second draft of your summary. Look back at the original question, and make sure that all your points are relevant to it, then check for spelling, punctuation or grammatical mistakes.

# Writing: descriptive composition (1) (experiences)

## About the exam

In **Paper 2** you may have to write a description of an experience or an event in the past and assess it or reflect on it in some way. You will be expected to write about 350 words.

## Exam Strategy

- Read the question carefully. How many parts are there?
- Plan your composition.
- Write your composition, following your outline closely.
- When you finish, check your work for grammar, punctuation and spelling mistakes.

**1**

1   Read the writing task.

> Describe an examination you once took, saying what you did, how you felt and why. (About 350 words.)

2   Now read the following outline, which was written in answer to the task. There is one detail, or set of details, in each paragraph of the outline which is irrelevant or repetitive. Find these details and cross them out.

## Exam Strategy

Spend at least **fifteen minutes** writing a detailed outline for your composition. If you do this, there will be no need for you to write the composition in rough first! Remember to:

- include all the main details of the composition
- indicate the paragraphs
- make notes about complex words and expressions you will use. Look at the outline and see how the information in brackets has been added **at the planning stage**
- check the plan against the title before starting to write, and make notes of any further ideas you have.

---

*Introduction (getting up)*
*alarm clock woke me up (knocked it off table/groaned)*
*day of history exam (dreading this day - Past perf)*
*examinations are very important in our lives - 3 reasons*
*got dressed, rushed downstairs (grabbed pens)*

*First supporting paragraph (in kitchen)*
*mother already waiting in kitchen*
*greetings - felt OK - will be question about Roman Empire (direct speech/bound to)*
*ate breakfast, but not hungry (went through the motions of eating)*
*set off for school*
*school is in modern building - over 1,000 students - good reputation*

*Second supporting paragraph (in exam)*
*in main hall - head teacher*
*head teacher only been at school for six months - everyone likes him*
*gave me paper - looked at it - no question about Roman Empire (glanced)*
*started to write - couldn't answer questions very well*
*other students doing well (gazed around)*
*clock = 5 minutes left (gasped)*

*Third supporting paragraph (after exam)*
*met friends outside - everyone cheerful (circled round me)*
*known my friends for many years - holiday together previous year (Past perf)*
*they mentioned great question about Roman Empire (shrieked/ stuttered - use direct speech)*
*question on back of paper!*

*Closing paragraph (going home/at home)*
*left friends, went home (turned on my heel/staggered)*
*at home - watched TV to comfort myself - favourite soap opera*
*another week before able to see funny side*

**2**  Read the following composition, which was written using the outline in Exercise 1. Ignore the numbered gaps for the moment. Check that your ideas about which information was irrelevant were correct.

*The alarm clock woke me suddenly. Knocking it off my bedside table, I lay back and groaned. The day I had been dreading, the day of my history exam, had finally arrived. I quickly got dressed, grabbed my pens, and rushed downstairs.*

*My mother was already waiting for me in the kitchen.*

*'Hello, dear. How are you feeling?'*

*'Fine. A bit nervous, but I think I'll be OK. There's bound to be a question about the Roman Empire - I know all about that at least.'*

*Not feeling in the least bit hungry, I went through the motions of eating my breakfast, then set off for school.*

*Before I knew it I was sitting in the main hall. (1) ............ as the head teacher gave me the paper. (2) ............ I glanced at the questions. They were all too difficult - and there was nothing about the Roman Empire! (3) ............, I reluctantly picked up my pen to write. I answered two questions I knew nothing about, but I really had little choice. Gazing around, I couldn't understand why everyone else seemed to be doing so well. It was then that I noticed the clock on the wall - only five minutes left! I gasped. Today was becoming a disaster!*

*Afterwards, my friends were waiting impatiently for me outside. (4) ............, they circled round me, demanding to know how I had done. They seemed horribly cheerful.*

*'What a great question about the Roman Empire!' shrieked one.*

*'What do you mean?' I stuttered, my mouth suddenly going very dry. I felt (5) ............ .*

*'The question on the back of the paper. Didn't you see it?'*

*That was the last straw! I stared at him (6) ............, turned on my heel and staggered off home. I felt shocked and disappointed, and couldn't bring myself to tell anyone about it. It took another week, before I could see the funny side of the whole situation. (308 words)*

**3**  The composition needs to be longer. Improve it by adding the following phrases in the appropriate gaps to make it more vivid and descriptive.

A  *as if I was stranded in the desert*
B  *my hands were shaking as*
C  *like vultures*
D  *in horror*
E  *I felt my heart pounding in my chest*
F  *taking a deep breath*

**4**  In your notebook, answer these questions about the composition.

1  How many parts were there in the composition title? Did the student who wrote this composition answer the task in full?

2  What method was used to organise the details within the paragraphs? (Look again at the list in Unit 1, page 15 for guidance.)

**5**

1  Now plan and write a composition in answer to the question below. Follow the procedure in the Exam Strategy boxes.

> Describe a classroom experience which was memorable in some way, explaining what happened, how you felt and why. (About 350 words.)

2  Use this checklist to help you prepare a detailed outline before you start writing. Useful things to include in this kind of composition are:

- an unusual or memorable incident
- comparisons, using *like* and *as if*
- a little direct speech, to add dramatic effect. Don't forget that you need to start a new paragraph with each new piece of speech. Use the composition above as a guide
- a range of descriptive verbs, adjectives and adverbs. Look again at the vocabulary exercise on page 19 to give you some ideas.

**6**  Exchange your composition with another student if you can. Evaluate each other's work and suggest improvements.

# 3 The moving image

## Vocabulary review: multiple-choice

Paper 1, Section A

Choose the word, **A**, **B**, **C** or **D**, which best completes each sentence. In this exercise, all the missing words have **similar meanings** or **similar forms** (they look the same but have very different meanings).

1   Her hands were swollen and wrinkled, but she still had her nails ............. regularly.
    **A** manufactured   **B** manicured
    **C** maintained   **D** managed

2   The girl's large, heavy earrings had ............. her earlobes permanently.
    **A** displaced   **B** dismayed   **C** disfigured
    **D** diseased

3   More and more people are having satellite dishes ............. on their roofs.
    **A** installed   **B** introduced   **C** implanted
    **D** inserted

4   Cut flowers may ............. through lack of water.
    **A** faint   **B** collapse   **C** wilt   **D** drop

5   The actor was so nervous that he could only remember small ............. of dialogue.
    **A** shreds   **B** pieces   **C** patches   **D** snatches

6   The ............. cheered when the final goal was scored in the match today.
    **A** viewers   **B** onlookers   **C** spectators
    **D** audience

7   Most people ............. family heirlooms and keep them safe.
    **A** cosset   **B** cherish   **C** nourish   **D** nurture

8   The man's laugh had a very cruel ............. to it.
    **A** ring   **B** boom   **C** resonance   **D** noise

9   The job you've been offered is a(n) ............. opportunity to travel and meet people.
    **A** sole   **B** only   **C** unique   **D** single

10  He ............. a yawn as the actor began yet another long speech.
    **A** squashed   **B** suffocated   **C** submerged
    **D** stifled

## Grammar: emphasis (1) (inversion)

**Watch Out!** *problem areas*

- *hardly/no sooner*
  Hardly had he arrived at the office *when* his boss summoned him to a meeting. ✔
  No sooner had we sat down to watch TV *than* the doorbell rang. (sooner *is a comparative, so we use* than *after it*) ✔

- **word order**
  Not ~~did~~ for one moment ∧*did* Sarah believe that the news she had heard was true.
  Not until ~~has your report been checked you will~~ ∧*your report has been checked will you* be allowed to publicise your views.

- **auxiliary verbs**
  Rarely did he ∧*do* his homework on time.
  Hardly ever did she ~~talked~~ ∧*talk* to anyone she didn't know.
  Because these inversions are emphatic, it's **impossible to use contractions** in the inverted verb.
  ~~Hadn't Peter~~ ∧*Had Peter not* helped us, we wouldn't have been able to cope.

- *little and few*
  *Little* and *few* usually have a negative meaning, and are often used to start inverted sentences.
  *A little* and *a few* have a positive meaning, and are never used to start these types of inversion.
  Little did she realise (= *she little realised*) what the results of her action would be. ✔
  In few cases do new actors find work easily. ✔
  In a few cases, new actors may find they have more work than they can cope with.
  (= *this occasionally happens*) ✔

### 1   Use of English: guided sentence transformations

1   Finish each of the following sentences in such a way that it is as similar as possible in meaning to the sentence printed before it, and uses an inverted verb form. In this exercise, the words which need to be changed or omitted are in italics, and the verbs to be inverted are underlined to help you.

EXAMPLE:

<u>You will</u> *only* be allowed to leave *when* you have finished the job.

*Not until you have finished the job will you be allowed to leave.*

1   It *never* <u>seemed</u> likely that the disagreement would be settled.
   At no ........................................................................

2   <u>We were</u> *not* <u>allowed</u> into the country *until* our visas had been double-checked.
   Only ........................................................................

3   <u>You are</u> *not* <u>to visit</u> the old part of town on your own, *whatever happens*.
   Under no ........................................................................

4   *This is the first time that* <u>television has played</u> such an important role in our lives.
   Never ........................................................................

5   <u>You do</u> *not often* <u>come across</u> someone as well-informed as Charles Osborne.
   Seldom ........................................................................

6   He would not have learned the news *if he hadn't* <u>been</u> listening to the radio.
   Had ........................................................................

7   <u>We had</u> *just* <u>sat down</u> to eat *when* the telephone rang.
   No sooner ........................................................................

8   I <u>refuse</u> to work for that company again.
   Never ........................................................................

9   <u>She did</u>*n't really* <u>realise</u> what was about to happen.
   Little ........................................................................

10  <u>He</u> *acts so well* that the audience hang on his every word.
   So ........................................................................

11  *It was to be another* six months *before* <u>Sally met</u> him again.
   Not ........................................................................

12  He *doesn't normally* <u>do</u> his fair share of the work.
   Rarely ........................................................................

 2   When you have checked the answers to Exercise 1.1, analyse any errors you made. Did you forget to:

*   add an auxiliary verb?
*   add or remove a negative?
*   invert the subject and verb?
*   change the order of other information?

### 2   Use of English: gapped sentences

1   Fill each of the gaps in the following sentences with a suitable word or phrase. In some, but **not all**, of the gaps you need to use an inversion.

1   The first night of the play was a disaster. Hardly ........................ a good word to say about it afterwards.

2   I thought my father would be pleased, but not once ........................ me on my exam results.

3   On no ........................ you to mention what happened to your colleagues.

4   Not ........................ the book, it is difficult for me to say what I think of the writer's views.

5   So ........................ with his performance, they offered to give him a permanent job.

6   Other students had poorer exam results – he is by no means ........................ in the class.

 2   When you have checked the answers to Exercise 2.1, analyse any mistakes you made. Did you forget:

*   that some sentences didn't need inversions?
*   which verb collocated with some of the dependent prepositions?

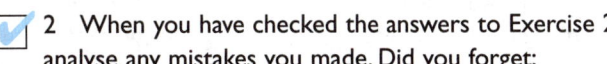

### Exam Tip!

Use inversions in **Paper 2** to make the register of your compositions more formal, for example in letters of complaint.

# Reading: literary text

## About the exam

In **Paper 1** you have to read three different texts and answer four to six questions on each text, choosing the correct answer from four options. There are usually two non-fiction texts and one fiction or literary text.

## Exam Strategy

- Read through the text to gain a general understanding of what it is about and what the author's attitude or tone is.
- Look at each question, or unfinished stem, and try to find and underline the information you need in the text **without looking at the four options**. Look at the options and choose the one which most closely resembles your answer from the text. This way you won't be confused by the many options or 'distractors'.
- Remember that the questions follow the order of the text. The last question normally asks about the text as a whole, often focusing on the attitude of the writer.

**1** Read the following text quickly. What type of novel could it be from? (More than one is possible.)

a) gothic horror
b) science fiction
c) historical
d) romantic
e) detective

Mandy Price, aged nineteen years two months, and the acknowledged star of Mrs Creasley's Nonesuch Secretarial Agency, set out on the morning of Tuesday, 14th September for her interview at the Peverell Press with no more apprehension than she usually felt at the start of a new job, an apprehension which was never acute and was rooted less in an anxiety as to whether she would satisfy the expectations of the prospective employer than in whether the employer would satisfy hers. She had learned of the job the previous Friday when she called in at the agency at six o'clock to collect her pay after a boring two-week stint with a director who regarded a secretary as a status symbol but had no idea how to use her skills, and she was ready for something new and preferably exciting, although perhaps not as exciting as it was subsequently to prove.

Mrs Creasley, for whom Mandy had worked for the past three years, conducted her agency from a couple of rooms above a newsagent and tobacconist's shop off the Whitechapel Road, a situation which, she was fond of pointing out to her girls and clients, was convenient both for the City and for the towering offices of Docklands. Neither had so far produced much in the way of business, but while other agencies foundered in the waves of recession Mrs Creasley's small and underprovisioned ship was still, if precariously, afloat. Except for the help of one of her girls when no outside work was available, she ran the agency single-handed. The outer room was her office in which she propitiated clients, interviewed new girls and assigned the new week's work. The inner was her personal sanctum, furnished with a divan bed on which she occasionally spent the night in defiance of the terms of the lease, a drinks cabinet and a refrigerator, a cupboard which opened to reveal a minute kitchen, a large television set and two easy chairs in front of the gas fire in which a lurid red light rotated behind artificial logs. She referred to her room as the 'cosy', and Mandy was one of the few girls who was admitted to its privacies.

It was probably the cosy which kept Mandy faithful to the agency, although she would never have openly admitted to a need which would have seemed to her both childish and embarrassing. Her mother had left home when she was six and she herself had been hardly able to wait for her sixteenth birthday when she could get away from a father whose idea of parenthood had gone little further than the provision of two meals a day which she was expected to cook, and her clothes. For the last year she had rented one room in a terraced house in Stratford East where she lived in acrimonious camaraderie with three young friends, the main cause of dispute being Mandy's insistence that her Yamaha motorbike should be parked in the narrow hall. But it was the cosy in Whitechapel Road, the mingled smells of wine and take-away Chinese food, the hiss of the gas fire, the two deep and battered armchairs in which she could curl up and sleep which represented all Mandy had ever known of the comfort and security of home.

Mrs Creasley, sherry bottle in one hand and a scrap of jotting paper in the other, munched at her cigarette holder until she had manoeuvred it to a corner of her mouth where, as usual, it hung in defiance of gravity, and squinted at her almost indecipherable handwriting through immense horn-rimmed spectacles.

'It's a new client, Mandy, the Peverell Press. I've looked them up in the publisher's directory. They're one of the oldest – perhaps the oldest – publishing firm in the country, founded in 1792.'

**2**   Find and underline the answers to these questions in the text. Here you are answering more than the four to six questions which you will have in the exam, to train yourself to deal with this type of text and question format.

1  Why was Mandy Price usually slightly apprehensive when going to a new job?
2  What was the main reason the director had hired Mandy?
3  Why did Mrs Creasley consider the agency's position in relation to the City and Docklands to be advantageous?
4  In what way could Mrs Creasley be considered a more successful businesswoman than others?
5  What was Mrs Creasley not supposed to do at the agency?
6  Why did Mandy continue to work for Mrs Creasley?
7  Why had Mandy wanted to leave home when she was sixteen?
8  What kind of relationship did Mandy have with the other girls in the house in Stratford East?
9  What impression does the author give us of Mandy's values and personality?

**3**   The multiple-choice options for the questions in Exercise 2 are given below. In each case, tick the option, **A, B, C** or **D**, which is closest to the answer you found in the text.

1  A  She was worried her new employer would not be pleased with her.
   B  She was afraid of being disappointed by her new employer.
   C  She felt uncomfortable with people she didn't know well.
   D  She had high expectations of herself and her performance.

2  A  He wanted an attractive secretary so that others would envy him.
   B  He didn't have the skills she had.
   C  He had a lot of work he needed her to do.
   D  He felt that a man in his position ought to have a secretary.

3  A  She expected business from the Docklands area.
   B  A lot of business came from these two areas.
   C  It was near potential employers.
   D  It was easy to go shopping in the City.

4  A  She had invested successfully in shipping.
   B  Business at her agency was thriving.
   C  She had remained in business while other agencies had closed.
   D  She ran the business virtually single handed.

5  A  cook meals
   B  receive clients
   C  sleep
   D  interview new girls

6  A  very few of the girls were allowed in the cosy.
   B  she liked the other girls who worked at the agency.
   C  she looked upon her as a mother figure.
   D  the cosy provided the kind of home she craved.

7  A  She wanted to live on her own.
   B  Her father showed little interest in her.
   C  She had to do all the cooking.
   D  Her mother was no longer there.

8  A  She always got on well with them.
   B  She often quarrelled with them.
   C  She found their company boring.
   D  She disliked them.

9  A  She had a much stronger attachment to places than people.
   B  Her independence was more important to her than anything else.
   C  She was more sentimental than she wanted to be.
   D  She didn't like to admit to things she had done.

**4**   For each question in a multiple-choice exercise there are four options: one option is the correct answer and the other three are 'distractors' or incorrect answers. **Distractors can be**:

• **wrong in relation to the text** (what they say is not exactly what the text says), **or**
• **wrong in relation to the stem or question** (they contain information which is in the text, but do not give a good and complete answer for the question stem).

Some distractors **both** fail to answer the question fully, **and** contain information not in the text.

For questions 1–9 above, option **A** in each case is one of the distractors. Look at the statements below, and match an option **A** distractor to each. (You won't have to use all of the distractors.)

a)  A word in the text has been repeated in the distractor, but here it is used differently, and has a different meaning. ............
b)  The statement in the distractor is the opposite of what is said in the text. ............
c)  The distractor gives us true information from the text, but only partly answers the question. ............
d)  The distractor may well contain information which is true, but the text doesn't actually tell us this – we are inferring it, and it is our opinion, rather than the truth. ............

## Use of English: guided key word transformations

For each of the sentences below, use a prepositional phrase containing the word in bold to write a new sentence as similar as possible in meaning to the original sentence. **You must not change the given word in any way**. If you are unsure what the prepositional phrase is, try looking up the key word you are given in a dictionary. In this exercise, the phrase you need to replace is in italics to help you.

EXAMPLE:

He can tell how much a picture is worth *immediately he sees it*. **glance**

*He can tell at a glance how much a picture is worth.*

1 She didn't want to leave the room *because she was afraid of* missing the beginning of the film. **fear**

.............................................................

2 *I don't want you to tell anyone else* what I am telling you now. **confidence**

.............................................................

3 *Whatever happens* we must avoid a scandal. **costs**

.............................................................

4 *As far as I know*, she is still working for the same company. **knowledge**

.............................................................

5 I wanted to find a new job because I felt *bored with my life*. **rut**

.............................................................

6 They *don't get on well* with their neighbours. **terms**

.............................................................

7 I *was thinking of* something particular. **mind**

.............................................................

8 We *couldn't possibly* sell this painting. **question**

.............................................................

### Study Tip

Although dependent prepositions and prepositional phrases are often tested directly in **Paper 1, Section A** and in **Paper 3**, it is important to have a good knowledge of such prepositions for **all** the papers of the Proficiency exam. Make sure you keep a record of dependent prepositions and prepositional phrases you come across, on a separate page in your notebook.

## Grammar: participle clauses

### Watch Out! *problem areas*

- **the subject of the participle clause**
  The subject of the participle clause is usually the same as the subject of the main clause, and a subject, noun or pronoun must appear in the main clause.
  Reading through the script, ~~there were~~ ∧*I noticed* lots of mistakes.
  ~~Not~~ ∧*Nobody* having any more questions to ask, the meeting came to a close.
  Not knowing what to say, ∧*he* fumbled with his papers and sat down.
  In some common expressions, however, the participle clause can be given its own subject. Generally speaking, women perform this task better than men. ✔

- **present, past and perfect participles**
  Present (*wanting to ...*), past (*wanted by ...*) and perfect participles (*having wanted to ...*) can all be used to make participle clauses.
  ~~Irritating~~ ∧*Irritated* by her remark, he glowered at her and started to shout.
  ~~Having wanted~~ ∧*Wanting* to catch his attention, she whistled shrilly.

- **double negatives**
  Not having read the book, ~~was he able~~ ∧*he was not able* to answer any of their questions.

**1** Read sentences 1–10, and the functions of participle clauses a)–e) on page 29. Now match each sentence with one of the functions. (You'll need to use some functions more than once.)

1 Sitting on his balcony, he watched the people below going about their business.
2 Putting down the telephone, he went into the lounge and made himself a drink.
3 Having already seen the play, he decided not to go with his friends to the theatre.
4 Wanting to forget the events of the evening, he turned on the television and watched a film.
5 Although thrilled by the good news, I decided not to celebrate until it had been confirmed.
6 Having been searched by the police, he was taken to a room for questioning.
7 He left the room, humming to himself as he went.
8 Not being a cinema buff, I am not able to comment on the quality of the film.

9  Allowed to leave the country, he would disappear without a trace.

10  Working as hard as he does, it's not surprising he's had a nervous breakdown.

The participle clause is used to describe:

  a)  events happening rapidly one after the other

  b)  events happening at the same time

  c)  a reason

  d)  a concession

  e)  a condition

### 2

1  Read the following extract, which features Tom Sloane, a spy who has lots of unusual adventures. Think about what types of extra information you could add to the story, in the numbered gaps, to make it more interesting and dramatic.

(1) ............ Tom Sloane kept his eye on the exceptionally fat man who was moving ponderously towards him. Something about the fat man was not quite right. Maybe it was the slightly insane grin which made Sloane feel uneasy. (2) ............ He naturally felt vulnerable He wondered what he should do. (3) ............ He stood up and strolled towards the man. (4) ............ . (5) ............ He understood that a moment's careless-ness could cost him his life. Sloane was ready for anything. (6) ............ Especially a fat man wearing a black bowler hat – the hat! Why hadn't he noticed it before? (7) ............ Sloane dived for cover. Zzzzzz! The bullet just missed him. (8) ............ The fat man continued to grin at Sloane. (9) ............ 'Good afternoon, Mr Sloane. How nice to see you,' he muttered. (10) ............

2  Read these sentences. How similar or different are they to your ideas?

1  Sloane was sitting under a palm tree and sipping his cocktail at the time.

2  He had not brought his gun with him to the beach.

3  He put his glass down.

4  He whistled nonchalantly as he went.

5  He understood this although he was exhausted from his previous mission.

6  He had been attacked by a knife-wielding nun the previous week.

7  He had just seen the man reach for the weapon on his head.

8  It buried itself in the sand beside him.

9  He was unperturbed.

10  He was clenching his teeth as he said it.

3  Add the information in sentences 1–10 to the story, using participle clauses and making any necessary changes.

EXAMPLE:

1  *Sitting under a palm tree, sipping his cocktail, Tom Sloane kept his eye on the exceptionally fat man ...*

### Exam Tip!

Use participle clauses to combine ideas dramatically in **Paper 2** narrative compositions and concisely in **Paper 3, Section B** summaries.

## Writing: descriptive composition (2) (people)

### Paper 2

### About the exam

In **Paper 2** you may be asked to write a description of someone you know. You will also be asked to provide details which justify the way you feel about them, or which give information about some aspect of their life or personality.

### Exam Strategy

As you write your composition, use reference pronouns such as *he*, *it*, *this*, etc. to refer to ideas already mentioned, and link ideas and details with connectors.

1  Read the following writing task.

> Describe someone you know, explaining how their leisure activities reflect their personality.
> (About 350 words.)

On page 30 there are two introductions to a composition written in answer to this question. The following questions will help you decide which one is more appropriate.

● What is the style and register of the writing? Is it appropriate for a descriptive composition?

● Is there a clear statement of topic? Is it relevant to the task (describing a person)?

● Are connectors used or are sentences disorganised and disconnected?

**1**

*I've always believed that the clothes a person wears and the way that person talks and behaves tell us a lot about what that person is like. I also think it's true that we can gain a glimpse of someone's personality from their interests and topics of conversation, and especially from the things they like doing in their free time. A particularly good example of the way someone's leisure activities reflect their personality is my brother, Peter.*

**2**

*In recent years, psychologists have discovered many interesting things about human personality. Such psychological investigations started with Freud in the nineteenth century. It has been demonstrated on many occasions that it is impossible to hide the kind of person we are. How exactly do a person's leisure activities reflect their personality?*

**2**   The student who wrote introduction 1 had lots of ideas for the description of his brother. Read his notes, and notice how he thought of **examples** of activities for each of the adjectives he uses to describe his brother's personality.

*a) watches videos over and over*
*    again in his room = obsessed*
*b) wants to be film director*
*    = ambitious*
*c) reads a lot of science fiction*
*d) makes model ships and aeroplanes*
*e) most of all loves the cinema*
*f) spends hours gluing and painting*
*    his models = patient/persistent*
*g) lives in another world*
*    = dreamer/vivid imagination*
*h) often doesn't eat with rest of family*
*    because watching a video*
*i) recently bought some expensive*
*    equipment to make his own*
*    films/results have been*
*    impressive = creative/talented*

**3**   Now read the student's outline for the descriptive composition, and decide where he should put each of the details a)–i).

Which detail seems to be particularly appropriate for the last paragraph? (Detail ….)

*Introduction*
*Clothes - way someone talks/behaves -*
*    tell us a lot*
*Also: topics of conversation - interests -*
*    leisure activities*
*Good example = Peter*

*First supporting paragraph*
*(3 main leisure activities, and examples*
*    of how they reflect personality -*
*    EMPHATIC ORDER)*

| Activity | Extra details |
|---|---|
| 1 ........................... | ........................... |
| 2 ........................... | ........................... |
| 3 ........................... | ........................... |

*Second supporting paragraph*
*(Details about most important activity.)*
*..................................................................*
*..................................................................*

*Closing paragraph*
*Hobbies and interests reflect*
*    energy/enthusiasm*
*Will one day achieve great things*
*..................................................................*

**4**   Now read the finished composition and check whether your ideas were similar to those of its writer.

*The clothes a person wears and the way that person behaves tell us a lot about what that person is like. Similarly, we can understand a lot about someone's personality from the way they talk, their interests and topics of conversation, and, of course, the things they like doing in their free time. A particularly good example of the way someone's leisure activities reflect their personality is my brother, Peter.*

*Peter likes to pursue interests which he considers 'constructive'. One of his hobbies is making model ships and aeroplanes, something which he takes very seriously. He often spends hours at his workbench gluing the parts together or painting models he has just finished. Not only does this require considerable patience and persistence, but it also clearly shows his desire to do things as carefully and conscientiously as he can. Another hobby my brother has is reading science fiction. He is a voracious reader of such novels. Maybe they are an outlet for his vivid imagination. His tendency to be a bit of a dreamer is certainly reflected in what he likes doing most in his free time - watching films on video or at the cinema.*

*Ever since he was a little boy, cinema has been the most important thing in Peter's life. So obsessed is he that he often spends hours locked in his room watching videos over and over again, even refusing to come down for meals with the rest of the family. He recently started making his own small-scale films and bought a lot of expensive equipment for this. The results so far have been very impressive, and prove that my brother possesses great talent and creativity.*

*Generally speaking, Peter's hobbies and interests reflect his tremendous energy and enthusiasm, and his unwillingness to waste time or do nothing. He is more than capable of fulfilling his ambition to become a famous film director. In fact, it would come as no surprise if he ended up like Spielberg one day, making blockbusters, earning huge amounts of money and living in an enormous mansion in Beverly Hills. (347 words)*

**5**   Look back at the composition again and underline:

- the statement of topic in the first paragraph
- the topic sentence in the second paragraph
- the topic sentence in the third paragraph
- the 'summing up' phrase in the closing paragraph.

**6**   Now answer the same task from Exercise 1, writing about a person you know. Use the questions below to help you.

**Details of their leisure activities**

- What does the activity involve?
- How much time does this person spend on the activity?
- Why does this person do this particular activity?
- Is the activity difficult in some way?
- Does this person have any ambitions with regard to this activity?

**Organising your composition**

- How many paragraphs will there be?
- How will you organise your information within the paragraphs? (Look again at Unit 1, page 15 for guidance.)
- How will you introduce and conclude your composition?
- How will you link the paragraphs together? (Use the composition above to give you ideas for useful expressions.)

**7**   Exchange your composition with another student if you can. Evaluate each other's work and suggest improvements.

**Exam Tip!**

When you write your conclusion do not simply repeat what you say in the introduction. Make sure you include some final thoughts (or a particularly interesting detail) as well. It is often a good idea to 'have something up your sleeve' for the conclusion!

## Vocabulary review: multiple-choice

Choose the word or phrase **A**, **B**, **C** or **D**, which best completes each sentence. In this exercise, all the missing words have **similar meanings**.

1 Most magazines on the market today contain lots of .............
   A commercials   B advertisements
   C propaganda   D manifestos

2 The government's anti-smoking ............. in the 1980s was particularly successful.
   A undertaking   B operation
   C campaign   D venture

3 You need to find a shop which sells electrical ............. if you want to buy a new plug.
   A wares   B units   C goods   D produce

4 Do you usually buy any particular ............. of instant coffee?
   A jar   B label   C mark   D brand

5 When Robert buys a tin of fruit he always reads the ............. carefully to see what preservatives have been used.
   A label   B sign   C ticket   D tag

6 Jenny always bought her bananas from the same ............. in the weekly market.
   A kiosk   B store   C stall   D stand

7 When Roger was at university he only went to shops that gave ............. to students.
   A discounts   B bargains   C sales
   D deductions

8 This supermarket's main priority is customer .............
   A happiness   B contentment   C satisfaction
   D complacency

9 The marketing department are creating a new ............. for this product which we hope will become recognisable worldwide.
   A mark   B logo   C design   D sign

10 These shoes are ............. this week at a special price of only £19.99.
   A for sale   B on retail   C on offer
   D for reduction

## Use of English: guided key word transformations

> **Paper 3, Section A, Question 4**

**About the exam**

In **Paper 3, Section A, Question 4** you have to rewrite eight sentences using a given word, **which you must not change in any way**, to produce sentences similar in meaning to the originals. This task tests your knowledge of verb patterns, phrases and idioms, rather than individual words.

### 1

1 Read this example carefully. It shows the sort of thing you need to consider when doing this type of task.

**EXAMPLE:**
They were well known for their fondness for practical jokes. **love**
*Their love of practical jokes was well known.*

*Love* here is a noun, not a verb. It has a dependent preposition *of*. Other changes: *were* changed to *was*; possessive *their*.

For each of the sentences in Exercises 1.2–1.6, write a new sentence as similar as possible in meaning to the original sentence using the word given in bold. **This word must not be changed in any way.**

2 In this exercise, which tests your knowledge of various **grammatical patterns**, you have been given several of the words required to answer the question, and gaps to show the number of words which are still missing.

1 A university education is very expensive these days. **cost**
   ............. cost ............. a university education is very ............. these days.

2 Over the past five years the number of people buying mobile phones has risen considerably. **increase**
   Over the past five years, ............. ............. been ............. ............. increase ............. the number of people buying mobile phones.

3  When the theft was discovered, Mike was dismissed immediately. **led**
The discovery of the theft led ............ ............
immediate ............

4  We only realised what had been happening after the accident. **unaware**
We ............ unaware ............ what had been happening ............ after the accident.

**3**  In this exercise, the part of the sentence to be transformed is in italics. The sentences test your knowledge of **phrasal verbs** and **dependent prepositions**.

1  I do*n't think you should get involved* in this argument. **keep**

........................................................

2  He did*n't really fancy going* on the climb. **reluctant**

........................................................

3  She's a very *reliable helper*. **relied**

........................................................

4  *One of the reasons* the enterprise *failed was that* the manager *was so inefficient*. **contributed**

........................................................

**4**  In this exercise, the sentences test your knowledge of **words and phrases expressing quantity**. Be careful with positives and negatives.

1  *A fairly large number of* people seem to be shopping at the new supermarket. **few**

........................................................

2  I spend *much less* money on groceries *than* she does. **nearly**

........................................................

3  Of all the stereo systems we have seen, this one is *easily the best*. **far**

........................................................

4  These two brands of ketchup are *almost the same*. **hardly**

........................................................

**5**  In this exercise, the sentences test your knowledge of **idiomatic expressions**.

1  I *suddenly* decided to take the bus home. **spur**

........................................................

2  The pickpocket appeared and *very suddenly* my wallet was gone. **flash**

........................................................

3  *I won't settle for anything less than* an exotic foreign holiday. **set**

........................................................

4  When he was lecturing us on our bad behaviour, I found it *difficult not to smile*. **face**

........................................................

**6**  As in the exam, the sentences in this exercise test your knowledge of a range of different language features.

1  Petrol catches fire very easily, so you mustn't smoke while filling your car. **highly**

........................................................

2  Would it bother you if I brought a friend with me to dinner? **put**

........................................................

3  It was only with the greatest difficulty that I could understand what he was saying. **virtually**

........................................................

4  When times are hard, we ought to think a little about the old and unemployed. **spare**

........................................................

5  I cannot understand why she needs so desperately to be popular. **craving**

........................................................

6  When we later returned to the shop, the manager was nowhere to be seen. **sign**

........................................................

7  Ten years ago this shop's profit was half of what it is today. **doubled**

........................................................

8  Can you check on my children while I go to the shops? **eye**

........................................................

9  A fight broke out almost immediately at the start of the match. **sooner**

........................................................

10  She was only thinking of your safety when she asked you to leave. **heart**

........................................................

☑  **2**  When you have checked your answers to Exercise 1, analyse any errors you made. Did you miss:

- a change of tense?
- the form of the key word (e.g. noun/verb)?
- a necessary dependent preposition?
- where an opposite or negative was necessary?
- a change of the form of a word (e.g. noun to adjective)?
- a phrasal verb or fixed expression?

# Grammar review: determiners and substitution

**Watch Out!** *problem areas*

- **the**

  The war is a terrible thing. It brings the terrible hardship to the people involved. ˰*The* Second World War is a prime example of this.

  ˰*The* computer has offered ˰*the* young all sorts of opportunities not available to their parents.

- **it and this**

  The photocopier has broken down again.

  *It* needs to be replaced. (= *the photocopier*) ✔

  *This* is bound to cause a lot of problems.

  (= *the breakdown*) ✔

  When referring to a previous sentence, *it* usually refers to the *subject* of that sentence. *This* usually refers to something *later* in the sentence.

  We can also use *this* to refer to an idea or to a *number* of things previously mentioned.

  There have been so many problems today. People shouting at each other, work piling up and customers complaining. All ~~these have~~ ˰*this has* been caused by the breakdown of the photocopier.

- **one(s)**

  Have you seen any good films recently? I saw ~~one really good film~~ ˰*a really good one* yesterday.

  Old people spend less money on clothes than young ~~ones~~ ˰*people*. (*or the young*)

  I couldn't find the new chair I wanted, so I bought several second-hand *ones* from the market. ✔

- **that and those**

  *The one* and *the ones* are often replaced by *that* and *those*.

  The book I'm reading now is far better than *the one/that* which I struggled to finish last month. ✔

  The books I bought in Germany are more useful than *the ones/those* I found in France. ✔

**1** Fill each of the gaps in the following sentences with one or more words from the box below. You do not need to use all the words, but you can use some words more than once.

| do | did | done | each | every | one | some |
|----|-----|------|------|-------|-----|------|
| none | so | both | either | neither | all | such |

1 James Joyce and T.S. Eliot are undoubtedly great writers, but ............. is easy to read.

2 Some of the films at the festival were very good, but ............. were outstanding.

3 John eventually got promoted, but he still isn't sure how he managed to ............. it.

4 A number of the students had a bit of a close shave, but ............. achieved a pass grade.

5 Did you like the film? You must be very sentimental if you .............!

6 When the customers entered the shop, ............. was given a questionnaire to complete.

7 She hurled the family china to the floor, shrieking as she .............

8 Alex is thinking of starting his own business – at least, he told me ............. last month.

**2** **Use of English:** guided cloze

Fill each of the gaps in the following passage with **one** suitable word. Most, but not all, of the words you need are **articles**, **determiners** or **reference words**.

## The value of marketing

When someone sees a new food product for sale in the supermarket, (1) ............. decision whether or not to buy (2) ............. depends on various factors. Among the most important of (3) ............., of course, are price and packaging. It is obvious that (4) ............. highly-priced product will not sell well. If a consumer is (5) ............. with two different brands of baked beans, one of which is twice as expensive as the other, he will probably choose (6) ............. which is cheaper. Nowadays, economic recession has made people even more reluctant to buy what (7) ............. be thought of as luxury items. Interestingly, however, (8) ............. is strong evidence to suggest that if the price of (9) ............. product is too low, the effect on sales will be the same. (10) ............. simply makes no difference whether the product is top quality or not. The public will not buy something it (11) ............. to be too cheap. Inevitably, (12) ............. comes as a surprise to most people, but market research has shown (13) ............. to be true. (14) ............. goes without saying that the colour and the quality of the packaging also (15) ............. a vital role in the success or failure of a new product. For example, people tend to opt (16) ............. brands of frozen vegetables in green or blue packets rather than (17) ............. packaged in red or yellow. The implications of all (18) ............. are obvious: it is essential that manufacturers and advertisers research the (19) ............. carefully before they (20) ............. a new product.

# Listening: note-taking

### About the exam

You may find in **Paper 4** that you are given headings and other notes to complete as you listen to a lecture or a talk. The information you need to listen for is usually factual and relates to the main points made by the speaker. You only need to write a few words each time – **not complete sentences**. As with the other listening tasks, the recording will be played twice.

### Exam Strategy

- Look at the incomplete notes and think carefully about the kind of information you are listening for (a name, a date, a verb form, etc.).
- The first time you listen to the recording fill in those parts you are sure of.
- When you hear the recording the second time, check what you have already written and fill in the remaining parts of the notes.
- Check the grammar, punctuation and spelling of what you have written carefully.

You will hear an interview in which a psychologist talks about the ways some big fashion stores encourage customers to spend money on clothes. Before listening, read the notes and try to predict the type of information missing. Then listen and for questions 1–10, complete the notes with a word or short phrase. Listen to the recording twice.

---

_Shop entrance_
Customer immediately notices:
- [_____1_____]
- [_____2_____]

_To the right of shop entrance_
Customer finds:
- most expensive clothes here
- [_____3_____] assistant
- clothes [____4____]
  carelessly on tables

_Central part of shop_
Customer moves along route known as

[_____5_____]

Accessories and rotating displays attract
  customer's attention

_Back of shop_
Customer drawn into areas known as
[_____6_____] spots
Two ways of achieving this:
- position of [_____7_____]
- display of bargains

_Changing rooms_
- Mirrors – make customer look tanned and
  [_____8_____]

- Make-up available
- Easy chairs
- Style consultants to give help and advice

_Other features of shop_
- Large amount of space
  Reason: sign of quality or luxury
- Use of particular colours
  Reason: [_____9_____]
- Use of particular smells
  Reason: [_____10_____]

# Grammar: structures with *it*

> **Watch Out!** *problem areas*
>
> - **it + adjective**
>   It must be difficult *to know* what brand of detergent to buy. ✔
>   It's amazing *that* she left the shop without paying. ✔
> - ***should***
>   *Should* can be used when referring to things which are important or must be done.
>   It is essential *that you (should)* do exactly what I say. ✔
>   It is also used to describe personal reactions.
>   It is amazing *that he should* speak to you like that. ✔
> - **sentence transformations**
>   She'll probably be late. = It's probable *that* she'll be late. (= *more formal*)
>   He's unlikely *to* arrive on time. = It's unlikely *that* he'll arrive on time.
>   We had difficulty *paying* the rent last week. = We found it difficult *to pay* the rent last week.
>   There's no point (in) *asking* her for help. = It's no use *asking* her for help.

**Use of English:** guided sentence transformations
Finish each of the following sentences in such a way that it is as similar as possible in meaning to the sentence printed before it. In this exercise you have been given the beginning and ending of each sentence to help you.

1 Nobody is expected to work during the lunch break.
There ........................ lunch break.
2 Her reluctance to take part in the event seemed rather strange to me.
I found it ........................ event.
3 The burglar appeared to have broken in through a window.
It looked ........................ window.
4 Your success or failure is of no interest to me.
It doesn't ........................ fail.
5 What time you decide to come to work is up to you.
I'll leave it ........................ work.

6 I'm surprised by the number of people who still believe whatever advertisements say.
It's ........................ say.
7 It seems futile for you to continue writing to him every week.
There ........................ to him every week.
8 Didn't you realise that he might be lying?
Didn't it ........................ the truth?

# Vocabulary: phrasal verbs and expressions: *set*

**1** Complete the sentences below with the correct form of *set up* or *set off*. Use a dictionary to help you if necessary.

1 It was six o'clock in the morning when we ............ for the monastery in the mountains.
2 One of the most memorable things which happened was when someone ............ a fire alarm by mistake and everyone rushed out of the hotel screaming.
3 The police have ............ road blocks everywhere in an attempt to catch the thieves.
4 She wore a black evening dress that ............ her pale complexion beautifully.
5 Could you come and help me ............ the video – I can't make head or tail of these instructions.
6 My wife and I are thinking of ............ a small business together.
7 The police were asking me lots of questions about something I knew nothing about. I think I've been ............
8 The officer in charge of the operation said that even someone slamming a door could ............ the bomb.

> **Study Tip**
>
> Some phrasal verbs have many meanings. Sometimes meanings change when the grammar is different (e.g. compare *set something up*, with *set somebody up*). Check typical contexts, grammar and usage in a good dictionary, and record example sentences like those in Exercise 1 in your notebook.

**2** Rewrite each of the following sentences using an expression with *set* and the word in brackets. Check these words in a dictionary if necessary. The sentences have been started for you.

1 I've never seen him before.
I've .............................................................. (eyes)

2 'I'll never enter this house again!' she screamed.
'Never .................................................... (foot)

3 She desperately wants to win the competition.
She's .................................................... (heart)

4 His ideas and habits are too fixed for him to cope with the changes.
He's too .............................................. (ways)

5 When I go to a restaurant I see the attentiveness of the waiters as being of prime importance.
When I go to a restaurant I ..................... (store)

## Vocabulary: connectors and adverbial phrases

In each of the following sentences, one or more of the words or phrases in italics is wrong. Decide which are **correct** and underline them.

1 *While/Despite/Even though* most people know that they have certain rights as consumers, very few people understand what these rights actually are.

2 Children are not usually taught about banking and insurance when they are at school. They are *thus/consequently/correspondingly* ill-equipped to deal with their money wisely when they grow up.

3 Passing lorries cause a lot of damage to roads in cities. *Also/Besides/Furthermore*, they shake and slowly destroy the foundations of old buildings.

4 *Since/Due to/Owing to* the lack of effective legislation controlling advertising, many companies still get away with misleading consumers about the qualities of their products.

5 People were not unwilling to support the new measures. *At least/As a matter of fact/Actually*, most people were extremely enthusiastic about them.

6 John told me that he was going to resign. *Or rather/At least/Besides*, that's what I thought he said – I might have been mistaken.

## Use of English: guided cloze

Fill each of the gaps in the following passage with **one** suitable word. Look again at Unit 1, page 13 for guidance on the best way to approach this task.

### The advertisers' challenge

Nowadays, it goes without (1) ............ that the success or failure of a new product depends, to a large (2) ............, on the ingenuity of the advertising campaign. In other (3) ............, money spent on advertising is preferable to money spent on efforts to improve the quality of the product. What exactly is it, (4) ............, that makes an advertisement 'ingenious'?

What (5) ............ innovations in packaging and product design, advertising as a 'science' has developed in leaps and (6) ............ over the past fifty years.

People have, (7) ............, become a lot more aware of advertising techniques and tricks. (8) ............, it is no longer enough to show men and women in white coats poring over microscopes or appearing in front of washing machines. (9) ............ is it enough to show photographs of Mrs X 'before and after'. (10) ............ the same token, advertisements which simply repeat the name of a product over and over again, or which play on people's feelings of guilt, are regarded as being rather old-fashioned these days. What is (11) ............, certain types of advertisement are no longer acceptable. Those which are thought to encourage anti-social or racist (12) ............, for instance, have been (13) ............ in many countries.

One of the problems (14) ............ face nowadays is that consumers are more sophisticated and demanding than they were in the past. They face the challenge of (15) ............ to promote products which are probably identical to an enormous number of others on the market. As a consequence, advertising agencies have to find ways to make the item they are promoting unique in (16) ............ way or other, or to create a particular image or association for that item. In the (17) ............ of modern advertising, it is essential to create an 'atmosphere' around a product which will (18) ............ to the consumer. (19) ............ is amazing, perhaps, is that (20) ............ the competition they face, advertisers can still find ways of making particular brand names seem more attractive than others.

# Writing: formal letter (complaint)

### About the exam

In **Paper 2** you may be asked to write a formal letter. There are many different types of formal letter and the exam question will give you an outline of the situation. You are expected to write **only 300** words for this task. This is because the examiner expects you to **spend longer on your planning** and organisation, to create a letter which is appropriate in style and content for the purpose outlined in the exam question.

### Exam Strategy

- Consider **who your reader is**, and **why you are writing**.
- Make an outline of what you need to say. Include the structures and vocabulary you intend to use **at the planning stage**. Check your outline against the task before you start writing.
- Check your letter for **register** and **style** as well as grammar, punctuation and spelling.

## 1

1   The following sentences come from a formal letter. Read them quickly to establish the situation: the writer of the letter, who the letter is written to, and the reason for writing. Make a note of these details in your notebook.

1   Had I known that the food and service in your restaurant would be so unsatisfactory, I would never have considered taking my wife there.

2   From the outset we were treated with indifference by the waiters who 'served' us.

3   I am writing to complain about the quality of service at your restaurant in Oxford Street.

4   Unless I receive an apology and some form of compensation, you will be hearing from the Association of Restaurants in due course.

5   To add insult to injury, the waiter insisted that the misunderstanding had been our fault.

6   Disgusted by the standard of the service, and not expecting the quality of the food to improve, I decided it was time for us to leave.

7   Surely the wine waiter should be able to open a bottle of wine correctly?

## 2

2   The list a)–g) below contains the functions you might need to use to write a successful letter of complaint. Match each function to one of the sentences 1–7 from Exercise 1 and write the number of the sentence in the space provided. One has been done for you as an example.

a) stating your reason for writing ......

b) mentioning the first in a list of complaints ......

c) asking a rhetorical question ..7..

d) mentioning something which was 'the last straw' ......

e) describing your response to the situation ......

f) expressing 'hindsight' (the wisdom of experience) ......

g) making a threat/demanding action ......

## 3

3   The following sentences are from a different letter of complaint. Rewrite each of them in such a way that the new sentence is as similar as possible in meaning to the original. In this exercise, you have been given both the beginning and the ending of the new sentence, and your changes should make the register **more formal**.

1   I visited your shop because I wanted to return a faulty mini CD player.
    My purpose ........................ a faulty mini CD player.

2   I was offended more by the attitude of the young man than by what was said.
    It was not so much ........................ of the young man.

3   I would have asked from the start to see the manager, if I had known I would be treated like this.
    Had ........................ to see the manager.

4   I'm writing to complain about the way the staff behaved in your shop.
    I am writing ........................ of the staff at your shop.

5   She seemed to find the whole situation amusing, and it was also obvious she didn't intend to do anything about it.
    Not ........................ intention of doing anything about it.

6   As far as these two members of staff are concerned, I want you to tell me what action you will take.
    I would like you to inform ........................ regard to these two members of staff.

7   I asked whether they could give me a cash refund.
    I asked ........................ be possible.

8   If inadequate action is taken, I shall be forced to publish this letter.
    Unless ........................ option but to publish this letter.

**4**   The sentences in Exercise 3 come from a composition written in answer to the following task.

> You were badly treated by the staff of a shop recently when you tried to return an item you had bought in a sale there. Write to the manager of the shop to complain, explaining what happened and what you would like her to do about it. (About 300 words.)

Read the composition below. Identify the sentences from Exercise 3 and check if your rewritten versions are correct. Ignore the numbered gaps for the moment.

Dear Madam

I am writing to complain about the behaviour of the staff at your shop last Thursday morning, 12th July.

My purpose in visiting the shop was to return a faulty mini CD player which I had bought the previous week in the sale.

(1) ............ the rather surly tone of voice of the young man who served me, I explained why I was returning the mini CD player and asked whether a cash refund would be possible. You can imagine my anger and amazement when he snatched the mini CD player out of my hands and walked away without saying a word. (2) ............, he told me in no uncertain terms that a cash refund was out of the question. He then walked away again, leaving the mini CD player on the counter.

Had I known that I would be treated like this, I would have asked from the start to see the manager. It was not so much what was said that offended me, as the attitude of the young man. (3) ............, I was treated with the same indifference by another member of staff. When I asked this assistant for the name of the first young man, she simply laughed. Not only did she seem to find the whole situation amusing, but it was obvious that she had no intention of doing anything about it. (4) ............, I decided to leave the shop immediately.

I feel that I must protest about such appallingly rude behaviour towards a regular customer of yours. Would a letter of apology be too much to expect? (5) ............, I would like you to inform me of the action you will take with regard to these two members of staff, and what you propose to do about the faulty mini CD player. Unless adequate action is taken, I shall have no other option but to publish this letter in the local newspaper.

I look forward to hearing from you.

Yours faithfully

Ronald Scott

**5**   Look at the numbered gaps in the letter. Choose the best word or phrase, **A**, **B** or **C**, to fill each gap.

1   **A**   Ignoring
    **B**   Having ignored
    **C**   On ignoring

2   **A**   Returning
    **B**   On returning
    **C**   Returned

3   **A**   To make matters worse
    **B**   To mention another matter
    **C**   As a matter of fact

4   **A**   Quite unexpectedly
    **B**   Somewhat reluctantly
    **C**   Not surprisingly

5   **A**   Last but not least
    **B**   To say the least
    **C**   At the very least

**6**   Read the following task and write a letter of complaint, including as many as possible of the elements from Exercise 2 and language from Exercises 3–5, where appropriate.

> A holiday you had arranged to go on was cancelled at the last moment. When you went to the travel agency to ask for your deposit back, the person you spoke to was rude and unhelpful. Write to the manager of the travel agency to complain about the behaviour of this employee, explaining the situation and what you expect the travel agency to do. (About 300 words.)

**7**   Exchange your letter with another student if you can. Evaluate each other's work and suggest improvements.

# 5 Tough justice

## Reading: non-fiction

### About the exam

**Paper 1** multiple-choice questions require you to think about:
- the main idea of the text
- details which support the main idea
- the purpose of the passage and the writer's message and attitude.

**1** The following text considers the place and purpose of punishment in British society. Read through the text quickly, to match each paragraph to one of the topics **A–E**.

**A** The need to review the system of punishment. (para. ...)

**B** How imprisonment is a form of punishment. (para. ...)

**C** The disadvantages of imprisonment. (para. ...)

**D** The justification for punishment. (para. ...)

**E** The purpose of imprisonment. (para. ...)

Punishment is a complex concept which arouses great emotion. It involves the infliction of pain on one person by another. This pain is usually
5 justified on the grounds that the first person has been guilty of some wrong-doing and that the second has a legal or moral right to respond by inflicting punishment. The right to
10 inflict pain in this way comes, it is argued, from the authority of one party in relation to another, whether it be parent to child, teacher to pupil or judge to offender. It is generally
15 accepted that any such punishment should be proportionate to the wrong which has been done.

The emotion surrounding this subject arises when one begins to
20 consider the nature of punishment and the purpose which it is meant to achieve. It is an emotion which has loomed large in recent years, particularly when the discussion is
25 about the punishment which is to be meted out to those who have been found guilty of breaking the criminal law. The most extreme form of punishment which can be imposed in
30 British society is imprisonment. One oft-quoted aphorism is that 'People are sent to prison as punishment, not for punishment'. In other words, the punishment consists solely of being
35 deprived of liberty. The only

additional punishment should come about as a direct consequence of loss of liberty and not through any added penalties imposed by the prison
40 system, such as restriction of diet or prohibition of contact with family or insanitary living conditions.

This debate very quickly leads on to a discussion about the purpose of
45 punishment. If it is purely retributive, one can argue that conditions of imprisonment should be as punitive and restrictive as possible. But most commentators wish to add an element
50 of reform or rehabilitation to the concept of punishment. One of its consequences, they argue, should be that the person who is subjected to the punishment will be less likely to
55 commit further offences or crimes in the future and will be helped to lead a useful life in society. The change in behaviour will come about either because of the deterrent effect of the
60 punishment or because it has led the person being punished to a greater awareness of the need to live differently in the future. The judge, like the parent of the wayward child,
65 punishes an offender for his or her 'own good', in order to help the offender to become a better person.

The difficulty with this worthy ambition is that the British criminal
70 justice system finds it very difficult to

cope with such complex objectives. The offender who goes to prison regards imprisonment primarily as retributive and is not convinced by
75 arguments about their potential for rehabilitation. The victim of the original offence is likely to be confused by a series of mixed messages about how he or she is
80 meant to benefit from the outcome of court proceedings. The public is at best ambivalent – unsure, that is, as to whether the process of justice is working or not. One of the unfortunate
85 results of this confusion is that all parties are left dissatisfied and in a state of ambivalence about the whole system.

As we begin a new century, it may
90 be that the time has come to review the place of punishment in society. In particular, we need to consider the extent to which any criminal justice process is used as a means of repairing
95 the harm which has been done by one individual to another. Certainly, this process is probably best equipped to deal with extreme acts of violence or breach of trust. However, there are
100 already a number of successful examples, both in Britain and internationally, of forms of justice in lieu of imprisonment which better meet the needs of the victim, of the
105 offender and of society.

## Exam Tip!

Try to deduce the meaning of difficult words **only** if you need them to help you to answer a question. For example, the words *arouses*, *loomed* and *aphorism*, all in the text, are not needed for general understanding, or to answer the questions on the text successfully.

When you do need to deduce the meaning of a word to complete the task, use the whole paragraph to help you, not just the one sentence containing the word.

**2**   You will need to understand the following words and phrases in the questions and text in order to answer the questions below. Try to work out the meaning of each of the words from the context – many clues are provided. Look for:

• a definition
• an example that makes the meaning clear
• repeated use of the word in other parts of the text
• words in the text that have a similar or opposite meaning.

1   infliction (line 3) ...........................................
(**HINT**: *This word appears in other parts of the first paragraph in verb form – inflict, inflicting. It collocates with both pain and punishment.*)

2   deprived (line 35) ...........................................
(**HINT**: *There is a word with a very similar meaning in the next sentence.*)

3   rehabilitation (line 50) ...................................
(**HINT**: *Look in the next sentence for a definition of this word, which relates to actions.*)

4   ambivalent (line 82) .......................................
(**HINT**: *This word occurs again as a noun in the last sentence of the paragraph. The prefix 'ambi-' (= both) may help you, together with the definition in lines 82–84.*)

5   parties (line 86) .............................................
(**HINT**: *This word obviously refers to people. You can work out its meaning by looking at the kinds of people mentioned in the paragraph as a whole.*)

6   in lieu (line 103) ...........................................
(**HINT**: *You will understand this if you speak French. If not, think about the meaning of the previous sentence and how the writer uses the connector 'however' to begin the sentence containing this phrase.*)

**3**   Find and underline the answers to these questions in the text.

1   How is the infliction of punishment usually justified?
2   How is prison generally seen to punish criminals?
3   What do most commentators see as the purpose of prison?
4   Why is the use of imprisonment unsatisfactory in many cases?
5   What changes does the writer want to see in the way criminals are punished?

**4**   Now read these possible answers to the questions in Exercise 3. In each case, tick the option which is closest to your answer, **A**, **B**, **C**, or **D**.

1   A   It is an ethical response to unacceptable behaviour.
    B   It is necessary in order to preserve people's authority.
    C   Society would collapse if people who broke the law were not punished.
    D   It is a natural emotional response to wrong-doing.

2   A   It imposes a variety of restrictions on them.
    B   It takes away their freedom.
    C   It makes them less likely to commit further offences.
    D   It does not allow prisoners contact with their families.

3   A   to be as punitive and as restrictive as possible
    B   to reform and rehabilitate prisoners
    C   to act as a deterrent against offending again
    D   to punish criminals and make them useful, honest citizens

4   A   Everyone involved is unsure of its value.
    B   The offender regards it only as a means of punishment.
    C   The victim receives no benefit from the punishment.
    D   The public doesn't trust the system to work.

5   A   the abandonment of prison as a form of punishment
    B   the introduction of alternative forms of justice for some crimes
    C   the opportunity given to criminals to repair the harm they have done
    D   the adoption of forms of justice which operate in other countries

# Grammar: modal verbs

> **Watch Out!** *problem areas* ←

- **must (have) and can't (have)**
  You ~~mustn't~~ ₍can't₎ have seen Anne yesterday –
  she's in America at the moment.
  You ~~can~~ ₍could/may/might₎ have seen her sister –
  she looks quite similar to Anne.

- **can and don't have to/don't need to/needn't**
  *Can* expresses freedom to do things we might
  choose to do, while *don't have to/needn't*
  expresses freedom from restrictions.
  In some open prisons, inmates *can* wear what
  they want. ✔
  They *don't have to/needn't* stay inside their cells all
  day if they don't want to. ✔

- **could(n't) (have) and might (not)(have)**
  The positive forms of *could* and *might* have very
  similar meanings.
  He *might* be guilty. = He *could* be guilty.
  But the negative forms have very different
  meanings.
  He *might not have* committed the crime.
  (= *I'm not sure if he did it or not*) ✔
  He *couldn't have* committed the crime.
  (= *I'm sure he didn't do it*) ✔

- **supposed to**
  I should do it. = *I'm supposed to* do it. ✔
  I shouldn't. = I ~~don't~~ ₍'m not₎ supposed to. ✔

- **could and was able to**
  We use *could* when talking about general ability
  in the past and *was able to* for specific success on
  one occasion.
  The robber *could* run like the wind (= *general
  ability*), and so he *was able to* escape (= *specific
  success on one occasion*) the policeman chasing
  him. ✔
  However, we use *couldn't* to express both general
  ability and specific failure on one occasion.
  The kidnapper *couldn't* read or write, so he
  couldn't make the ransom note himself, and had to
  get an accomplice to help. (= *general ability and
  specific failure*) ✔

**1  Use of English:** gapped sentences
Fill each of the gaps in the following sentences with a
suitable word or phrase.

1  How on earth ........................ told all those lies to
the police?

2  You ........................ sense than to buy that gold
watch from him. It's probably stolen.

3  The witness is almost blind, so he ........................
seen what happened.

4  The judge was satisfied with my written statement,
so I ........................ give evidence in person.

5  You ........................ trusted him if you gave him your
cheque book!

6  I wouldn't walk on those floorboards if I were
you – ........................ be safe.

**2  Use of English:** key word transformations

1  For each of the sentences below, write a new sentence
as similar as possible in meaning to the original sentence,
but using the word given in **bold**. **This word must not
be altered in any way**.

1  Although I should have telephoned my boss today,
I just didn't have time. **supposed**

........................................................................

2  Registration with the police was obligatory for us.
**were**

........................................................................

3  It was in your power to have him arrested for
behaving like that. **could**

........................................................................

4  It was remiss of you not to warn me that your
plane was delayed. **might**

........................................................................

5  Her trying to help was pointless, as they rejected
her suggestions. **bothered**

........................................................................

6  It was unnecessary for the robber to use the gun, as
the cashier handed over the money. **there**

........................................................................

7  Before I managed to ask him his name, he had left.
**was**

........................................................................

8  You don't have to stay here if you don't want to.
**under**

........................................................................

 2  When you have checked your answers to Exercise 2.1,
analyse any errors you made. Did you have to:

- use a passive form?
- find the right verb pattern to follow a noun or
  adjective?
- change from positive to negative, or negative to
  positive?

# Vocabulary: multiple-choice

**Paper 1, Section A**

### Exam Strategy

- Don't just put down the first one you see which looks right.
- Think about both meaning and grammar.
- Look for clues before and after the gap.
- Always guess if you're not sure. You don't lose marks for incorrect guesses.

**1**   Choose the word or phrase **A**, **B**, **C** or **D**, which best completes each sentence.

1   In this exercise, the sentences focus on words with **particular grammatical patterns**.

1   Did you hear that Robert has been ............. with illegal possession of firearms?
   **A** accused   **B** convicted   **C** arrested   **D** charged

2   The lack of evidence ............. me question the testimony of the police.
   **A** prompted   **B** caused   **C** forced   **D** made

3   The judge ............. the jury to take their time over reaching the verdict.
   **A** suggested   **B** advised   **C** demanded   **D** insisted

2   In this exercise, the sentences focus on **connectors** and **adverbial phrases**.

1   ............. the trial has finished, she is free to do whatever she wants.
   **A** Since when   **B** At last   **C** Now that   **D** Just now

2   The court accepted his evidence, ............. of his reputation as an unreliable witness.
   **A** even though   **B** besides   **C** in spite   **D** despite

3   ............., most of the crimes investigated by the police involve people in their twenties.
   **A** In retrospect   **B** By and large   **C** To a degree   **D** All things considered

**2**   In this exercise, as in the Proficiency exam, the sentences contain a mix of types of vocabulary.

1   Henricks is alleged to have ............. a number of serious crimes.
   **A** done   **B** made   **C** committed   **D** discharged

2   Many people thought that the sentence he received was unnecessarily ............. .
   **A** heavy   **B** strong   **C** big   **D** weighty

3   The defendant pleaded not guilty, claiming he had been ............. .
   **A** set up   **B** set down   **C** set off   **D** set to

4   He was caught ............. stealing money from the cash-box.
   **A** red-handed   **B** heavy-handed   **C** light-fingered   **D** heavy-set

5   You can't have burgled the house alone, so who was your ............. .
   **A** ally   **B** accomplice   **C** assistant   **D** associate

6   She will shortly ............. trial for the part she played in the recent robbery.
   **A** give   **B** perform   **C** make   **D** stand

7   Detectives are said to be ............. into the causes of the recent fire.
   **A** looking   **B** investigating   **C** checking   **D** searching

8   The villagers ............. the law into their own hands by organising armed patrols of the area.
   **A** took   **B** seized   **C** grabbed   **D** put

9   ............. the conflicting evidence, the court had no alternative but to acquit the leader of the gang.
   **A** By means of   **B** With a view to   **C** In view of   **D** In response to

10   The Prime Minister is currently ............. charges of corruption and perjury.
   **A** standing   **B** confronting   **C** facing   **D** undergoing

# Use of English: comprehension and summary

**Paper 3, Section B**

### About the exam

In **Paper 3, Section B** you normally have to answer eleven to fourteen comprehension questions about a passage of approximately 600 words, before writing a summary.

These questions usually focus on:
- the relationship between the main ideas and supporting detail
- the meanings of specific words or expressions
- what is implied in certain parts of the passage
- what pronouns such as *it* and *this* refer to in the passage.

43

### 1

1   In your notebook write a list of as many different ways of protecting your home against burglary as you can. Do they have any (dis)advantages?

2   Read the title of the following passage and predict what it will be about.

3   Now read quickly through the passage, which is designed to advise British homeowners about the police support and burglar alarms available to them. Make a quick note of the differences between the role played by alarms in Britain, and in your country.

# Modern technology comes to the aid of the British homeowner

For those who have suffered at the hands of burglars, it is usually a shattering experience. As well as losing valuables, there is the trauma of having had your home invaded, and often the loss of items of great sentimental value can be far more distressing than the theft of cash or
5   electrical goods.

Modern technology has come to the aid of the homeowner in the fight against crime, as ever more sophisticated devices are peddled to the security conscious. But do these alarms make much difference? Or is installing them, at best, no more than a self-deceptive gesture
10   towards peace of mind?

The police are strong advocates of alarms to protect against crime, and the first thing to do is to call in your local crime prevention officer for advice. Not all flats or homes would benefit from an alarm, and a crime prevention officer is among the best-placed to give you impartial
15   advice. What's more it's free.

One thing to keep in mind is that one of the biggest problems for the homeowner and the police is the 'false alarm' syndrome. Last year, a crackdown by the police was launched to combat this now endemic problem, which is the bane of many a street, with unwelcome alarms
20   more of a nuisance than a deterrent. Alarms should meet local environmental regulations on noise, and automatically switch off after 20 minutes.

The key to avoiding false alarms lies in the installation, and official police guidelines for registered companies to follow have been laid
25   down. For this reason 'do-it-yourself' kits are frowned on. But while the 'DIY' option is at the bottom end of the market, it can still have a deterrent effect.

Most alarm-systems rely on infra-red sensors which detect heat emissions. A burglar in the room should trigger them. But infra-red
30   sensors are extremely sensitive and changes in room heating can set them off, so they may have to be programmed precisely to your needs. You may want the alarm set automatically for the night time – in which case it should be set up to cope with someone getting up in the night to visit the kitchen without the entire system having to be shut
35   off and then reset.

The next step up is the alarm system connected to a monitoring station. Contrary to popular myth, such alarms are not connected directly to the police, but are monitored by private security companies. Here costs can escalate quite sharply. As well as an annual monitoring
40   fee, the company will often insist on twice-yearly service visits, for which it will also charge.

Finally there is an odd array of other hi-tech gadgets coming on to the market, designed to target the thief, though it's hard to know if any of these will bring home the goods in the long run. A smoke
45   system can emit clouds of dense but harmless smoke into a room where an intruder has been detected. Another system relies on miniature cameras to send photographs of any burglar back to the monitoring station. There is even one company which can install electric fencing, although this walks a fine line between the need to
50   protect your property and your duty to protect other people, be they trespassers or not, from coming to any harm.

**2**  Answer the following questions about the passage. In this exercise there are hints to help you, although you will get no extra help in the real exam.

1  In your own words, explain why losing valuables can be the least distressing aspect of burglary.

...........................................................................

(**HINT**: *You need to mention two things here.*)

2  Explain in your own words who is involved in the 'peddling' of sophisticated alarm systems (line 7).

...........................................................................

(**HINT**: *Look at the context – can you deduce the meaning of the unknown word? Rephrase the answer.*)

3  Explain in your own words how installing an alarm might be 'a self-deceptive gesture towards peace of mind' (line 9).

...........................................................................

(**HINT**: *Rephrase the words of the question. You may find it helpful to look at the previous sentence.*)

4  What is meant by the phrase 'strong advocates of alarms' (line 11)?

...........................................................................

(**HINT**: *Look at the whole sentence.*)

5  In your own words, explain why the police recently launched a crackdown.

...........................................................................

(**HINT**: *Look at the context to decide what a 'crackdown' is and what it was aiming to combat.*)

6  What were two results of the 'crackdown' by police referred to in line 18?

...........................................................................

(**HINT**: *You do not need to explain 'crackdown' – just look for two results.*)

7  What was the intention of laying down guidelines on the installation of alarms?

...........................................................................

(**HINT**: *Look at the first part of the sentence in which the word 'guideline' occurs. Use your own words.*)

8  Why might DIY alarm kits be 'frowned on' by police? (line 25)

...........................................................................

(**HINT**: *Think about what the previous sentence means. The phrase for this reason also helps here.*)

9  Explain in your own words what the disadvantages of infra-red alarm systems are.

...........................................................................

(**HINT**: *What follows the connector 'but'?*)

10  What do most people believe about alarms connected to a monitoring station?

...........................................................................

(**HINT**: *Look at the next sentence. Be careful to mention **only** what people believe.*)

11  Why might someone be reluctant to install an alarm system connected to a monitoring station?

...........................................................................

(**HINT**:*Look at what the writer says at the end of the paragraph.*)

**3**

1  Read the summary question below. Which paragraphs do you need to refer to for the summary? (paras. .............)

> In 60-80 words, summarise what the passage says about the devices available for protecting property and the disadvantages they may have.

2  Make notes of the information you need to include and write the first draft of your summary. Remember to use connectors and try not to use the same grammatical structures in each sentence. Look again at Unit 2, page 21, for guidance on methods of summary editing.

3  Read through the second draft of your summary and check for spelling, punctuation or grammatical mistakes.

# Writing: narrative composition (1)

**Paper 2**

### About the exam

In **Paper 2** you may have to write a narrative composition or story. You may be given the first line, the last line or the title.

### Exam Strategy

- Read the question and make notes. Think of an interesting beginning, and a clear, strong ending before you start. What background details will you have to supply to interest your reader?
- Include details which tell the reader how the main characters feel and react. Use a range of descriptive verbs, adjectives and adverbs, comparisons using *like* (+ noun) and *as if* (+ clause) and direct speech (but not too much!).

## 1

1 Read the composition below, which was written in answer to the following task.

> Write a story which finishes with the sentence:
> *He vowed that he would never take something which didn't belong to him again.* (About 350 words.)

2 Put paragraphs **A–E** in the correct order. Write your answers in the spaces provided.

**A** .............

*He didn't take the wallet out of his pocket and examine the contents until he had reached the safety of his bedroom. He gasped when he realised that there was probably more than £200 inside, in crisp, clean notes. He had never before seen so much money. Since his parents were not particularly well-off, he had always had to make do with just £5 pocket money a week. This money would make the motorbike he had been wanting to buy for the past couple of years a possibility. The smile which had appeared on his face faded rapidly, however, when he noticed the crumpled letter squashed next to the notes.*

**B** .............

*All he could say was, 'I've found your wallet. Tell me where you live and I'll bring it round.' He knew immediately that he had made the right decision and felt a wave a relief sweep over him. He stuffed the wallet back into his pocket and set off for the woman's house.*

**C** .............

*'Olga – here's a little present from me to give to Mum when she comes out of hospital. She'll be over the moon when you give it to her,' he read. He turned the letter over because he couldn't continue, then spotted a telephone number scrawled on the back. He felt the sweat on his face and hands suddenly turn cold. How could he possibly keep the money? There was only one thing to do. Picking up the telephone, Peter dialled the number and waited for what seemed like an eternity. Eventually a young woman picked up the phone.*

**D** .............

*That evening, after he had returned the wallet, he thought about the events of the day. He would never have been able to live with himself if he had kept the money! How fortunate that he had noticed the letter. He vowed that he would never take something that didn't belong to him again.*

**E** .............

*Peter's heart was thumping in his chest and the sweat was rolling down his face as he bent down to pick up the wallet from the pavement. He knew that what he was about to do was wrong, but he just couldn't help himself. He looked to the left and right to make sure that nobody was watching him, then snatched the wallet up, stuffed it into his pocket and walked away.*

**2** The following sentences summarise what the paragraphs of a good narrative should achieve, but they are in the wrong order. Match each paragraph of the story above to one of the summaries below. Write the letter of the paragraph in the correct box.

☐ involves a decision or turning point in the story

☐ develops the action further and moves towards the conclusion

☐ sets the scene of the story

☐ reflects on the events of the story as a whole, showing us the feelings and imagination of the main character

☐ gives the action an immediate background or context

**3** Match the structures with their function in a narrative. Use the story to help you.

| structure | function |
|---|---|
| 1 Past simple | setting the scene |
| 2 Past perfect | adding action to the story |
| 3 Hypothetical structures | providing background information |
| 4 Past continuous | reflecting on the action and its significance |

**4**

1 Read the outline of the composition below. Note how the student who wrote it made choices about the verb forms and vocabulary he wanted to use **at the planning stage**.

---

*Para. 1*
Peter sees wallet on pavement,
  (past cont. - sweat rolling, chest
    thumping = nervous)
picks it up, (snatch / stuff into
  pocket = excited) walks away.
Looking forward to going to party in the
evening.

*Para. 2*
At home, he looks at the contents.
  (gasp = amazed)
Finds £200  (crisp notes)
- motorbike now possible   (past perf. cont)
Notices letter.
  (crumpled, squashed - smile fades)
Remembers that he must write to his
grandmother.

*Para. 3*
Reads letter, sees telephone number.
  (rhetorical qu. how could he possibly …?)
Decides to return letter, so phones
woman, who sounds very busy.

*Para. 4*
Talks to woman on the phone.
  (wave of relief - right decision)
Goes to return the money - meets a friend
on the way.

*Para. 5*
Reflects on the events of the story.
  (would never have … live with himself)
Goes out to celebrate.

---

2 There are some details which are irrelevant to the action. Cross them out on the outline above.

**5** Parts of the composition he wrote could be improved and made more dramatic by varying the grammatical structures used. Rewrite the relevant parts in your notebooks.

1 Improve paragraph **E** by using a participle clause in one of the sentences.
2 Improve paragraph **A** by using inversions in two of the sentences.
3 Improve paragraph **C** by using a participle clause (starting with the verb *feel*) in one of the sentences.
4 Improve paragraph **D** by using an inverted third conditional.

**6** The composition is good because it contains a lot of 'vivid' and descriptive vocabulary. Find the words and phrases in the composition which mean:

1 beating loudly (para. E) .....................................
2 pushed quickly and carelessly (para. E) ....................
3 disappeared (para. A) .....................................
4 breathe in quickly, because surprised
   (para. A) .....................................
5 crushed and bent (para. A) .....................................
6 extremely happy (para. C) .....................................
7 written quickly and carelessly (para. C) ....................
8 a very long time (para. C) .....................................
9 noticed (para. C) .....................................
10 felt relieved (para. B) .....................................

**7**

1 Now write a complete composition using the following task and initial outline.

> Write a story which ends with the words: *Never again would she accept a gift without wondering where it had come from.* (About 350 words.)

---

*Outline*

man approached by a stranger in a café –
café best in town

stranger shows him some jewellery – he buys
a necklace

stranger also selling watches and cigarette
lighters

gives the necklace to his wife – wife already
has about twenty

wife puts away necklace for a few weeks –
then she wears it to a party

a friend recognises the necklace – stolen
recently in burglary, burglars also stole
wedding ring

---

2 Use your answers from Exercises 2–6 to improve the outline and write the composition.

**8** Exchange your complete outline and composition with another student if you can. Evaluate each other's work and suggest improvements.

# 6 Bright lights, big city

## Vocabulary review: multiple-choice

Choose the word or phrase, **A**, **B**, **C** or **D**, which best completes each sentence. In this exercise, all types of vocabulary are tested.

1  We followed a ............. street up to the walls of the castle overlooking the town.
   **A** turning  **B** curving  **C** winding
   **D** swirling

2  The Council's decision to allow traffic back into the old part of the town ............. to be a huge mistake.
   **A** turned out  **B** ended up  **C** came off
   **D** wound up

3  In the ............. of time, we'll get used to all the skyscrapers that have sprung up.
   **A** passage  **B** course  **C** flow  **D** path

4  The part of the city near the sea is ............. to flooding.
   **A** apt  **B** likely  **C** prone  **D** capable

5  This building ............. witness to the brilliance of the architect who designed it.
   **A** supports  **B** makes  **C** holds  **D** bears

6  The conservatism of many local people has been a major ............. block to the development of this town.
   **A** tripping  **B** staggering  **C** stumbling
   **D** slipping

7  Save for the ............. of a street lamp the alleyway was shrouded in darkness.
   **A** glow  **B** glitter  **C** sparkle  **D** flame

8  Traffic ............. in the centre is just one of the problems facing the town.
   **A** constipation  **B** congestion
   **C** conflagration  **D** contamination

9  Experts have been ............. the city's fourteenth century church for over five years.
   **A** renewing  **B** reclaiming  **C** reforming
   **D** restoring

10 I used to live in a small village on the West ............. of Scotland.
   **A** beach  **B** shore  **C** seaside  **D** coast

## Grammar: the passive

**Watch Out!** *problem areas*

- **avoiding continuous passive tenses**
  Continuous passive tenses are not incorrect, but sound 'clumsy', and so are often avoided.
  We will be ~~being~~ met in five minutes.
  ~~It will have been being done by Robert.~~ *Robert will have been doing it.*
  The town has been ~~being attacked~~ *under attack* for three days now.

- ***make* and *let***
  They made me do it. = I was made ˄*to* do it.
  They let me see her. = I was allowed to see her. ✔

- **sentence transformations**
  They heard him complain about the service at the restaurant. = He was heard ˄*to* complain about the service at the restaurant.
  Information about the hotel is available at the reception desk. = Information about the hotel ~~is found~~ *can be found* at the reception desk.
  New anti-pollution measures will be introduced next month. = Next month will ~~be~~ *see* the introduction of new anti-pollution measures.
  If we want to do something about the traffic problem, we should act now. = If the traffic problem is ˄*to be* resolved, we should act now.

**1  Use of English:** guided sentence transformations
1  Finish each of the following sentences in such a way that it is as similar as possible in meaning to the sentence printed before it. In this exercise, all the transformations require **passive forms**.

1  The mayor will present a prize to the best architect.
   The best architect ...........................................................

2  The police have arrested more drivers than usual this year for drunken driving.
   An increased ...........................................................

3  Chemical dust from nearby factories is slowly covering the town.
The town ..................................................................

4  The ban on smoking in the city's restaurants takes effect from next month.
Smoking is ..................................................................

5  Refusal to obey the local laws about noise in the street could lead to your arrest.
You ..................................................................

6  They insisted that he should fill in all the application forms again.
He ..................................................................

7  The completion of the project should have taken place last month.
The project was to ..................................................................

8  A quick solution to the housing problem is an urgent priority.
The housing problem needs ..................................................................

**2**  When you have checked the answers to Exercise 1.1, analyse any mistakes you made. Did you forget to:

- use the correct preposition?
- use *number* (not *amount*) for a plural countable noun?
- change the form of a word (e.g. noun to verb)?
- include all necessary auxiliaries?

**2  Use of English:** gapped sentences
Fill each of the gaps in sentences below with a suitable word or phrase.

1  The disused chimney ........................ up by demolition experts last week.
2  The decision whether or not to proceed with the plan ........................ by the end of today.
3  It was suggested that an attempt ........................ to save the old Town Hall building.
4  'Where's your daughter?' – 'She ........................ after at the day care centre today.'
5  Since we last met, another sentence ........................ to the contract, to avoid any possible misunderstanding.
6  Six months' free insurance ........................ in the purchase price.

**Exam Tip!**

Use passive forms in **Paper 2** discursive compositions, reports and formal letters to lend your writing an impersonal tone.

# Reading: non-fiction

**Paper 1, Section B**

**Exam Strategy**

In **Paper 1** there are four multiple-choice options for each question on the reading texts. Only one option is correct, while the other three are 'distractors'. When evaluating the options, look for:
- options which are not true, according to the text
- options which use similar words or phrases as those in the text, but have different meanings
- options which don't answer the question fully, although they may be true.

**1**

1  Read the following extract about the role of the architect in society, and answer this question: *In what way are architects different from painters and musicians?* Make a note of your answer.

..................................................................
..................................................................

It is the job of architects to create and shape the urban environment in which we live. For this reason, it is quite impossible to escape the products of their often fertile imaginations. Unlike other forms of artistic expression, such as painting or music, which are appreciated only by a select paying few in concert halls and galleries, the art of architects is all around us, demanding a response. You cannot simply leave the exhibition behind, disdainfully toss your programme into the litter bin, grumble about the nonsense of modern art – and go home to watch television. Because architects have built the world we live in. They are responsible for what we see and most likely hear every day of our waking lives.

**2** Now compare the answer you noted down for the question on page 49 with the following four multiple-choice options, **A–D**. Use the hints and questions below each option and the extract on page 49 to help you decide which option is correct, and which are 'distractors'.

**A** Their modern art is not considered to be 'nonsense'.
(**HINT**: *Look for the words 'modern art' and 'nonsense', and what these words refer to. Does this part of the text compare architects with painters and musicians?*)

**B** They often have fertile imaginations.
(**HINT**: *Look for the phrase 'fertile imaginations' and who it refers to. Is this phrase used to draw any comparisons between architects and other types of artist?*)

**C** Their artistic creations affect everybody.
(**HINT**: *Look for this phrase in the text – if you can't find the same words, can you find this idea expressed in different words? What is the relevance of the sentence about leaving an exhibition, throwing away the programme, etc? Which words, contrasting with 'everybody', does the text use to describe people who consume other types of art?*)

**D** Their art is not selected by a few paying consumers.
(**HINT**: *Look for the words 'select', 'few' and 'paying', and who these refer to. Do the words have the same meaning in the text as in the option?*)

**2** You're going to read an article written by Prince Charles, son of the British Queen, expressing his feelings about architecture in Britain today. Before reading, think of a city you have lived in, or know well, which has a number of modern buildings. How do you feel about them? Make a brief note of your thoughts. Now read the article and see if your views about modern architecture are similar to those of Prince Charles.

For far too long, it seems to me, some planners and architects have consistently ignored the feelings and wishes of the mass of ordinary people. Perhaps, when you think about it, it is hardly surprising, as architects tend to have been trained to design buildings from scratch – to tear down and rebuild. Consequently, a large number of people in Britain have developed a feeling that architects tend to design houses for the approval of fellow architects and critics, not for the tenants.

It has been most encouraging to see the development of Community Architecture as a natural reaction to the policy of decamping people to new towns and overspill estates where the extended family patterns of support were destroyed, and the community life was lost. Now we are seeing the gradual expansion of housing co-operatives, particularly in the inner-city areas of Liverpool, where the tenants are able to work with an architect of their own who listens to their comments and their ideas and tries to design the kind of environment they want.

This sort of development, spearheaded as it is by such individuals as Rod Hackney and Ted Cullinan – a man after my own heart, as he believes strongly that the architect must produce something that is visually beautiful as well as socially useful – offers something very promising in terms of inner-city renewal and urban housing, not to mention community garden design.

What I believe is important about Community Architecture is that it has shown 'ordinary' people that their views are worth having; that architects and planners do not necessarily have the monopoly of knowing best about taste, style and planning. On that note, I can't help thinking how much more worthwhile it would be if a community approach could be used in more new projects in London.

It would be a tragedy if the character and skyline of this capital city were to be further ruined, and St Paul's dwarfed, by yet another giant glass stump in Trafalgar Square, better suited to downtown Chicago than the City of London. It is hard to believe that before the last war, London must have had one of the most beautiful skylines of any great city, if those who recall it are to be believed.

Those who do, say that the affinity between buildings and the earth, in spite of the City's immense size, was so close and organic that the houses looked almost as though they had grown out of the earth, and had not been imposed upon it – grown moreover, in such a way that as few trees as possible were thrust out of the way.

What, then, are we doing to our capital city now? What have we done to it since the bombing during the Second World War? What are we shortly to do to one of its most famous areas – Trafalgar Square?

Instead of designing an extension to the elegant façade of the National Gallery, which complements it and continues the concept of columns and domes, it looks as if we may be presented with a kind of municipal fire station, complete with the sort of tower that contains the siren. I would understand better this type of high-tech approach if you demolished the whole of Trafalgar Square and started again with a single architect responsible for the entire layout, but what is proposed is like a monstrous carbuncle on the face of a much-loved and elegant friend.

Apart from anything else, it defeats me why anyone wanting to display the early Renaissance pictures belonging to the Gallery should do so in a new gallery so manifestly at odds with the whole spirit of that age of astonishing proportion. Why can't we have those curves and arches that express feeling in design? What is wrong with them? Why has everything got to be vertical, straight, unbending, only at right angles – and functional? As Goethe once said, 'there is nothing more dreadful than imagination without taste.'

**3** Read the following questions and unfinished statements about the passage. In each case, choose the answer, **A**, **B**, **C** or **D**, which you think fits best according to the passage.

1 Why do modern architects frequently ignore the wishes of ordinary people?
   A They do not care about what ordinary people think or want.
   B They have not been trained properly.
   C They have been taught to design new buildings to replace older ones.
   D They are interested only in impressing fellow-architects.
2 How does the writer explain the development of Community Architecture?
   A People did not like living on camp sites while their new homes were built.
   B As an objection to the disruption of families and communities.
   C People have designed the environment they want.
   D People tried it out in Liverpool and it was seen to be very successful.
3 Community Architecture has shown that
   A ordinary people's ideas are worth more than those of architects.
   B ordinary people should always be consulted by architects.
   C architects should not have monopolies.
   D architects are not the only ones with good design ideas.
4 How was pre-war architecture in London different from modern architecture?
   A Many people recall it as being beautiful.
   B Environmentally-friendly building materials were used.
   C Trees were planted around houses.
   D Houses blended in with the surroundings.
5 The writer would prefer Trafalgar Square to
   A have new architecture in harmony with existing buildings.
   B be left completely untouched by new architecture.
   C be re-designed entirely by one architect.
   D have more curves and arches than it currently does.
6 In general, what are the writer's views about architects?
   A They should be controlled by local communities.
   B They should be more sensitive to the environment and to people's wishes.
   C They should look to the Renaissance for inspiration when they design buildings.
   D They should avoid the use of concrete and glass.

**4** The writer of the passage uses several words **metaphorically**.

1 Which verb in paragraph 3 suggests 'leading a purposeful attack'?
2 Which verb in paragraph 5 emphasises the idea of something being very small next to something very big?
3 Which noun in paragraph 5 is used to suggest that a building is short and ugly, and appears to have been cut off, or not allowed to grow naturally?
4 Which adjective in paragraph 6 suggests that pre-war houses grew out of the ground like plants?

# Grammar plus: relative clauses

**1** **Use of English:** guided cloze

Fill each of the gaps in the following passage with one suitable word. Some, but not all, of the missing words are parts of **relative clauses** or **participle clauses**.

# Highs and lows of city life

In many countries of Europe there has been a steady drift of people away from villages to large cities. These people, many of (1) ............ have grown up in great poverty and deprivation, hope to improve their standard of (2) ............., and see the metropolis as the answer to all their (3) ............. . In many ways, they find what they are looking for. Large cities do offer a huge number of facilities, (4) ............ which better education, better health care and improved housing are perhaps the most important. Large companies and factories, the vast (5) ............ of which pride themselves on looking after the interests of their (6) ............, open huge numbers of career opportunities for those (7) ............ to work hard, and the money (8) ............ from hours of hard toil can be happily spent in huge supermarkets and chain-stores, (9) ............ people of modest means to steadily improve the material quality of their lives. Inevitably, (10) ............, there comes a time when people begin to yearn for the simplicity and natural lifestyle of the village or small town. They become aware of the problems of big city life.

Traffic problems and pollution, (11) ............ of which affect most large cities today, cause the most unhappiness. For people (12) ............ whom fresh air, unpolluted water and beautiful countryside are distant, (13) ............ none-the-less clear, memories of a previous, peaceful life in a village, the city must at (14) ............ feel unbearable. The pressure of overpopulation has meant that, in the last thirty or forty years, thousands (15) ............ thousands of new (16) ............ of flats have been (17) ............, often with (18) ............ regard for architectural beauty, and the surrounding countryside has (19) ............ but disappeared in many cases. It is no (20) ............ such an easy matter to escape the noise and turmoil of the streets and find a field or a forest where adults can relax and children can play in safety.

**2** **Where possible**, shorten the following sentences, using participle clauses instead of relative clauses, or by omitting relative pronouns.

1 People who work in large cities often long to escape from 'the rat race'.
2 Most houses which were built more than a hundred years ago have problems with damp.
3 The tram starts from the castle, which is the oldest surviving building in the town.
4 The house which I lived in as a child has just been knocked down.
5 The City Council, which is well known for its radical ideas, recently developed this dock area.
6 Visitors who are caught taking photographs inside the church are usually asked to leave.
7 The mosaic was discovered by workmen who were digging in the street.
8 The square is surrounded by old buildings, which are now on the verge of collapse.
9 The river which flows through the town centre is liable to flood in winter.
10 The man who I have been talking to used to live in this neighbourhood.

# Listening: multiple-choice

## About the exam

In **Paper 4** you may have to answer multiple-choice questions. These test your understanding of factual details, abstract ideas and the opinions of the speakers. They follow the order of the information in the passage, although the final question may be about the passage as a whole. You will hear the recording twice.

## Exam Strategy

- Read the questions and multiple-choice options before listening. Sometimes, a number of options seem to mean similar things. It is vital to notice the differences between them before you listen.
- The first time you listen, eliminate those answers you are sure are wrong.
- Sometimes there are questions about a speaker's feelings. Pay careful attention to the way the speaker talks, as well as to what they actually say.

**1**   You will hear three people talking about their reactions to a council proposal to pedestrianise the centre of the town where they live. Listen to their comments about the proposal and decide how each speaker feels. Choose one adjective for each speaker.

| | | | |
|---|---|---|---|
| enthusiastic | bitter | indifferent | overjoyed |
| depressed | concerned | aggressive | resigned |
| | determined | confused | |

1 is ............   2 is ............   3 is ............

**2**   Now you will hear a journalist conducting a short interview on the same topic. Read question 1 and the multiple-choice options which follow it. Options **B, C** and **D** contain statements, shown in **bold**, which can't all be true. Listen carefully and decide which option is correct.

1   How does the young man account for the traffic problem in the town centre?
   A   An increased number of lorries are passing through the town.
   B   People are lazy and **want to use their cars** for even the shortest journey.
   C   People are **forced to** drive into town because there are **no buses**.
   D   People **rely on their cars** rather than the **infrequent bus service**.

**3**   You will now hear all the interviews conducted by the journalist. Before listening, read the following questions, note the number of people you will hear, and make sure you understand the differences between the multiple-choice options for each question.

Now listen to the recording and for each of the following questions, choose which of the alternatives **A, B, C** or **D**, is the most appropriate response. Listen to the recording twice.

2   The young man believes that pedestrianising the centre will mean the Council will have to
   A   do nothing more at all.
   B   build a modern bypass.
   C   provide a tram service.
   D   divert traffic to existing roads.
3   According to the older man, what does the city centre lack at present?
   A   trees and vegetation
   B   a main square
   C   public works of art
   D   historic buildings
4   The Gregory Building
   A   is situated on the High Street.
   B   is a rather unusual shape.
   C   has been the Post Office since the 1940s.
   D   was built in the nineteenth century.
5   What is the woman's main concern about the Council's plan?
   A   She may have to sell her shop.
   B   Shops will lose the custom of people who are travelling through the town.
   C   Local people will go to other towns to do their shopping.
   D   The restoration of old buildings will cause disruption.
6   The woman's tone is
   A   resigned.
   B   aggressive.
   C   determined.
   D   sarcastic.
7   Overall, the journalist found people's opinions
   A   predictable.
   B   uninteresting.
   C   informative.
   D   shocking.

# Writing: formal letter (2)

### Study Tip

To write successfully, you need to be aware of the **register, or degree of formality**, of the words you use. When you write a letter, being either too informal or too formal can make you seem aggressive, disrespectful or unnatural. The main factors which affect formality are **your status as the writer** (as a customer, an employee, or the manager of a restaurant, secretary of a club, etc.), and the **status of the reader of your letter** (an editor, a councillor, a manager, etc.). Think of this issue first when planning how formal your letter should be.

Add notes about the formality of new words and expressions when you record them in your notebook, and keep phrases of a similar register together, grouped under composition types.

The exercises in this section are designed to help you to recognise the formality of different structures and expressions, to think about how tone affects register, and to create vocabulary records which you can refer to when writing letters.

**1** Read the following reasons for writing a letter. Decide what register would be most appropriate and mark each one **I** (informal and personal), **N** (neutral, polite and not really personal) or **F** (for very formal, impersonal letters).

Reasons for writing:
1 to complain to the train company about a train which was three hours late
2 to make suggestions to the local Council about spending on leisure facilities
3 to congratulate a close colleague on her new baby
4 to recommend your area for a newspaper feature on local history
5 to ask for a refund after a disastrous holiday
6 to congratulate your town council on improvements made to a local service
7 to explain to parents why your theatre club's trip to an adult play is unsuitable for their young child
8 to apologise to a furious customer who had a miserable stay in your hotel
9 to apologise for missing a friend's wedding
10 to demand an explanation from your local council for noisy roadworks in your street.

## 2

**1** Read the following list of phrases, and put them into pairs which mean approximately the same thing. Record these pairs in your notebook.

1 I feel you should be aware that …
2 Unless I hear from you in the coming week, I shall be obliged to …
3 I thought you might like to know that …
4 I am writing to express my feelings about …
5 If you have difficulty in finding …
6 I look forward to your early reply.
7 Should you be unable to locate …
8 It would be helpful if you could send me information about …
9 Looking forward to hearing from you soon.
10 I am writing to pass on my response to …
11 I would be most grateful for details of …
12 If you don't get in touch, I will have to …

**2** Now decide which phrase in each pair is the more formal, and underline it.

**3** The following sentences could be used in a neutral letter. Rewrite them more formally, using the word given in brackets. Remember that this means changing both the vocabulary and structures. The beginning of the new sentence is given to help you.

1 I shall do anything which is needed to solve this problem.
Whatever measures …………………… (taken)
2 Unfortunately, I can't see my lawyer next week.
I regret that …………………… (unable)
3 If you won't co-operate, I shall have to consult your manager.
Should you refuse to co-operate, …………………… (alternative)
4 I'm writing to you because I think the action you are planning is disgusting.
I am writing to you to express …………………… (propose)
5 Nobody should let this situation get any worse than it already is.
This situation should …………………… (further)
6 I don't really believe you are being sincere.
I have serious …………………… (about)
7 We should be trying extremely hard to prevent such situations from developing.
We should be making …………………… (every)
8 I will be at home all weekend, if you need to get in touch with me.
Should …………………… (wish)

**4**

1   Read the following writing task.

> The Planning Committee of your local council has caused considerable controversy recently by granting permission for a large hypermarket to be built on the outskirts of your town. Write to the council to express your concern about what they plan to do, explaining the effect the hypermarket would have on the community and the environment, and outlining what action you are prepared to take. (About 300 words.)

2   Now read the following letter, which was written by a student in answer to the task. The underlined parts are too informal and make the register inconsistent. Rewrite these parts using more formal expressions, and making any other necessary changes.

Dear Sir
(1) _I am writing to you because I am really worried about_ the proposals for building a hypermarket on the outskirts of the town.
(2) _As I am sure you know_, the proposed hypermarket would totally change the character of the town. It is almost certain that small local shops (3) _couldn't_ compete with such an enormous enterprise and, as a result, would be forced to close down. (4) _You can't let this happen._ Many of us would miss the personal service offered by these smaller businesses, and resent the fact that we would now be expected to travel more than four kilometres to do our shopping. What would happen to those people who do not own a car?
This area is famed for its natural beauty. It is an area of abundant wildlife and a popular weekend destination for both visitors to the town and local people. I am amazed that you could even have considered siting the hypermarket here. Surely we should be (5) _trying hard to_ protect the countryside rather than destroying it?
(6) _I am not at all sure that this project would benefit_ the community. Were you to go ahead with the building of the hypermarket the damage both to local people and to the environment would be enormous.
(7) _If you decide to_ ignore the opposition of a large number of local people to this scheme, then (8) _we shall have to_ take the matter higher. Many of us are already considering bringing legal action against the council's Planning Committee. We shall also organise demonstrations and (9) _do whatever else we have to_, to prevent the hypermarket from being built.
I look forward to hearing from you.
Yours faithfully
Andreas Papadopoulos

(287 words)

**5**

1   Now write a letter in response to the following task.

> The local authorities are considering demolishing a number of historic buildings in your town, suggesting that a large car park might be more useful. Many people think this would be a disastrous mistake. Write a letter to the authorities outlining your concerns and suggesting what else could be done with the buildings. (About 300 words.)

2   To help you get started, read these comments, which were made by local residents.

> Those buildings date from the seventeeth century!

> They're a tourist attraction, even though they're empty.

> A car park would be so ugly. What about the pollution?

> How about restoring them and turning them into a museum?

> They could offer them to local artists, to use as studios and put on exhibitions.

**6**   Exchange your letter with another student if you can. Evaluate each other's work and suggest improvements.

## Vocabulary review: multiple-choice

> **Paper 1, Section A**

Choose the word or phrase **A**, **B**, **C** or **D** which best completes each sentence.

1 Scientists are amazed at the sheer ............. of the animal kingdom.
   **A** division **B** divinity **C** diversity
   **D** diversion

2 The ............. of poisonous gases into the atmosphere is largely responsible for recent climatic changes.
   **A** emission **B** eviction **C** ejection
   **D** evacuation

3 The natural ............. of the bear in Greece is slowly being destroyed by man.
   **A** habitat **B** habitation **C** residence
   **D** lodging

4 Radioactive ............. is often dumped at the bottom of disused mine shafts.
   **A** rubbish **B** remnants **C** waste
   **D** left-overs

5 While diving, we encountered many large ............. of brightly-coloured fish.
   **A** herds **B** shoals **C** flocks **D** swarms

6 Doctors found several harmful ............. in the food of the local people.
   **A** intoxicants **B** nutrients **C** substances
   **D** solids

7 The polar ice ............. are slowly melting as a result of global warming.
   **A** caps **B** fields **C** regions **D** areas

8 Holes in the ozone ............. are thought to be increasing in size.
   **A** blanket **B** level **C** layer **D** cover

9 Much of the mineral wealth of Siberia has yet to be ............. .
   **A** exploded **B** exploited **C** excavated
   **D** exposed

10 The wound in his foot had not been dressed properly and quickly became ............. .
   **A** contaminated **B** polluted **C** infected
   **D** marred

## Grammar: mixed and open conditions

> **Watch Out!** *problem areas*

- **unreal past**
  It was only when I spoke to her that I realised we were very similar. ✔ → If I hadn't spoken to her, I *wouldn't/might not/would never* have realised that we ~~had been~~ ˄*were* so similar.

- **mixed conditionals**
  If he hadn't been *so* careless during the experiment, he might not ~~have been~~ ˄*be* in hospital now.
  If he ~~hadn't been~~ ˄*wasn't/weren't* *such* a good reporter, he wouldn't have been promoted last week.
  If you hadn't listened to me, you wouldn't be doing *so* well now. ✔

- **inversions**
  These structures are rather formal.
  Should you see Alice, give her my regards. ✔
  If he doesn't let me go, I don't know what I'll do. ✔ = ~~Shouldn't I~~ ˄*Should I not* be allowed to go, I don't know what I'll do. ✔
  Were you to go on the expedition, you wouldn't be able to complete your research. ✔
  If I could help you, I would do so. ✔ = Were I able to help you, I would do so. ✔

- ***but for***
  ~~Hadn't you~~ ˄*Had you not* helped me, I wouldn't have known what to do. = But for your help, I wouldn't have known what to do. ✔

- **open conditions**
  The tenses used in open conditionals are no different from the tenses which would be used if the clauses were separate.
  Have you finished your work? + you can go = If you have finished your work, you can go. ✔
  In the past hunters didn't catch anything + they went hungry = In the past, if hunters didn't catch anything, they went hungry. ✔

**1** Combine the information in the following pairs of sentences to make sentences with conditional forms. Put the verb(s) in brackets in the correct form, and make any other necessary changes. You have been given the beginning of each sentence to help you.

1 You didn't go on the expedition. You are still alive. (might/kill)
If .....................................................................

2 The government took little action. The disaster occurred. (could/avoid)
The disaster ......................................................

3 I visited the Congo last year. I now have malaria. (would/catch)
If .....................................................................

4 He is not innocent. He was acquitted last month. (should/send)
If .....................................................................

5 Few people listened to the warnings of the ecologists. Some species of animals have disappeared. (could/save)
Had ..................................................................

6 I may not be allowed to enter the USA. I'll have to reconsider my options. (prevent)
Should ..............................................................

7 They may make me take the exams again. I'll probably stop doing the course. (make)
Were I ..............................................................

8 The Minister of Agriculture listened to the advice of so-called 'experts'. Large tracts of farmland are no longer productive. (ignore)
Had ..................................................................

**2** Use of English: key word transformations
For each of the sentences below, write a new sentence as similar as possible in meaning to the original sentence, but using the word given. **This word must not be altered in any way.**

1 If you obey the regulations, you will be permitted to fish in this river. **long**
..........................................................................

2 Taking the necessary precautions, you shouldn't have any health problems. **provided**
..........................................................................

3 He'll give you the sack if you are late for the meeting! **otherwise**
..........................................................................

4 If we took effective action now, we could still save the rainforests. **were**
..........................................................................

5 Your refusal to co-operate would cause immediate expulsion from the country. **should**
..........................................................................

6 The ban on hunting was only imposed because the minister insisted. **but**
..........................................................................

**3** Use of English: gapped sentences
Fill each of the gaps in the following sentences with a suitable word or phrase.

1 Nobody needs to leave their houses ........................ river seems likely to flood.

2 If we are to save the whale from extinction, we ........................ action now.

3 If you really have seen the film, why ........................ me what happens in the end?

4 If you don't have a jeep, don't even ........................ crossing the Sahara.

5 If ........................ a way of saving the giant panda, we need to start looking now.

# Vocabulary review: multiple-choice

**Paper 1, Section A**

Choose the word or phrase, **A**, **B**, **C** or **D**, which best completes each sentence. This task revises some of the vocabulary from previous units of the course.

1 The population of some countries has ............. slightly over the past twenty years.
A fallen   B waned   C descended   D sunk

2 My father was ............. disappointed when the lecture was cancelled.
A strongly   B completely   C bitterly
D absolutely

3 'DDT' is a ............. used by many farmers to kill insects which destroy their crops.
A patricide   B genocide   C herbicide   D pesticide

4 I discovered that we had been told a(n) ............. of lies by the manager of the factory.
A set   B array   C pack   D quantity

5 They are determined to ............. war on those who pollute the rivers and seas of this country.
A wage   B undertake   C bring   D set

6 I've been ............. my brain all day trying to come up with a solution to our problem.
A stretching   B racking   C twisting   D rattling

7 ............., I'm not interested in what you have to tell me.
A Doubtless   B Without question   C At the least
D Frankly

8 Environmentalists ............. the government to do something about the factory waste.
A suggested   B insisted   C urged   D made

# Use of English: comprehension and summary

**1** Read the following passage and underline the words which best describe the purpose of the piece. More than one answer may be possible.

> to entertain    to publicise    to sell something
> to inform    to persuade    to explain

# The monkey man

Jordi Casamitjana, the 33-year-old research co-ordinator at the Monkey Sanctuary in Cornwall, needs no encouragement to talk. It doesn't really matter what the subject is – he will speak rapidly, enthusiastically and, if you
5  don't interrupt, at length on almost anything. And if you ask this irrepressible ethnologist about the social life of the Spanish wasp (something of a speciality) or woolly monkeys (something of an obsession) there is no stopping him.

This is just as well, as this summer he will attempt to set the
10  world record for the longest uninterrupted science lecture – at least 12 hours.

Casamitjana and about 15 other conservationists live and work with 23 Amazonian grey woolly monkeys at the Monkey Sanctuary, near Looe in Cornwall. The listed
15  Victorian mansion has been cleverly joined to several large monkey enclosures and houses both sets of primates in idyllic surroundings.

This pioneering conservation centre was set up in 1964 by Len Williams (father of John Williams, the classical guitarist)
20  and soon afterwards produced the first woolly monkeys bred successfully in captivity – its first world record. Now it is a

leading force in developing practical methods to rehabilitate captive monkeys which were once kept as pets or caged zoological exhibits.

25  Over the next two to three years, the centre aims to relocate all the Cornish monkeys back to Brazil. The plan is to house them on some of the 3,600 forested islands which pepper Lake Balbina about 180 kilometres north of the city of Manaus.

30  Rather than introduce them into the wild, where they might perish because of habitat destruction (woolly monkeys live in the tree tops of primary forest) or endanger indigenous monkeys by carrying human diseases into their midst, they will be living in an environment which is large enough for
35  them never to realise any geographical limits but which is nevertheless protected and allows for the monkeys to be monitored and observed.

The project will also help the Brazilian authorities in their campaign against the large illegal pet trade. Seizing illegally
40  captured monkeys, known as orphans, creates a problem as there is no obvious place to put them.

They have some experience of the forest but, since capture, no social experience. On the other hand, the Cornish monkeys have developed the social skills but in enclosures.
45  The idea is that they should be able to teach each other – a hypothesis that received strong verification when two socialised Cornish monkeys 'adopted' several orphans and were then able to 'learn' (through mimicry) how to negotiate the forest environment.

50  All this, of course, involves raising large amounts of money, which is where Casamitjana and his verbal gift come into their own.

'It will be very interesting to see not just if I can physically do it but how it can be done,' he enthuses, revealing a
55  promising array of gesticulation. 'It is a lecture so it needs to be structured, but over 12 or more hours, and there will also be a level of interaction with the audience.' He has thought through every angle right down to possibly getting a radio mike if he has to answer the call of nature.

60  The lecture is due to take place this summer at a venue to be announced. In the meantime, you can visit the Monkey Sanctuary (open all week except on Friday and Saturday), where Casamitjana gives regular talks which last a mere hour about the woolly monkeys and the Sanctuary's work.

**2** Now answer the following questions about the passage.

1 Which word in the first paragraph is echoed by the phrase 'there is no stopping him'? (line 6)

.........................................................................................

2 Explain what the writer means in this context when he says 'this is just as well'? (line 9)

.........................................................................................

3 Which two phrases in the fourth paragraph show that the work of the conservation centre is indeed 'pioneering'?

.........................................................................................

4 What does the word 'pepper' (line 27) suggest about the islands of Lake Balbina?

.........................................................................................

5 Explain in your own words what might happen to the Cornish monkeys which are returned to the wild.

.........................................................................................

6 What does the writer mean by 'indigenous monkeys'? (line 32)

.........................................................................................

7 Why were the islands of Lake Balbina chosen as a suitable environment for the monkeys?

.........................................................................................

8 Using your own words, explain what 'they' (line 42) refers to.

.........................................................................................

9 Explain in your own words what the Cornish monkeys and the orphan monkeys could 'teach each other'. (line 45)

.........................................................................................

10 What is meant in the context by the phrase 'Casamitjana and his verbal gift come into their own'? (line 51)

.........................................................................................

11 What does the writer imply when he mentions that Casamitjana's 'array of gesticulation' is 'promising'? (line 55)

.........................................................................................

12 In your own words, explain what is meant by the phrase 'he has thought through every angle'. (line 58)

.........................................................................................

**3**

1 Read the following summary question.

> In a paragraph of 70–90 words, summarise the advantages of setting up a sanctuary for the Cornish woolly monkeys on the islands of Lake Balbina.

2 Look at paragraphs 6–8 again. Underline the relevant parts of the passage, and then write a list of the points you need for this summary. Be careful to include only those points which are relevant.

3 Now write the first draft of your summary.

**4** Read the following first draft and compare the notes you made in Exercise 3 with the points made in this student's summary. Ignore the sentence numbers for the moment. Have you included the same information?

(1) The islands of Lake Balbina are ideal as a monkey sanctuary because they are large enough for the monkeys to live on, the monkeys would not be restricted and they would also be protected. (2) As well as this, they could be monitored. (3) Illegal pet monkeys, known as orphans, which have been seized by the Brazilian authorities could also be sent to the islands to live with the Cornish monkeys. (4) It is strongly believed that the pet monkeys would successfully teach the Cornish monkeys how to live in the rainforest. (5) On the other hand, the Cornish monkeys, which have developed social skills but in cages, would teach these to the 'orphan' monkeys.
(113 words)

**5**

1 The summary is still too long. Read the following instructions, which refer to the sentence numbers in Exercise 4, to edit the summary to an appropriate length.

- **Sentences 1 and 2** Remove the phrase which repeats one of the points and combine the two sentences by removing the connector.
- **Sentence 3** Remove two phrases which add unnecessary detail, and reduce the relative clause, by using a participle clause instead.
- **Sentences 4 and 5** Remove any extra adjectives or adverbs and the relative clause, which all add unnecessary information. Then combine the two sentences, by replacing the connecting phrase with a single-word connector.

2 Look again at Unit 2, page 21 for guidance on further things you can do to edit a summary.

## Vocabulary: dependent prepositions and prepositional phrases

**1** Fill each of the gaps in the following passage with the correct preposition.

According to the World Wide Fund for Nature, the polar bear could be faced (1) ............ extinction and a large number of other animals reduced (2) ............ very small remnant populations by global warming in Arctic regions.

Warmer winters are responsible (3) ............ the thinning or disappearance of ice sheets in many parts of the Arctic, resulting (4) ............ a situation where polar bears are (5) ............ risk of starvation because they cannot travel to their normal breeding and hunting grounds.

Even in places where there is still much ice around, polar bears are (6) ............ threat because they rely (7) ............ snow caves to rear their young. Due to the warmer weather, these caves are prone (8) ............ sudden collapse, burying the youngsters (9) ............ . Other effects of the changes (10) ............ climate are also being noticed. Animals such as reindeer (also known (11) ............ 'caribou' in North America) have adapted (12) ............ the extreme cold and are able to cope (13) ............ the Arctic climate. For millions of years they have been migrating to places where they can breed and find food. These migrations coincide (14) ............ the growing season for the plants they feed (15) ............ . Ecologists have found, however, that they are now arriving (16) ............ their spring feeding grounds too late. The plants they eat have grown and gone to seed. This is having a serious impact (17) ............ the herds of caribou. A substantial number of calves are being lost and there is already a substantial reduction (18) ............ herds. Scientists are concerned, but powerless to do anything (19) ............ response to the situation – everything they have tried has been (20) ............ vain. It is simply one of the unforeseen consequences of global warming.

**2** Use of English: key word transformations
For each of the sentences below, write a new sentence as similar as possible in meaning to the original sentence, but using the word given. **This word must not be altered in any way**.

1 He was arrested, when police found the stolen painting in his home. **possession**
.......................................................................

2 Don't panic – I'm in control of the situation. **hand**
.......................................................................

3 Bad weather led to the cancellation of the trip yesterday. **account**
.......................................................................

4 You have to book specially if you want to tour the Olympic stadium. **arrangement**
.......................................................................

5 The fine he paid was much too heavy for the offence he had committed. **proportion**
.......................................................................

## Vocabulary: descriptive verbs

Choose the word or phrase **A, B, C** or **D**, which best completes each sentence.

1 The rock was so heavy that it was only with the greatest difficulty that the climbers could ............ it out of their way.
   **A** heave  **B** fling  **C** throw  **D** cast

2 The barriers suddenly collapsed and the crowd of supporters ............ forward onto the pitch.
   **A** swirled  **B** gushed  **C** surged  **D** trickled

3 The crowed roared with excitement when Benson ............ his partner off her feet and carried her above his head around the skating rink.
   **A** skimmed  **B** ripped  **C** hurtled  **D** swept

4 After several ferocious punches both boxers were ............ unsteadily on their feet.
   **A** bouncing  **B** lunging  **C** swaying  **D** swinging

5 A burst tyre caused the car to ............ off the road and into the river.
   **A** swerve  **B** fire  **C** curve  **D** skate

6 It is not yet known what made the aeroplane stall and then ............ into the sea.
   **A** swoop  **B** dip  **C** hurl  **D** plummet

# Listening: multiple-choice

**Paper 4**

> **Exam Tip!**
>
> Watch out for multiple-choice options with the same wording as that used by the speaker on the cassette. The meaning could be very different.

You will hear an interview in which a scientist talks about how stars in space may have been responsible for a number of environmental catastrophes on the Earth.

For each of the following questions, tick which of the alternatives **A**, **B**, **C** or **D** is the most appropriate response. Read the questions first and notice the difference between the options. Underline any key differences, to make sure you don't forget them. Listen to the recording twice.

1  What do many scientists believe caused the dinosaurs to disappear?
  **A**  large amounts of iridium in the Earth's crust
  **B**  a meteorite crashing into the Earth
  **C**  an asteroid which passed very close to the Earth
  **D**  changes in the Earth's climate

2  What convinced Arnon Dar that collapsing neutron stars have been the cause of the mass extinction of life on Earth?
  **A**  Nothing else would be powerful enough.
  **B**  There is no evidence for volcanic activity.
  **C**  Supernova explosions are far too rare.
  **D**  The two events happen with the same frequency.

3  According to Dar, muon particles cause
  **A**  much heavier rain than normal.
  **B**  cosmic rays to be created.
  **C**  radiation which kills animals and plants.
  **D**  showers of high energy particles.

4  Why does Dar consider the evidence about marine life to be significant?
  **A**  It shows how dangerous muon particles are to life.
  **B**  It suggests that muon particles caused the death of marine life.
  **C**  It produced a valuable fossil record for scientists.
  **D**  Scientists have always ignored it.

5  How does Dar explain the survival of many insects?
  **A**  Radiation does not affect insects.
  **B**  They can survive any environmental disaster.
  **C**  The environment was ideal for insects 251 million years ago.
  **D**  They are more resistant to radiation than large animals.

6  When Dar talks about the possibility of another mass extinction happening, he sounds
  **A**  optimistic.
  **B**  sarcastic.
  **C**  indifferent.
  **D**  slightly concerned.

# Vocabulary: phrasal verbs and expressions: *run*

**1**  Rewrite each of the following sentences using a phrasal verb with *run*, making any necessary changes. Use a dictionary to help you if necessary.

1  By chance I met someone I hadn't seen for years.
  I ........................ for years.
2  'Soon we'll have no more fuel,' she said.
  She said we ........................ fuel.
3  He spent much more money than he could afford while he was at college.
  While ........................ debt.
4  There was a lot of unexpected opposition to the government's proposal.
  The government's ........................ unexpected opposition.
5  A car hit and seriously injured an old woman today.
  An ........................ today.

**2**  Rewrite each of the following sentences using an expression with *run*. You have been given key parts of each expression in brackets.

1  Don't eat those mushrooms because I think they may be poisonous.
  If you ........................ poisoned. (risk)
2  There will be enough supplies if we are careful.
  As long ........................ of supplies. (short)
3  The woman's scream really frightened me.
  My ........................ the woman's scream. (blood)
4  The problems we've been having are very ordinary, and we'll have no problems solving them.
  These problems are very ........................, and we can solve them easily. (mill)

# Writing: report (1)

### About the exam

In **Paper 2** you may have to write a report. A report is normally written for a specific reason, and tends to summarise and explain facts, often for the purpose of **making suggestions and recommendations for action**. The layout and organisation of a report is very important, as is the register of the language used. Reports should have information organised into sections with **headings**, and a formal, impersonal tone. Clear and thorough planning is essential to writing a successful report.

**1** Read the following task and decide what points you will cover in your answer. Make a list in your notebook of at least four.

The City Council is considering a proposal made by the Nuclear Energy Advisory Group, to build a nuclear power station nearby. As the councillor in charge of energy policy, write a report for the other members of the Council, detailing the potential effects this might have on the environment and local people. Make any recommendations you think appropriate. (About 300 words.)

**2** Now read the following report, which was written in answer to the task. Ignore the numbered gaps for the moment. Are the ideas included similar to your own?

_Report on the Nuclear Energy Advisory Group's proposal for a nuclear power station at Shenkly Point._

_For: Shenkly Council_
_From: Anna Mytakidis_

1. _____

_A proposal to build a nuclear power station near the city was recently made by the Nuclear Energy Advisory Group. It was suggested that the use of nuclear energy would solve several problems presently affecting the city._

2. _____

_Atmospheric pollution around the city is currently very high. There is the additional problem of acid rain, which is responsible for widespread damage to nearby forests and lakes, and is steadily destroying many of the city's historic buildings and monuments. It has been pointed out that nuclear energy does not add to the greenhouse effect or produce acid rain, so its use would result in a much cleaner environment._

3. _____

_The Nuclear Energy Advisory Group stated that fears about health or the environment were unfounded. Very strict safety measures would be taken and there would be no question of nuclear waste being dumped near the city. The NEAG ruled out the possibility of an accident ever occurring._

4. _____

_Available figures suggest that, were we to use nuclear energy, the cost of electricity would decrease significantly. Apparently, once the power station was in operation, we could expect reductions in the cost of electricity of up to 30 per cent. Another community benefit would be the creation of several hundred jobs._

5. _____

_The proposal has much to recommend it. Most people, however, would be worried about potential accidents. These fears are not altogether unfounded - there have been several such disasters in recent years. I feel that we should not reject the proposal outright, but would recommend that the question of safety be considered more carefully. At the very least, the advice of nuclear scientists not connected with the NEAG should be sought and efforts made to consult environmentalists from areas where there are already nuclear power stations in operation._

**3**   Give each paragraph of the report an appropriate heading. One of the paragraphs is not in the most logical place. Which one?   (para. .......)

**4**

1   Read the following extract from a different report, ignoring the numbers and underlining for the moment. What is the main purpose of this extract?

(1) *The proposal to build a car factory in the suburb of Westham <u>sounds really good</u>. (2) <u>It would provide unemployed people with jobs</u> and <u>make the whole area wealthier</u>, because it would offer over 2000 jobs. (3) <u>Another thing is that</u> it would not only provide opportunities for work, but it would also offer <u>lots of</u> other services, <u>which would include</u> baby-sitting facilities, a free health-care scheme and a company pension. (4) <u>The biggest problem, though</u>, would be that the factory is <u>going to be</u> 30 miles from the town centre. (5) This would <u>without a doubt</u> be a problem for <u>the people who don't have their own car</u>, as bus and train services <u>don't run very often</u>. (6) If the factory management <u>didn't want</u> to provide company transport, the Town Council would have to <u>think about</u> improving the services which already exist.*

2   Although there are no grammatical mistakes, this piece of writing would not be very successful in the exam because the register is too informal and the tone too personal. Rewrite the extract in your notebook using the following suggestions.

1   This phrase is too informal and personal in tone. Replace it with an expression containing the words *much* and *recommend*.
2   Rewrite the whole of this sentence. Start with the present participle *Offering* ... and then rewrite the underlined phrases, using the words *solve*, *unemployment* and *increase*.
3   The connecting phrase is inappropriate, so replace it with a more formal expression, and rewrite the clauses which follow using an inversion. Replace *which would include* with a present participle.
4   The first part of this sentence is rather informal, so replace the underlined words with *major drawback*, and use a more appropriate connector. *Going to be* is also too informal, so use a future passive structure with the word *located*.

5   Replace the first underlined phrase with one word and the second one with a more formal phrase, starting with *for those*, and ending with *transport* (as a noun). *Don't run very often* is informal, and can be replaced by an adjective.
6   Rewrite the whole sentence starting with *Should* ... Replace *didn't want to* with a suitable adjective, and the phrasal verb *think about* with a more formal verb.

**5**

1   Now write a report answering the following task.

You attended a meeting recently in which various measures were proposed to make your city 'greener'. As an assistant to the city mayor, you have been asked to write a report of the plans, giving your opinion of the suggested measures and making any recommendations you think appropriate. (About 300 words.)

2   Here are some of the ideas which were suggested in the meeting to help you.

- fining people who drop litter
- tree-planting programme and creation of parks
- cleaning up the river
- recycling of rubbish
- imposing restrictions on traffic

**Exam Strategy**

- Decide which points you want to include. Write an outline of what each paragraph should contain, and its heading. Organise everything you want to say, and how it will be linked, **at the planning stage**.
- Think about the consequences of the various measures proposed – what language will you use to connect the two? (E.g. more trees → healthier atmosphere, city more attractive to tourists = *Were more trees to be planted, the atmosphere would ... and the city ...*)
- Check your outline against the composition title, and see that it answers the question fully, and relevantly, **before you start writing**.

**6**   Exchange your report with another student if you can. Evaluate each other's work and suggest improvements.

# UNIT

# 8 A sporting chance

## Vocabulary review: multiple-choice

**Paper 1, Section A**

Choose the word or phrase, **A**, **B**, **C** or **D**, which best completes each sentence.

1 When the archaeologist picked up the map it ............. to dust in his hands.
   **A** crumbled   **B** dissolved   **C** disintegrated
   **D** decomposed

2 You must win this race – your whole career as an athlete is ............. stake.
   **A** on   **B** at   **C** in   **D** to

3 The machine hadn't been oiled for ages, so it's not surprising it ............. .
   **A** held out   **B** wound down   **C** seized up
   **D** caught up

4 Such a scandal could ............. disaster for the government.
   **A** make   **B** spell   **C** anticipate   **D** speak

5 The climb had to be abandoned, as a result of the ............. weather conditions.
   **A** diverse   **B** inverse   **C** perverse   **D** adverse

6 On arrival at the airport, the football team was ............. by coach to the hotel.
   **A** transferred   **B** transported   **C** transmitted
   **D** transformed

7 She didn't ............. the idea of having to go to the party on her own.
   **A** savour   **B** agree   **C** relish   **D** delight

8 Many athletes have reached their ............. by the time they are twenty.
   **A** summit   **B** top   **C** point   **D** peak

9 Many famous people resent their private lives being held up to public ............. .
   **A** observation   **B** deliberation   **C** scrutiny
   **D** investigation

10 You could make a formal complaint to the committee, but I wouldn't go down that ............. if I were you.
   **A** lane   **B** street   **C** avenue   **D** road

## Grammar: intensifiers

> **Watch Out!** *so* and *such*
>
> - **articles**
>   *Such* only needs an indefinite article when used with a singular countable noun.
>   We've been enjoying such ~~a~~ good weather lately.
>   *So* can be used with an adjective, an article and a noun, often in preference to *such*, in formal situations.
>   He was such an adventurous climber, that ... ✔ =
>   He was so adventurous a climber, that ... ✔
>   ~~He was a so adventurous climber, that ...~~
> - **inversions**
>   *Such* is not generally used in inversions which have an auxiliary verb. It can be replaced by *so* + adjective + article.
>   ~~Such a good time did we have that we didn't want to leave.~~ = *So* good *a* time did we have that we didn't want to leave. ✔
> - **conditionals and wishes**
>   *So* and *such* often appear in conditionals and wishes, meaning *as much as is/was true*.
>   If we hadn't received so much money, we wouldn't have ... (= *as much money as we did*) ✔
>   I wish my neighbours weren't so noisy! (= *as noisy as they are*) ✔

**1** **Use of English:** key word transformations
For each of the sentences below, write a new sentence as similar as possible in meaning to the original sentence, but using the word given. **This word must not be altered in any way**.

1 It terrifies me just to think about climbing that mountain. **mere**

   .........................................................................

2 I feel deep gratitude for your help. **indeed**

   .........................................................................

3 I'm not surprised at all that you won the race. **least**

   .........................................................................

4  Absolutely no-one in the team is a better player than Jack Carlton. **exception**

..................................................................................

5  He's the quickest learner I've ever met. **so**

..................................................................................

6  I've told you this on innumerable occasions. **time**

..................................................................................

7  He's good at nothing except long distance running. **one**

..................................................................................

8  On looking around we realised that we were totally lost. **well**

..................................................................................

9  I'm afraid that a rematch is completely impossible. **whatsoever**

..................................................................................

10  The opposition were just too strong to beat. **such**

..................................................................................

**2  Use of English:** gapped sentences

Fill each of the gaps in the following sentences with a suitable word or phrase.

1  There ........................ indeed that doctors could do for her injury, and she was forced to retire from competition.
2  Why on ........................ me that you didn't want to take part?
3  We were forced to abandon the match, so ........................ weather.
4  Although they are a very good team, they are ........................ means the best.
5  Don't tell her, ........................ do – she'll be horrified if she finds out.
6  All the training he had done didn't seem to ........................ of difference to his performance.
7  I hadn't expected quite ........................ a wind. It blew us miles off-course.

> ### *Exam Tip!*
>
> Use emphatic structures in **Paper 2** to make narrative compositions more dramatic, and to organise and distinguish arguments in discursive compositions.

**3  Use of English:** guided cloze

Fill each of the blanks in the following passage with **one** suitable word. Most, but not all, of the words you need are **emphatic words** or part of **emphatic expressions**.

# ICE-FISHING

Every weekend, hundreds of Russians trudge for miles across snow and ice to indulge in (1) ............ one thing which they really enjoy: ice-fishing.

(2) ............ finding a suitably desolate spot of (3) ............ own, they drill a hole in the ice, dip in their line and wait for the fish to bite. With (4) ............ company whatsoever, save that of the relentless howling of the wind, they sit for hours huddled over the frozen Moscow river, never exchanging more than the (5) ............ of grunts or nods with a fellow fisherman, should one pass by. (6) ............ the practitioners of this bizarre sport may say, the rewards of ice-fishing do not include the fish they hope to catch. To say the (7) ............ , these are inedible. Could it be, then, that they do it (8) ............ and simply for the challenge? Yet another case of man battling against the elements?

In fact, the majority of Russians do not understand why so large (9) ............ number of their countrymen can waste the precious hours of winter daylight on (10) ............ appears to be such a pointless activity. (11) ............ all, they cannot understand why anybody should risk life and limb to catch fish which are usually thrown back into the river. For (12) ............ ice-fishing may appear to be safe, it can be (13) ............ dangerous indeed. In fact, (14) ............ unpredictable are the movements of ice-floes, that every year lives are put in danger or (15) ............ altogether.

Fishermen can find themselves swept away and stranded on sheets of ice, and, (16) ............ if rescued by helicopter within a few hours, will perish in the sub-zero temperatures. Such is the expense of these rescue operations that there have been signs of a backlash among non-fishermen recently, many of (17) ............ have demanded that fishermen be fined for recklessly endangering their lives and the lives of others. Some have even suggested that the stranded fishermen (18) ............ not be given the (19) ............ bit of help – after all, they have only themselves to blame for their unhappy predicament. (20) ............ to say, the fishermen themselves do not seem to care one way or the other. For them, the risk and sacrifices they make are part and parcel of the mysterious allure of ice-fishing.

# Reading: literary text

**1** Read the following text quickly. What impression do you get of the voyage the *Stormchild* is about the make?

*Stormchild* sailed on the next tide, just after midnight. She slipped unseen down the river with her navigation lights softly blurred by the small rain. Instead of the champagne parting and the
5 paper streamers there had only been David and Betty calling their farewells from the pontoons, and once their voices had been lost in the night there were only the sounds of the big motor in *Stormchild's* belly, the splash of the water at her stern
10 and the hiss of the wet wind. That wind was southerly, but the forecast promised it would change to easterly by dawn and if the forecast held good then I could not hope for a better departure wind. It was blowing hard, but the big, heavily laden steel
15 *Stormchild* needed a good wind to shift her ponderous weight.

I raised sail at the river's mouth, killed the engine, and allowed the wind to take over. The wake from the boat foamed white into the blackness
20 behind us as the coastal lights winked and faded in the rain that still pattered on the deck and dripped from the rigging. The green and red lights of the river's markers vanished, and soon the only mark to guide *Stormchild* was the flickering gleam of the far
25 Portland light. I had lost count of how many times I had begun voyages in just this manner: slipping off on a fast tide, making my way southerly to avoid the tidal rips that come off the great headlands of southern England, then letting my boat tear
30 westwards towards the open Atlantic. Yet however many times I had done it, there was always the same excitement.

'Gee, but it's cold,' Jackie Potten said sullenly.

'If you're going to moan all the way across the

**2** Read the following questions and unfinished statements about the passage. In each case, choose the answer, **A**, **B**, **C** or **D**, which you think fits best.

1 The writer implies that the departure of *Stormchild* was
  **A** an anticlimax.
  **B** very worrying.
  **C** a cause for celebration.
  **D** unexpected.

35 Atlantic,' I snapped, 'then I'll turn round now and drop you off.'

There was a stunned silence. I had surprised myself by the anger of my voice, which had clearly made Jackie intensely miserable. I felt sorry that
40 I had snapped at her, though I also felt justified, for I was not at all sure that I wanted her on board *Stormchild*, but the notion of Jackie coping on the boat had energised David and Betty with a vast amusement and they had overridden my objections
45 with their joint enthusiasm. Betty had taken Jackie shopping, returning with a car-load of vegetarian supplies and armfuls of expensive foul-weather gear that I had been forced to pay for. I had ventured to ask the American girl whether she had any sailing
50 experience at all, only to be told that she and her mother had once spent a week on a Miami-based cruise ship. 'But you can cook, can't you?' David had demanded.

'A bit.' Jackie had been confused by the question.

55 'Then you won't be entirely useless.' David's characteristic bluntness had left Jackie rather dazed.

Dazed or not, Jackie was now my sole companion on *Stormchild*, which meant that I had the inconvenience of sharing a boat with a complete
60 novice. I could not let her take a watch or even helm the ship until I had trained her in basic seamanship, and that training was going to slow me down. Worse, she might prove to be seasick or utterly incompetent. All in all, I was sourly thinking, it had
65 been totally inconsiderate of David and Betty to have encouraged her to join the ship.

2  How did the writer view the weather conditions?
   A  They were worse than he had expected.
   B  They could have been better.
   C  They would soon be ideal.
   D  They were likely to improve slightly.
3  What was surprising about the writer's sense of excitement on setting sail?
   A  There was no good reason for it.
   B  He had set sail from England many times before.
   C  The lack of navigational lights made conditions extremely dangerous.
   D  He had a companion he disliked.
4  The writer lost his temper with Jackie Potten because
   A  he hated people who complained.
   B  he wanted to be on his own.
   C  he disliked Americans.
   D  he resented her presence on the boat.
5  Why had David and Betty persuaded the writer to take Jackie Potten?
   A  They thought she would make him laugh.
   B  They didn't realise she knew nothing about sailing.
   C  They wanted to play a trick on him.
   D  They thought the situation would be funny.
6  What do we learn about the writer's dealings with Jackie Potten?
   A  They disliked each other.
   B  He had known her for some time.
   C  He knew very little about her.
   D  She was paying him to teach her the basics of sailing.

**3**

1  Find the following words in the first and second paragraphs of the passage, and try to deduce their meaning from the context. The sounds of some of the words can help you to understand their meanings.

1  slipped (line 2)
2  splash (line 9)
3  hiss (line 10)
4  shift (line 15)
5  winked (line 20)
6  faded (line 20)
7  pattered (line 21)
8  dripped (line 21)
9  flickering (line 24)
10  tear (line 29)

2  Make three lists: words connected with movements, sounds or lights.

| movements | sounds | lights |
|---|---|---|
|  |  |  |

**4**  Use one of the words from Exercise 3, in the correct form, to complete each of the following sentences.

1  We listened to the rain as it ............. on the roof of the caravan.
2  I don't understand how he managed ............. away from the party unnoticed.
3  The fluorescent light started ............. and then went out completely.
4  There was a long slow ............. from the fire, as it started to rain and we abandoned the barbecue.
5  Sandra rushed out of the house and ............. down the road towards the bus stop.
6  All we could see in the darkness were the lights of the houses as they ............. at us in the distance.
7  Everyone laughed when David fell off the boat into the river with a huge ............. .
8  I had terrible problems trying ............. the piano on my own, and eventually gave up – it was just too heavy.
9  The rainwater seeped through the ceiling and started ............. onto the floor beneath.
10  As we drove away, the lights of the village gradually ............. and then disappeared altogether.

**Study Tip**

Deducing the meaning of words from context is an important reading skill which you need to develop. It is probably the best way of building up your **passive vocabulary**: words that you can recognise and understand when listening or reading, but don't necessarily use (or even need to know) when you are speaking or writing. Look again at Unit 5, page 41 for guidance on techniques you can use to help you understand unknown words.

## Listening: multiple-choice

### Exam Strategy

Sometimes you have to answer questions which focus on the **attitude** of one or more of the speakers you hear or what is **implied** by what they say. For these questions, pay attention not just to **what** is said, but **how** it is said.

 You will hear two friends, Jenny and Susan, arguing about Jenny's decision to go hang-gliding at the weekend.

For each of the following questions, tick which of the alternatives **A**, **B**, **C** or **D**, is the most appropriate response. Listen to the recording twice.

1 According to Susan, since Jenny took up hang-gliding
   A at least six people have been badly injured.
   B her conversation has become maddening.
   C she has talked all the time about it.
   D at least six people have lost their lives.

2 When Jenny says 'come on', she is
   A inviting Susan to go out to eat with her.
   B showing she understands Susan's point of view.
   C suggesting that Susan is exaggerating.
   D encouraging her to continue talking.

3 Jenny reminds Susan that after her fencing match she had not wanted to
   A go out to eat.
   B drop in to see her.
   C talk to her.
   D hang around with her.

4 Susan is a
   A nurse.
   B trainee teacher.
   C doctor.
   D medical student.

5 When Jenny says 'you might land up in hospital', she is
   A warning her friend.
   B being pessimistic.
   C teasing her friend.
   D commenting on fencing.

6 When Jenny says that she is a 'grown woman', she is
   A stating that her parents allow her to go hang-gliding.
   B saying that she can do what she wants.
   C saying she knows what she wants.
   D suggesting that hang-gliding makes her feel important.

## Vocabulary: phrasal verbs and expressions: *bring*

**1** Rewrite each of the following sentences using a phrasal verb with *bring*, making any necessary changes. Use a dictionary to help you if necessary.

1 Someone should have mentioned this matter at the meeting yesterday.
   This ........................ yesterday.
2 It's unlikely that he'll manage to perform such a difficult dive in the competition tomorrow.
   His chances ........................ slim.
3 Sponsorship is responsible for more than half of most athletes' earnings.
   Sponsorship ........................ most athletes earn.
4 She regained consciousness when an old lady put some smelling salts under her nose.
   An old ........................ putting some smelling salts under her nose.
5 There has been a huge change in smoking habits, as a result of this anti-smoking campaign.
   This campaign ........................ people who smoke.
6 I'm sure we can convince him that our way of thinking is better.
   I'm sure he ........................ thinking.

**2** Rewrite each of the following sentences using an expression with *bring*. You have been given key parts of each expression in brackets to help you.

1 It's unlikely that the adverse publicity will make her behave more sensibly in the future.
   I doubt ........................ publicity. (senses)
2 His failure in the championships made him realise how important regular training was.
   His ........................ training. (home)
3 This scandal will damage the reputation of the government.
   The government ........................ scandal. (disrepute)

4 Nothing could have persuaded me to talk to him again after what he did.

After ........................ again. (myself)

5 The audience clapped and cheered ecstatically at the end of the performance last night.

The performance ........................ last night. (house)

## Vocabulary: dependent prepositions and prepositional phrases

Fill each of the gaps in the following passage with **one** appropriate preposition.

The hazards of extreme weather conditions discourage most walkers (1) ............ venturing into the hills in winter. The mere thought of having to contend (2) ............ snow and ice on mountain slopes, or even being confronted (3) ............ an avalanche, is enough to dampen the spirits of even the most experienced of climbers. For those few adventurous souls who do insist (4) ............ climbing in winter, however, a course in winter mountaineering skills lessens the dangers.

John White's Mountain School in Cumbria offers a short course which introduces beginners (5) ............ winter climbing. Anyone is eligible (6) ............ the Winter Walking Skills course, provided they are (7) ............ good health. Those who participate (8) ............ the sessions are taught basic navigation skills, winter skills (such as how to dig a snow hole), the use of ice-axes and crampons, and mountain first aid. This last subject, of course, is (9) ............ particular importance. The necessity (10) ............ learning how to recognise and deal (11) ............ hypothermia and frostbite effectively, for example, is impressed (12) ............ all the students who enrol (13) ............ the course.

More advanced courses are also (14) ............ offer at John White's school. The Winter Mountaineering course, for example, is geared (15) ............ those who are experienced (16) ............ climbing. This course covers many of the subjects taught on the basic course, but also includes climbing techniques and more complicated navigation. Much (17) ............ demand is the Ice Climbing course – the equivalent perhaps (18) ............ learning to drive a lorry after having learnt to drive a car – which caters (19) ............ experienced climbers and covers more specialised ice-axe and crampon techniques, rope work and other essentials for those determined to gamble (20) ............ fate. By the end of the course, climbers will have sampled their first proper ice-climbing route. Weather permitting, of course.

## Writing: discursive composition (1)

> ### Paper 2

### About the exam

In **Paper 2** you may have to write a discursive composition in which you present an argument. You may have to:

- present both sides of an argument in a balanced discussion
- present one point of view, giving supporting evidence.

### Exam Strategy

- Read the question carefully and decide if a balanced or a one-sided argument is required.
- Make a clear, organised outline. Make sure you have:
  1 an introduction – give some general information about the topic 'as it is today', and introduce the discussion; using a rhetorical question is one common way of doing this
  2 notes about the evidence you will use to support your points, and the connectors you will use to link them
  3 a genuine conclusion, which summarises your argument and, if possible, refers back to the composition title and your introduction.

### 1

1 Read the following task and underline the key words.

> Encouraging children to take part in team sports at school is the best way of developing their characters. Discuss. (About 350 words.)

2 Look at the statement, and decide:
- whether you agree with it or not
- what evidence you could use to support your view.

Note down at least four or five points which you could use to support your ideas.

1 Read the following detailed outline written by a student preparing to answer the task. Are any of your ideas included?

> ### Introduction
> Opening comments: the situation as it is today.
> 1 Children encouraged to take part in team sports, in some cases forced.
> 2 Underlying philosophy of this participation = team sports good for the body, build character.
> 3 This may be true - true that it's the <u>best</u> way?
>
> ### First supporting paragraph
> Main idea: promoting focus and self-sacrifice.
> Team sports involve lots of physical training.
> 1 Children train hard before inter-school matches - physically fit for 'big day'.
> 2 Such a rigorous programme demands self-sacrifice
> Other activities and non-team sports involve self-sacrifice/perseverance - tennis, chess.
>
> ### Second supporting paragraph
> Main idea: developing co-operation.
> 1 Team sports are character-building - encourage co-operation.
> Success of team depends on co-operation of individuals.
> 2 Valuable training for later life - but not only activities which encourage this. Plays and concerts encourage co-operation between children.
>
> ### Third supporting paragraph
> Main idea: criticising competitive attitudes.
> 1 Team sports are about winning - enhance the competitive spirit. Non-team sports do the same - whether this is character-building or not is open to question.
> 2 Many problems today - 'me-first' attitude.
> 3 Teach children there's more to life than winning?
>
> ### Closing paragraph
> 1 Team sports one way of developing children's characters - wrong to consider them to be the best way.
> 2 Should encourage children to develop personalities in ways they think best.

2 Underline any parts of the student's outline which you think would be useful, but you didn't think of when making your own notes.

3 Look again at Unit 1, page 15 for guidance on common methods of organising information in paragraphs. Which method has been used in this outline?

.............................................................................

**3** Read the finished composition, and choose the best word or phrase from the list on page 71 to fill each of the numbered gaps. Remember that you need to pay attention to the **whole composition**, not just the words immediately around each gap, in order to do this effectively.

In many schools in the world today children of all ages are encouraged, and (1) ............ forced in some cases, to take part in team sports. The underlying philosophy is that team sports are (2) ............ good for the body ............ that they build a child's character. This may well be true, but is the suggestion that team sports are the best way of developing a child's character (3) ............ true?

Participation in a team sport, (4) ............, usually involves a lot of physical training. Before important events children may have to train very hard (5) ............ be well-prepared and physically fit for the 'big day'. (6) ............, such rigorous training demands dedication and self-sacrifice on the part of the child. (7) ............, there are other activities which also involve a high degree of perseverance. (8) ............, non-team sports such as tennis or even activities like chess require equal preparation and discipline.

Team sports are also considered to be character-building, (9) ............ encourage co-operation between individual team members. (10) ............, the success or the failure of the team depends not so much on the individual skills of the players as on their ability to co-operate. This is valuable training for later life, (11) ............, but team sports are not the only activities which encourage children to do this. Plays and concerts, (12) ............, also encourage co-operation between children.

Teachers frequently point out that team sports are about winning. They enhance the 'competitive spirit' of the boys and girls who take part. (13) ............ that non-team sports do the same. Whether this is character-building or not, (14) ............, is open to question. So many of the problems we face in society nowadays (15) ............ the 'me-first' attitude found in so many people. (16) ............ schools aim to teach children that there is much more to life than winning and being first?

(17) ............, clearly team sports are one way of developing children's characters, but it would be wrong to consider them to be the best way. (18) ............, we should encourage children to develop their characters and personalities in ways they themselves feel are best. (355 words)

| | | |
|---|---|---|
| 1 | a) indeed | b) whereas |
| 2 | a) on the one hand ... on the other hand | b) not only ... but also |
| 3 | a) actually | b) basically |
| 4 | a) of course | b) however |
| 5 | a) as a result | b) in order to |
| 6 | a) without doubt | b) nevertheless |
| 7 | a) however | b) furthermore |
| 8 | a) Not to mention | b) For instance |
| 9 | a) so as to | b) in that they |
| 10 | a) as a matter of fact | b) obviously |
| 11 | a) of course | b) similarly |
| 12 | a) for example | b) such as |
| 13 | a) although | b) it goes without saying |
| 14 | a) however | b) in fact |
| 15 | a) result in | b) are the direct result of |
| 16 | a) couldn't | b) shouldn't |
| 17 | a) in conclusion | b) in the final analysis |
| 18 | a) instead | b) naturally |

**4** The language used in discursive compositions is usually objective and impersonal. Match each of the following phrases 1–10 with its function a)–c), below.

**Impersonal language for discursive compositions**

1 the underlying philosophy is that …
2 … is/are often considered to be …
3 this may be due to …
4 according to recent research, …
5 it would be wrong to suggest/claim that …
6 … is/are frequently regarded as …
7 it is sometimes suggested/pointed out/ claimed that …
8 it seems unlikely that …
9 the idea behind this is that …
10 … this is open to question

a) explaining the reasons for something ............
b) reporting an opinion in an impersonal way ............
c) disagreeing with an opinion, or suggesting that it may not be well-founded ............

**5** Now write a discursive composition in answer to the following task.

'There is no justification whatsoever for participation in dangerous sports.' Discuss. (About 350 words.)

**6** Exchange your composition with another student if you can. Evaluate each other's work and suggest improvements.

# The mind's eye

## Vocabulary review: multiple-choice

> **Paper 1, Section A**

Choose the word or phrase, **A**, **B**, **C** or **D**, which best completes each sentence.

1   There's absolutely no point in ............. against the injustice of the situation.
    **A** railing   **B** complaining   **C** shrieking
    **D** berating

2   Take your boots off immediately – they are ............. in mud!
    **A** caked   **B** cemented   **C** gripped   **D** clasped

3   Some mystics claim to be able to see ............. of the future in water or crystal.
    **A** dreams   **B** fantasies   **C** visions
    **D** hallucinations

4   Dogs can hear sounds which to human beings are ............. .
    **A** inexplicable   **B** inaudible   **C** indelible
    **D** intangible

5   He did not have the slightest ............. to visit the zoo.
    **A** yearning   **B** craving   **C** desire   **D** longing

6   The explorers were devastated when they realised that the desert oasis was only a(n) ............. .
    **A** mirage   **B** image   **C** illusion   **D** icon

7   After five weeks the wound in his leg started to ............. .
    **A** heal   **B** cure   **C** treat   **D** recover

8   Many people have lost faith in doctors and are turning to ............. medicine.
    **A** altered   **B** alternating   **C** alternate
    **D** alternative

9   The old man could be heard ............. to himself about people's ingratitude.
    **A** groaning   **B** whimpering   **C** muttering
    **D** yelling

10  I could tell from the ............. on her face that she was deep in thought.
    **A** glare   **B** frown   **C** scowl   **D** glance

## Vocabulary: verb + noun collocation

In the following sentences, only one of the nouns in italics collocates with the verb **and** fits the meaning of the sentence. Underline the correct noun in each case.

1   She gave him a sharp *hit/slap/punch* across the face and walked away.

2   She made several *gestures/faces/waves* to gain the attention of the waiter.

3   Yesterday, the management took an important *conclusion/decision/plan* regarding payment of part-time staff.

4   This pizza's new – would you like to give it a *try/chew/bite*?

5   Could you have a quick *glimpse/read/glance* at this letter I've written?

6   Do you have any *memory/recollection/thought* at all of what he said to you?

7   After the operation, he made a remarkable *recovery/improvement/progress*.

8   Realising I was late, I took a quick *suck/gulp/drink* of my drink and left.

9   He made me a(n) *offer/suggestion/plan* I couldn't refuse.

10  What *influence/effect/consequence* do you think his resignation will have on the company?

11  As soon as he saw me, he gave me a big *grimace/smile/frown* and waved the tickets triumphantly in the air.

12  I can't decide now – I need to have a *reflection/thought/think*.

13  When he saw the body, he gave a heart-rending *gasp/cry/murmur* and sank to his knees.

14  She has no *intention/aim/plan* of giving you back the money you lent her.

---

### Study Tip

Record collocations on separate pages of your notebook, so that you can add to them when you meet new ones. Be careful! Some of the nouns may be wrong in the context of a particular sentence but still collocate correctly with the verb. Use a good English–English dictionary to help you check appropriate contexts for using your vocabulary.

# Grammar: verb patterns (-*ing* and infinitive)

> ### Watch Out! *problem areas*
>
> - **verb + *to* infinitive or -*ing* form**
>   Several verbs have one meaning when they are
>   followed by a *to* infinitive and a different meaning
>   when followed by an -*ing* form.
>   I *tried to cut up* the chicken, but without success.
>   (= *attempted*) ✔
>   You ought to *try cutting up* the chicken with a
>   cleaver. (= *to see if it works*) ✔
>   We *regret to tell* you that your application
>   has been turned down. (= *we know this is
>   unfortunate*) ✔
>   I really *regret not telling* him what I was planning
>   to do. (= *I made a mistake*) ✔
>   After describing the work of his colleagues,
>   he *went on to talk* about his own research.
>   (= *he changed the subject*) ✔
>   She *went on talking* even when the meeting had
>   finished. (= *she continued*) ✔
> - ***begin* and *start***
>   These can both be followed by a *to* infinitive or
>   an -*ing* form, with little change in meaning. A *to*
>   infinitive must be used, however, when the form is
>   *beginning* or *starting*.
>   Oh dear! It's beginning ~~raining~~ *to rain*.
> - **preposition + -*ing* form**
>   Prepositions should be followed by an -*ing* form.
>   She congratulated me *on passing/having passed* my
>   driving test. ✔
>   After some verbs, *to* is a preposition and
>   therefore must be followed by an -*ing* form.
>   She objected to ~~have~~ *having* to get up so early in
>   the morning.
>   (also *be/get used to, look forward to, confess to*)
> - **infinitives: continuous/passive/perfect**
>   I expect *to be working/to be promoted/to have
>   finished* by next week. ✔

### *1* Use of English: key word transformations

For each of the sentences below, write a new sentence as
similar as possible in meaning to the original sentence, but
using the word given. **This word must not be altered
in any way**.

1 The builders don't think they will still be doing the
renovations at the end of next week. **hope**

..........................................................................

2 The police didn't mention whether or not the
suspects were armed. **omitted**

..........................................................................

3 Although we sent a message, there was no reply.
**tried**

..........................................................................

4 I have no memory of when I found this book.
**remember**

..........................................................................

5 You must take notice of the school rules. **ignored**

..........................................................................

6 I really don't like it when I have to work overtime.
**object**

..........................................................................

7 She insisted that I had to leave immediately. **my**

..........................................................................

8 I will definitely not lend you any more money!
**refuse**

..........................................................................

### *2* Use of English: sentence transformations

Finish each of the following sentences in such a way that it
is as similar as possible in meaning to the sentence printed
before it.

1 Perhaps finding someone to replace her is proving
difficult for him.
He appears ....................................................

2 I'm excited that the new theatre will be completed
soon.
I'm looking ....................................................

3 I wish I'd paid more attention to his warnings.
I regret ....................................................

4 The travel agent is going to send us the tickets
when they arrive.
I've arranged ....................................................

5 Just lately, money has become more of a problem
for me.
I'm starting ....................................................

6 'I admit that I forgot to turn on the alarm system,'
said Robert.
Robert confessed to ....................................................

7 She took extra night classes, so as not to have to
repeat the course.
She avoided ....................................................

8 He said that nobody had given him money.
He denied ....................................................

9 It's not normal for me to have to work this hard.
I am not ....................................................

10 The censors regarded the film as not being suitable
for young children.
The film was considered ....................................................

## About the exam

You are usually asked to summarise one or more aspects of the writer's argument, not all of it. Frequently, you will need to look for the required information in more than one place in the passage.

### Exam Tip!

Always work your way through the comprehension questions **before** you attempt the summary. This will help you to gain a better understanding of the passage in general, and may also give you one or two of the points required for your summary.

**1** What skills do you think children can learn from playing games? Make a note of your thoughts. Now read the following passage quickly, to see if any of your ideas are mentioned.

# The importance of children's games

In child development there is an important phenomenon that shows very clearly the process of preparation for the future: play. Games must not be considered as the haphazard creations of parents or educators.
5 They should be seen as educational aids and as stimuli for the child's psyche, imagination and life skills. Every game is a preparation for the future. The manner in which children approach a game, their choice of game and the importance they place upon it, show their attitude and relationship to their environment and how they relate to their fellow human beings. Whether they are hostile or whether they are friendly,
10 and particularly whether they show leadership qualities, are evident in their play. In observing children at play we can see their whole attitude towards life; play is of the utmost importance to every child.

But play is more than preparation for life. Games are above all communal exercises that enable children to develop their social feeling.
15 Children who avoid games and play are always open to the suspicion that they have not adjusted satisfactorily to life. These children gladly withdraw from all games, or when they are sent to the playground with other children usually spoil the pleasure of others. Pride, lack of self-esteem and the consequent fear of 'getting it wrong' are the three main
20 reasons for this behaviour. In general, by watching children at play, we can determine with great certainty the extent and quality of their social feeling.

The goal of superiority, also revealed in play, betrays itself in the child's tendency to be the leader and organizer. We can discover this tendency
25 by watching how children push themselves forward and to what degree they prefer those games that give them an opportunity to satisfy their desire to play the leading role. There are very few games that do not incorporate at least one of these factors: preparation for life, social feeling, or the striving for dominance.

30 There is, however, one other factor that is present in play: the opportunity for children to express themselves. Children are more or less left to their own devices in play, and their performance is stimulated by their interaction with other children. There are a number of games that especially emphasize this creative bent. In the preparation for their
35 future profession, those games providing the opportunity for children to exercise their creative spirit are especially important. In the life stories of many people, it is not uncommon that some who made dresses for dolls in childhood went on to make dresses for adults in later life.

Play is indivisibly bound up with the psyche. It is, so to speak, a kind
40 of profession and must be considered as such. Therefore it is not a trivial matter to disturb children in their play. Play should never be considered merely as a way of passing the time. With regard to the goal of preparing for the future, all children have in them something of the adult they will become. Thus in the appraisal of individuals we can reach more accurate
45 conclusions when we have knowledge of their childhood.

**2** Answer the following questions about the passage.

1 Explain in your own words why the writer describes games as the 'haphazard creations of parents or educators' (line 3).

...........................................................

2 Describe in your own words the two roles games can play in preparing children for the future.

...........................................................

3 Find three aspects of a child's approach to game playing which might reveal that child's social attitude.

...........................................................

4 What attitude might a child who is not socially well-adjusted have towards games?

...........................................................

5 Explain in your own words why some children may worry about 'getting it wrong' when playing games.

...........................................................

6 What does the writer suggest about the goal of superiority when he says that it 'betrays itself'? (line 23)

...........................................................

7 What need is satisfied by the tendency for children to want to be the leader in a game?

...........................................................

8 What is the effect of the fact that children are 'more or less left to their own devices' during play? (line 31)

...........................................................

9 What precisely is meant by the word 'bent' in line 34?

...........................................................

10 Explain in your own words why it is 'not a trivial matter to disturb children in their play' (line 40).

...........................................................

**3**

1 Read the following summary task.

In a paragraph of 60–80 words, summarise what adults can learn about children from watching them play, and the assumptions they should try to avoid in their treatment of children's games.

2 Read the passage again and underline any information which relates to the summary question. Identify and list the points required **in your own words**.

**4** Write the first draft of your summary. Remember to use connectors and try not to use the same grammatical structures in each sentence.

**5** Check and edit your summary.
Look again at Unit 2, page 21 for guidance on methods of summary editing.

**6** Read the second draft of your summary and check for spelling, punctuation and grammar mistakes.

## Vocabulary: dependent prepositions and prepositional phrases

Fill the gaps in the following text with the correct prepositions.

### The power of the unconscious mind

Suddenly you find that you have lost all awareness (1) ............ what you were going to say next, though a moment ago the thought was perfectly clear. Or perhaps you were (2) ............ the verge of introducing a friend, and his name escaped you, as you were about to utter it. You may say you cannot remember; (3) ............ all probability, though, the thought has become unconscious, or (4) ............ least momentarily separated from consciousness. We find the same phenomenon (5) ............ our senses. If we concentrate hard (6) ............ a continuous note, which is (7) ............ the edge of audibility, the sound seems to stop (8) ............ regular intervals and then start again. Such oscillations are the result of a periodic decrease and increase (9) ............ our attention, not due to any variation (10) ............ the note.

But when we are unconscious (11) ............ something it does not cease to exist, any more than a car that has disappeared round a corner has vanished into thin air. It is simply (12) ............ of sight. Just as we may later see the car again, so we come across thoughts that were temporarily lost (13) ............ us.

Thus, part of the unconscious consists of a multitude of temporarily obscured thoughts, impressions, and images that, in spite of being lost, continue to have an influence (14) ............ our conscious minds. A man who is distracted or 'absent-minded' will walk across the room (15) ............ search of something. He stops, in a quandary – he has forgotten what he was (16) ............ . His hands grope (17) ............ the objects on the table as if he were sleepwalking or (18) ............ hypnosis; he is oblivious (19) ............ his original purpose, yet he is unconsciously guided by it. (20) ............ the end, he realises what it is that he wants. His unconscious has prompted him.

# Grammar: emphasis (2) (cleft sentences)

Very often, the **way** we speak reinforces the meaning of the grammatical structures we are using. In Exercises 1 and 2 below, the **intonation** and **stress** used by the speakers are at least as important as the actual words they say.

## 1

1  For each of the following sentence endings, 1-6, you will hear two possible **beginnings A** or **B**. These beginnings have slightly different **stress** and **intonation**, which affects the meaning. Listen and write the letter of correct beginning, **A** or **B**, in the spaces provided. The first one has been done for you as an example.

1  1 ..*A*.. not important, so it seems.
   2 ..*B*.. how on earth did they do it?
2  1 ....... she did.
   2 ....... to fix the car.
3  1 ....... is why he didn't ask her to marry him.
   2 ....... is this problem on page 66.
4  1 ....... at the cinema.
   2 ....... not a thriller.
5  1 ....... doesn't concern you at all.
   2 ....... is that more and more people are breaking the law.
6  1 ....... I suddenly broke out in a cold sweat.
   2 ....... was when he didn't come to work on time.

2  Now listen again to check your answers.

## 2

1  For each of the following statements you will hear a reply. Tick which statement, **A** or **B**, you think the reply is referring to.

1  **A**  Wasn't it that meeting that Peter was late for?
   **B**  I think it was Peter who waltzed in over an hour late for the meeting.
2  **A**  It was his dishonesty which amazed me more than anything else.
   **B**  I was really taken aback by his dishonesty.
3  **A**  All he ever does is moan about how much studying he has to do.
   **B**  He always seems to have his head buried in a book.
4  **A**  What he really wanted to do was go abroad to study.
   **B**  It was Paris that he had his heart set on visiting.
5  **A**  Anna's the one who can't make it to the party tomorrow night.
   **B**  I think it's tomorrow night that Anna can't come to the party.

6  **A**  What's new is that this test is being done on a human subject.
   **B**  This is the drug being tested for the first time on humans.

2  Now listen again to check your answers.

**3**  Cleft sentences are common in both written and spoken English. For each of the following extracts, 1-5, rewrite the sentence in italics in a way which makes it more emphatic or persuasive.

1  People's lifestyles are changing. The majority of people are no longer concerned just about making money, or about moving on in their careers – they are beginning to pay attention to the way they live. *More and more people are leaving big cities to go and live in small towns and villages. This is particularly interesting.*
   What ......................................................................

2  I like going out with friends – you know, to cafés and fast food restaurants and I'm keen on music ... um ... but *I really like going to parties!*
   What ......................................................................

3  I'm sick to death of my husband! *He just complains about the weather!*
   All ......................................................................

4  I have wonderful memories of my childhood. Long summer days spent out on the veranda with my brothers and sisters, the excitement of Christmas or going on holiday, the magic of birthday parties spent with all my friends ... *I remember my father playing the piano in the evenings most, though.*
   What ......................................................................

5  You know, I can hardly remember a thing about the operation I had yesterday. It seemed to be over before I knew what had happened. *I can remember the doctor giving me the injection though.*
   The only ......................................................................

**4**  **Use of English:** sentence transformations
Finish each of the following sentences in such a way that it is as similar as possible in meaning to the sentence printed before it.

1  Janice is in America, so you probably saw her twin sister in town yesterday.
   Janice is in America, so it ..............................

2  I can't understand why you didn't telephone me when you heard the results.
   What ......................................................................

3  What I find particularly offensive is his arrogant attitude.
   It's ......................................................................

4  Going out to parties is the only thing you think
   about.
   All ................................................................

5  I'm baffled by his lack of enthusiasm for the
   project.
   What ...........................................................

6  I'm more concerned about the state of your health
   than about your finishing the job.
   It's not .......................................................

7  I am not interested in what they have decided
   to do.
   What ...........................................................

8  They will ask you to attend an interview.
   What ...........................................................

9  You should complain to the manager.
   The person ...................................................

10 I first realised that something was wrong when one
   of the cheques bounced.
   The first .....................................................

## Listening: sentence completion

Paper 4

### About the exam

The prompt sentences in sentence completion
exercises focus on the main ideas in the text.
Normally there are between ten and twelve
sentences to be completed. The prompt sentences
always follow the order of information in the
recording. As with all of the listening tasks, you will
hear the recording twice.

Look again at Unit 2, page 18 for guidance on the best way
to approach sentence completion exercises.

You will hear part of a radio show in which a psychologist
talks about what makes people lucky or unlucky. Read the
prompt sentences before listening, and try to predict what
kind of information you will need to listen out for. When
you have done this, listen to the recording and complete
each sentence with a word or short phrase. Listen to the
recording twice.

A recent study in Iowa suggests that there is a
[_____ 1] for good
and bad luck.

The study involved the choice of cards which
[_____ 2] to the
participant

Researchers concluded that the 'intuition part' of
some people's brains was not
[_____ 3]

Not only are some people rich and wealthy, but
[_____ 4] also go in
their favour.

Lucky people are usually much
[_____ 5] than unlucky
people.

People who believe that good things
[_____ 6] find their
expectations fulfilled.

Luck and unlucky people also
[_____ 7] in different
ways.

Many individuals gain
[_____ 8] being
particularly lucky or unlucky.

Some people possess
[_____ 9] which brings
good things to them.

Lucky people often say that
[_____ 10] is
responsible for their good fortune.

Irrational decisions, however, are often based on
[_____ 11]

In business, someone who is 'lucky' is good at
making [_____ 12]
decisions.

# Writing: narrative composition (2)

## Exam Strategy

A good narrative requires a careful outline! Make sure yours includes:

- a clear idea of what will happen, and how you will integrate the first or last line into the story logically, if this is provided in the exam task
- a dramatic **beginning** or **ending**, which will grab the reader's attention
- enough **description** and **plot** to make a focused story which is interesting to read, but not over-complex
- **flashbacks**, to explain the background to events and the feelings of characters in your story
- sophisticated language, including vivid verbs, adverbs and a wide variety of structures, so you don't repeat yourself when writing.

### 1

1   Read the following task, and make brief notes about what the old woman might have said.

> Write a story which finishes with the sentence: *How grateful she felt that she had listened to the old woman.*
> (About 350 words.)

2   Now read the following outline, which was written by a student in preparation to answer the task above. Ignore the numbers and underlining for the moment. Is there anything wrong with the outline, in your opinion? Make a note of your thoughts in your notebook.

*Introduction*
*In the morning – Ruth at home with her unwell mother*
*Her mother is encouraging her about job interview.*
*(1) Feels very close to her mother (only person who understands her)*

*First supporting paragraph*
*Goes to station*
*4 o'clock – still waiting for train. Standing all alone on platform/(2) waiting impatiently. (Disaster if train is late.)*

*Second supporting paragraph*
*Suddenly someone taps her on shoulder. Turns round and sees old woman.*
*(3) Woman tells her she must go home at once – something is wrong.*

*Closing paragraph*
*(4) Ruth rushes home. Finds her mother unconscious in kitchen.*
*As she brings her round she thinks about the day's events. How grateful she felt that she had . . .*

2   As you read the outline, you will notice that this student put all the events of the story in chronological order. Obviously, the beginning of such a story would not really **grab the attention** of the reader. Read the four possible starting points, 1–4, which are underlined in the outline above. Match each starting point to one of the following comments, a)–d), and write the number in the space provided.

a) This is an interesting point in the narrative, but it might be a confusing place to start the story, as there is too much to explain (why, who, etc.). ............
b) This would be good, as it focuses on the feelings of the central character, but it's not a very dramatic opening. ............
c) This would be a dramatic start, but happens rather late in the story – nearly all of the other events would have to be in *flashback* form. ............
d) This opening is ideal – it's dramatic, creates sympathy with the feelings of the main character, and a certain amount of suspense – the reader is drawn into the story, and the background to the situation. ............

3   Now read the composition which the student wrote. Does it start where you thought it should? Ignore the underlining for the moment, but think about any improvements which you might make. Note down any ideas in your notebook as you read.

Standing alone on the platform, Ruth began to feel her spirits sinking. It was already 4 o'clock. If the train didn't arrive in the next ten minutes, she would be late for her job interview – and that would be a disaster. *She suddenly thought of her unwell mother and felt unbearably sad.* Her mother really was the only person who understood what this job meant to her.

Her thoughts were suddenly interrupted by someone's hand tapping gently on her shoulder. She turned round quickly and looked into the face of an old lady. *There was something familiar about her. What was it?* 'I'm sorry to frighten you, my dear,' she said, 'but you must go home immediately. Something is wrong.' Amazed, Ruth stared at the old lady, got up quickly and rushed out of the station.

Five minutes later she was standing at the front door. As she looked for the key in her handbag, *she began to feel rather angry with herself for listening to the woman.* Immediately she opened the door, though, she noticed the smell of gas in the house. She ran to the kitchen to find her mother unconscious on the floor and the door of the oven open. She had obviously had one of her 'dizzy spells'. Fortunately, though, she was still alive. Taking hold of her quickly, she pulled her out into the garden and brought her round. As she did so, she thought about the day's events. How grateful she felt that she had listened to the old woman.
*(256 words)*

**4**  The composition is well written, but too short for the exam. One way of adding length and interest to this story would be to give the reader more insight into the feelings of the young woman, with the use of **flashbacks**.

Read the three parts of the composition which are underlined and write a flashback for each one in your notebook, using the following notes. The first one has been done for you.

1  *She suddenly thought of her unwell mother and felt unbearably sad.*
Notes: Sadly she remembered ... morning – mother encourages her/looks on admiringly/makes suggestions as to what she should wear, etc.
Flashback: Sadly she remembered how much her mother had encouraged her that morning, how she had looked on admiringly, reassuring her and making suggestions as to what she should wear and what she should say.

2  *There was something familiar about her. What was it?*
Omit the question *What was it?* and add the following.
Casting her mind back ... when child – often saw woman outside church/railing against injustice of life/appearance not changed.
(Use *remembered* in your sentence.)

3  *She began to feel rather angry with herself for listening to the woman.*
Add three short sentences.
How ... stupid to believe her.
She ... obviously drunk.
How ... know something wrong?
(Change verb forms as necessary.)

**5**  Now read the following task.

> Write a story which starts with the words: *Sitting on her own in the busy restaurant, Susan looked again at her watch and sighed.* (About 350 words.)

Use the Exam Strategy box on page 78 and the language in Exercise 4 to help you. You can also refer to Unit 5, pages 46–47 for guidance on the basic structure of narrative compositions.

**Useful expressions for introducing flashbacks**

... she cast her mind back to ...

... it called to mind the time when ...

... this was not the first time she had ...

... only once before had she ever ...

... it brought it all back to her: the time she had ...

**6**  Exchange your composition with another student if you can. Evaluate each other's work and suggest improvements.

# *10* The world of work

## Vocabulary review: multiple-choice

**Paper 1, Section A**

Choose the word or phrase, **A**, **B**, **C** or **D**, which best completes each sentence.

1 The baby can't even crawl yet, ............. walk!
   **A** let alone   **B** not to mention   **C** least of all
   **D** by and large

2 This part of the museum is strictly .............
   limits to the public.
   **A** beyond   **B** off   **C** above   **D** out of

3 Her new novel is written from the ............. of a small child.
   **A** view   **B** prospect   **C** regard   **D** perspective

4 There is a pressing ............. for better facilities in this area.
   **A** need   **B** requirement   **C** movement
   **D** desire

5 We are considering ............. up our own import-export business.
   **A** putting   **B** taking   **C** setting   **D** making

6 At first ............., the place seemed utterly deserted.
   **A** look   **B** regard   **C** view   **D** glance

7 I am so busy these days that I don't have much time for household .............
   **A** tasks   **B** chores   **C** jobs   **D** labours

8 Most of the people who live in this town ............. to London every day.
   **A** commute   **B** transport   **C** impute
   **D** mutate

9 The government is thinking of introducing a(n) ............. ban on the use of certain pesticides.
   **A** blanket   **B** umbrella   **C** carpet   **D** curtain

10 Only a cunning and ............. businessman could amass such a fortune so quickly.
   **A** unkempt   **B** unscrupulous   **C** unpalatable
   **D** unseemly

## Grammar: determiners and pronouns

**Watch Out!** *problem areas*

- **use of the definite article**
  Many of the people don't agree with the changes which have been made. (= *people in general*)
  Many (of the) people I have spoken to would like to have a greater say in matters. (= *a specific group*) ✔
  All the people want *Everyone wants* better working conditions.
  I managed to read all the *the whole* report in a day.

- ***each* and *every***
  When we use *each* we look at people or things separately or 'one at a time'. *Every*, on the other hand, puts people or things into groups (like *all*).
  *Each/every* manager we get seems to want to make us work harder. ✔
  She had a child on *each/either* side of her. ✔
  (= *only two sides*)
  There were enemy soldiers on *every* side. ✔
  (= *many sides*)
  *Each/Every one* of the customers who came into the shop was given a questionnaire ✔ = they were every *each* given a questionnaire.

- ***neither* and *none***
  *Neither* applicant who applied for the job was successful. ✔ = Of the two applicants who applied for the job, *neither* was successful. ✔
  *None* of the applicants who applied for the post was accepted. ✔ = Of the many applicants who applied for the post, *none* was accepted. ✔

**1** **Use of English:** gapped sentences
Fill each of the gaps in the following sentences with a suitable word or phrase

1 How dare you interfere! What I do in my private life is ........................ yours!

2 No ........................ you say to him, he never listens.

3   You have every ........................ angry about how you were treated.
4   Although neither sister was a high flyer, ........................ them managed to pass their exams.
5   The help desk should be ........................ who has a problem with their computer.
6   There's no ........................ a fuss – things will only get worse if you do.
7   I asked two colleagues, but found ........................ could help.
8   I got lots of feedback, ........................ unfortunately turned out to be useful.

# Grammar: adjectives

> **Watch Out!** *problem areas*
>
> - **gradable and limit adjectives**
>   Gradable adjectives, which can exist in different degrees, can be modified with a range of adverbs.
>   She is a(n) very/extremely/fairly *friendly* person, isn't she? ✔
>   Limit adjectives, which have strong meanings and cannot exist in different degrees, can only be modified by adverbs with very strong meanings.
>   That meal was ~~very~~ ∧*absolutely* delicious!
>   We were ~~extremely~~ ∧*utterly* exhausted when we arrived.
>   *Really* can be used with both gradable and limit adjectives.
>   I think he's really *intelligent/brilliant.* ✔
>   She's a really *good/wonderful* teacher! ✔
>
> - *almost, nearly, virtually* **and** *practically*
>   These intensifiers can only be used with ungradable adjectives which have a **fixed meaning**.
>   This bottle of wine is *almost* empty. ✔
>   The book she is writing is *nearly* complete. ✔
>   The building was ~~virtually~~ ∧*absolutely* enormous.
>
> - *quite*
>   *Quite* has two different meanings.
>   The film was *quite interesting*, I suppose. (= *reasonably*) ✔
>   His contributions to science have been *quite remarkable*. (= *absolutely*. We stress *quite* when we use it with this meaning.) ✔

**1**   Look at the following sentences and choose the correct alternative, **A, B, C** or **D**, to fill each of the gaps.

1   We were ............ amazed that nobody had thought of the idea before us.
    **A** virtually   **B** almost   **C** quite   **D** extremely
2   They were ............ devastated by the news of his death.
    **A** extremely   **B** very   **C** really   **D** rather
3   Unlike you, I find him ............ friendly.
    **A** slightly   **B** virtually   **C** practically   **D** fairly
4   Apparently, they need someone for the job whose French is ............ fluent.
    **A** rather   **B** practically   **C** somewhat   **D** slightly
5   I found the assistants in the shop ............ rude and unhelpful.
    **A** somewhat   **B** virtually   **C** absolutely   **D** almost
6   He has lived in Paris for so long that he is ............ French.
    **A** quite   **B** fairly   **C** almost   **D** rather

**2**   **Use of English:** key word transformations
For each of the sentences below, write a new sentence as similar as possible in meaning to the original sentence, but using the word given. **This word must not be altered in any way**.

1   Hardly anyone turned up to watch the football match. **nobody**
    ............................................................................................
2   I know you can produce good work when you put your mind to it. **capable**
    ............................................................................................
3   Meeting the professor tonight will be a real honour for me. **proud**
    ............................................................................................
4   He only wants to join the project because he thinks he'll make some money out of it. **sole**
    ............................................................................................
5   The chances of our finding someone to replace Mr Jones are incredibly slight. **virtually**
    ............................................................................................
6   I cannot understand why you are unwilling to give Max a job. **baffled**
    ............................................................................................
7   In some countries people under the age of sixteen are not allowed to buy tobacco. **restricted**
    ............................................................................................
8   There were a few tiny mistakes in Harry's homework. **quite**
    ............................................................................................

# Reading: non-fiction

**1** Read the following passage about the construction of a traditional wooden building in Gloucestershire, in southwest England and answer the questions below.

Where do you think the passage was taken from?

- an encyclopaedia
- a school textbook
- a poster
- a magazine
- a newspaper

Many people would quail at the idea of having to construct an open-plan building 70ft long and 24ft wide out of freshly cut oak, using nothing but their hands and traditional tools. But to a master-craftsman like Henry Russell, the task of creating the Great Oak Hall at Westonbirt, the Forestry Commission's arboretum, or botanical tree garden, in southwest England, is no more than an agreeable challenge. A tousle-haired beanpole of 32, Henry is a versatile fellow, and for the past few years has been at the forefront of the revival in green woodworking. For years he has dreamt of building a big hall at Westonbirt, and now he has his chance.

Even though many of the materials have been given, and much of the work will be done by trainees, the building will cost over £300,000. So that work can start at once, a third of this sum has been underwritten by the charity Friends of Westonbirt Arboretum, and a fund-raising campaign will open later this year. When the project was launched at a reception in a marquee by the site of the hall, a number of oaks, contributed by local woodland owners, already lay on the ground outside, and 50 more mature oaks had been felled in the Silk Wood, one area of the arboretum. In a celebratory speech, the chairman of the Forestry Commission emphasised that nobody should see the cutting-down of ancient trees as an act of destruction or vandalism. On the contrary, he said: the harvesting was merely the latest move in centuries of careful woodland management, and the flora of the forest floor was already responding to the light which the felling of the trees had let in.

His words were very much to the point, but he rather gave away his own lack of practical skills when Henry Russell, handing him a sledge-hammer and wedges, invited him to split a round of oak as a token start. For Henry, in contrast, cutting, splitting and shaping green wood is second nature. He is well capable of tackling an entire oak on his own, cutting it to size with handsaws and axes; but in this case, to save time, the initial preparation of the trunks will be done mechanically by Henry, using a portable power-saw, and the cedar tiles for the roof will also be cut by machine; but thereafter, hand-tools will be the order of the day.

The aim is that much of the preliminary work will be done by volunteers, whether skilled workers or novices. Starting on 29th May, five week-long courses, for 12 trainees a time, will be held under the supervision of Gudrun Leitz, another pioneer of the green wood revival.

Taught by her and Henry, students will learn the techniques of cutting and shaping the wood. All they need bring with them, she says, is energy, enthusiasm, suitable clothes, and a pair of boots with steel toecaps. If they behave like most latter-day woodworkers, they will live on site in tents or homemade shelters. They will also need to be fairly impervious to scrutiny, for the site is in a commanding position, near the entrance, and visitors to the arboretum – around 300,000 a year – will doubtless flock round.

From models and drawings, it looks as though the hall will be a striking blend of ancient and modern. Like all its main timbers, the furniture will be made of oak, but the windows will be of high-tech glass. As to which will last longer – the wood in the building, or the oaks growing outside it – no one can say; but there is no doubt that the hall will be the most striking innovation at Westonbirt since the arboretum was founded in 1829.

**2**   Look at the following questions and unfinished statements about the text. In each case, choose the answer, **A**, **B**, **C** or **D**, which you think fits best, according to the passage.

Look again at Unit 3, page 27 and Unit 6, page 49, for guidance on how distractors operate, and of the best way to approach this type of question.

1   Green woodworking is a way of constructing buildings which
   **A**   is often used in the building of traditional houses.
   **B**   is coming back into fashion again.
   **C**   has been developed only in recent years.
   **D**   requires master craftsmen like Henry Russell.

2   The felling of trees for this project
   **A**   happened at the site of the new building.
   **B**   was essential for the other life on the forest floor.
   **C**   was seen as controversial by many.
   **D**   was funded entirely by the Friends of Westonbirt Arboretum.

3   The chairman of the Forestry Commission
   **A**   wanted more traditional woodland management.
   **B**   initiated the project with a public speech.
   **C**   had very pointed things to say about the project.
   **D**   was better at public speaking than woodworking.

4   The volunteer workers will
   **A**   have to construct their own accommodation.
   **B**   only be working with hand tools.
   **C**   stay on the site for over a month.
   **D**   be involved in the preparation of trunks.

5   What will the workers on the project have to get used to?
   **A**   being looked at closely by visitors
   **B**   meeting vast numbers of tourists
   **C**   being made to live in tents on site
   **D**   supervising visitors to the site

6   The Great Oak Hall at Westonbirt will
   **A**   be something new and original that will attract attention.
   **B**   use fashionable high-tech materials.
   **C**   be unusual, because built entirely of wood.
   **D**   be more durable than most modern buildings.

## Use of English: cloze

**Paper 3, Section A, Question 1**

**1**   Fill each of the blanks in the following passage with one suitable word or phrase.

Look again at Unit 1, pages 12–13, for guidance on the best way to approach this task.

## Keeping an eye on the staff

Big Brother could soon be watching from the inside. Several international companies are (1) ............ scientists on (2) ............ of developing microchip implants for their workers to measure their timekeeping and whereabouts.

The technology which has been tested (3) ............ pets and human volunteers, would enable firms to track staff all around a building or complex. The data could help them to (4) ............ up estimates of workers' efficiency and productivity.

Professor Kevin Warwick, a leading British scientist (5) ............ in developing the new technology, (6) ............ the headlines recently when he (7) ............ a silicon chip transponder surgically implanted in his forearm. He was subsequently (8) ............ to show how a computer could monitor (9) ............ every move, using detectors that were (10) ............ around the building in which he worked.

In his experiment, Warwick showed how the system could also benefit workers by programming (11) ............ to switch on lights, computers and heating systems as he entered a room – and turning them off when he (12) ............ .

The technology is likely to have a great (13) ............ to companies with high labour costs, for whom small increases in staff productivity can have a big (14) ............ on profits. At just a few pounds for each person, it is also relatively (15) ............ .

(16) ............ into the use of implants follows (17) ............ from earlier experiments by companies that showed how 'smart badges' (18) ............ by staff could be programmed to relay a worker's (19) ............ back to a central computer. These badges use ultrasound to tell the computer exactly where the wearer is, (20) ............ their desktop computers and phone calls to track them around the building.

## Vocabulary: adverb + adjective collocation

**1** Match the adverbs in box A to the adjectives in box B. The first one has been done for you.

| A | B |
|---|---|
| wildly | dull |
| widely | guarded |
| highly | available |
| deeply | skilled |
| closely | convinced |
| deadly | forbidden |
| entirely | moved |
| strictly | exaggerated |

**2** Complete each of the following sentences with the appropriate adverb + adjective combination from Exercise 1.

1 The lecture was ......................... and I almost went to sleep.
2 The gameplan of the winning team remained a ......................... secret.
3 She was ......................... by all the letters of support she received.
4 The report was published last week and is now ......................... in all leading bookshops.
5 Smoking in the work area is ......................... .
6 Osborne quickly gained the reputation of being a ......................... negotiator.
7 The details of the scandal have been ......................... .
8 I am not ......................... that we need to make so many workers redundant.

---

### Study Tip

Watch out for collocations like these when you are reading. Read with a pencil in your hand, mark interesting language that you come across, and transfer it to your notebook.

Few students learn and use adverbs really effectively; successful use of collocations like these in **Paper 2** compositions and **Paper 5** speaking will impress your examiner.

---

## Vocabulary: phrasal verbs and expressions: *work*

**1** Fill the gaps in the following sentences with the correct form of the phrasal verbs *work up* or *work out*. Make any necessary changes to complete each sentence. Use a dictionary to help you if necessary.

1 I can't ......................... he left so suddenly without telling anybody. It really baffles me.
2 Here's a calculator – can you ......................... much money we owe the part-time staff, please?
3 I'm afraid it's just not ......................... me and my new boss. We've had three rows already.
4 I can't ......................... enthusiasm for his plan. It just seems to me like a real waste of time and money.
5 Come on, calm down. It's not worth getting yourself all ......................... such a small issue.
6 Sarah ......................... the gym three times a week. I don't know where she finds the energy.

**2** Choose the correct alternative to complete each of the following sentences.

1 The assessment wasn't much of a challenge to Sarah, and she made *short/small* work of it, finishing the whole thing in a matter of hours.
2 You'll have your work *cut/pulled* out to change the filing system here. I don't see how on earth you can do it.
3 I see that the firemen are working to *regulation/rule* again. I know they deserve a pay rise but I don't think this is the way to get it.
4 I'm working my fingers to the *skin/bone* trying to make enough money to live on. I don't think I can carry on like this.
5 Calm down! Don't work yourself into a *frenzy/fuss*, simply because you think you may lose your job!
6 I'm trying to work up the *courage/bravery* to go and tell my boss what happened.

# Grammar: the future

## Watch Out! *problem areas*

- **will and going to**
  *Going to* is frequently over-used where *will* would be more appropriate.
  I'll help you with your suitcase, if you like. ✔
  I'm going to help you with your suitcase.
  (= *sounds aggressive*)
  Will/Would you help me with this? ✔
  Are you going to help me with this?
  (= *sounds angry/sarcastic*)

- **predictions**
  The Present continuous is not generally used for predictions about events which are outside a person's control.
  I'm ~~getting~~ *going to get* really angry with you soon!
  ~~He's having~~ *He'll have/He's going to have* an accident one of these days if he's not careful.

- **Future continuous**
  This future form is commonly used when we want to ask a favour of someone. Here, *will* or *going to* would appear too direct.
  *Will you be going* to the bank? Could you give them this letter, please? (= *are you planning to do this anyway?* ) ✔

- **other future forms**
  Modal verbs can be used to refer to the future, as can structures such as *likely to*, *bound to*, etc. These tend to add something to the meaning.
  The plane *is due to/should* leave in half an hour.
  (= *it is expected to leave*) ✔
  She was *on the verge of* tears when I arrived.
  (= *very close to tears*) ✔
  The Prime Minister *is to* visit Spain next week.
  (= *formal engagement*) ✔
  We're *about to* go – are you ready? (= *we'll go in a few minutes*) ✔

## 1

1   Choose the appropriate ending, a) or b) for each sentence. Indicate your choice in the spaces provided.

1   I'm playing tennis with Roger tomorrow, .......
    a) if the weather is good.
    b) so I'm afraid I can't come with you on the picnic.
2   Are you going to you marry me, .......
    a) if I promise to give you whatever you want?
    b) or do I have to wait for *another* five years?

3   The train is due to arrive at six o'clock this evening, .......
    a) but I expect it'll be late.
    b) owing to the bad weather conditions.
4   He is on the verge of resigning, .......
    a) by the end of this month, I'm sure.
    b) though I don't think he's told the boss yet.
5   That tree's going to fall down, .......
    a) so get away from it quickly!
    b) by the time we return.
6   I'll be wearing a red pullover, .......
    a) if you'd prefer that.
    b) so I'll be easy to spot.
7   I'll be going to the supermarket later, .......
    a) so if you want something, let me know.
    b) if you can't be bothered to.
8   You'll be working overtime every day next week, .......
    a) because three members of staff are ill.
    b) if you don't listen to what I'm telling you!

2   Now rewrite the stems 1–8 above, so that they are appropriate for the **other** ending.

EXAMPLE:
*I'll play tennis with Roger tomorrow if the weather is good.*

## 2   Use of English: sentence transformations

Finish each of the following sentences in such a way that it is as similar as possible in meaning to the sentence printed before it.

1   He'll be getting promoted soon.
    It won't ................................................................
2   He doesn't stand a very good chance of winning the race on Saturday.
    He is ................................................................
3   When he refuses to work overtime, I'm certain there'll be problems.
    His ................................................................
4   Scientists are very close to discovering a cure for cancer.
    Scientists are on ................................................................
5   I have to renew my licence next month.
    My licence is ................................................................
6   Everyone thinks the sale of the house will be complete by the end of the week.
    The house ................................................................

# Writing: report (2)

## Exam Strategy

- Read the question carefully. Make a quick note of **who the reader will be**, and the **purpose** of your report (e.g. to summarise / justify / make recommendations, etc.).
- Plan your report, using **headings** and thinking about what information you intend to include in each paragraph.
- Keep the language you use **impersonal** and **formal**. If you mention the views of other people about a particular matter, make sure you do so using words and phrases of an appropriate register.

### Exam Tip! ◀

As you write, avoid the temptation to turn your report into a discursive composition. A report 'reports' on a situation – it is not a discussion of a topic.

**1** Exercises 1 and 2 focus on the differences between a report and a discursive composition.

1 Read the following two extracts from student compositions. One comes from a discursive composition and the other comes from a report. Tick the one which comes from a report.

**1** ☐

*Income and status*
*The majority of students thought that income and status were inseparable. Interestingly enough, however, only about 40% of those present expressed a wish to become doctors or lawyers – careers which offer both a high income and high social status. Money was thought to be important, but not the most important factor in choosing a career.*

*Job satisfaction*
*Most students regarded job satisfaction as the most important factor in their future careers. The opinion was expressed by a number of participants that since work comprised a large part of most people's lives, it was essential that this area should bring fulfilment. Job satisfaction was seen to include other factors such as prospects of promotion and . . .*

**2** ☐

*It is interesting that large numbers of people nowadays have become disillusioned with the system whereby career status and income are seen as the most important aspects of a person's life. There has even been a tendency among young people in recent years to reject the values of materialism altogether and to embrace alternative lifestyles. The fact that the 1960s are viewed with nostalgia by many today, and that the songs of the Beatles and Jim Morrison are once more in vogue, shows that young people have not lost their idealism. In fact they are probably just as idealistic as their fathers and mothers were when they were young. How exactly does this idealism express itself today however?*

*What is certain is that students and young people have grown just as tired of politics as they have with the values of materialism. They find politicians difficult to take seriously and prefer to become involved in ecological or 'green' issues, such as campaigning against the destruction of the rainforests or modern farming methods, or even . . .*

2 Cross out the items in the following list which you would be **unlikely** to find in a report.

a) direct speech
b) phrases like 'it is interesting that ...', 'remarkably, ...'
c) rhetorical questions
d) examples to support ideas
e) a general or abstract discussion of a topic
f) use of the passive voice

**2**

1 Extract 1 in Exercise 1 was written in answer to the following task.

> You attended a conference at your school or college recently in which students discussed the factors they considered to be important in their future careers. Income, prospects, job satisfaction and social life were among some of the points covered.
>
> Using these points or others you consider to be appropriate, write a report summarising their views and comment on what they reveal about the hopes and aspirations of young people in your country. (About 300 words.)

**2** Read extract 1 again, and the alternative conclusions below. Decide:

- which conclusion is most appropriate for the task, and extract 1
- which conclusion is most appropriate for a discursive composition.

**A** ☐

The conference was a great success. Those who participated benefited enormously from the opportunity it presented to exchange opinions and to discuss issues of importance to young people today. I would recommend that further conferences be held in the future on subjects such as the attitude of European countries towards poverty, the problem of environmental pollution or the place of music and art in a modern society.

**B** ☐

In conclusion, it is clear that young people demand much more from a job than just money or status. Even though there is little job security these days, the youth of today is looking for something more than just 'landing a better job' or buying a bigger house. Should we not consider changing the education system to bring it more in line with these hopes and aspirations? A system which encouraged creativity and social awareness would be more valuable than the one we have at present, which appears to actively encourage only selfishness and greed.

**C** ☐

The conference was extremely worthwhile and gave young people an opportunity to express their feelings about a number of issues relevant to the world of work. It is particularly significant that income is no longer considered to be the most important factor in a career. This seems to suggest that young people today are less materialistic than the previous generation. It is also significant that most young people do not see their social life as being a priority – something which would indicate that older people have seriously misunderstood the younger generation.

**3**

**1** Write a report in answer to the following task.

You work voluntarily as a librarian in a school or college library. Recently a number of students have made complaints about the service and facilities offered, some of which are detailed below. Write a report to the Finance Director, who decides how funds for improvements are allocated. Outline what you feel to be the most serious problems and suggest what should be done to improve the situation. (About 300 words.)

> *The books I need for my course are always out on loan!*

> I can't understand why they allow people to talk and even smoke in the library!

> *Why doesn't the library have photocopying facilities?*

> Wouldn't it be a good idea if we could sit down somewhere and have a cup of coffee?

**2** Plan your composition, deciding which problems you intend to include, and the headings you will use for your paragraphs.

**3** Now write your report, making sure that the language you use is formal and impersonal.

### Useful expressions for report writing

this report will describe …
the aim of this report is to …
it has been mentioned/pointed out/suggested
   that …
the opinion has been expressed (by many students)
   that …
is/are seen to be …
it is apparent that …
I (would) recommend/suggest that … be done …
I feel (strongly) that …

**4** When you have finished, check your report carefully for errors.

**4** Exchange your report with another student if you can. Evaluate each other's work and suggest improvements.

# UNIT
## 11  The monster in the machine

## Vocabulary review: multiple-choice

> **Paper 1, Section A**

Choose the word or phrase, **A**, **B**, **C** or **D**, which best completes each sentence.

1 Radiation is known to cause changes to the genetic ............ in most organisms.
   **A** material   **B** fabrics   **C** matter   **D** stuff

2 Some European countries seem to attach little importance to their architectural ............ .
   **A** heritage   **B** inheritance   **C** heredity
   **D** heresy

3 The success of Dr Rogers' experiments made quite an ............ on the scientific community.
   **A** influence   **B** impact   **C** impulse   **D** effect

4 In much biological research the electron microscope is an ............ piece of equipment.
   **A** indiscernible   **B** indisputable
   **C** indiscriminate   **D** indispensable

5 It was only when he examined the diamond more carefully that he noticed it contained a slight ............ .
   **A** fault   **B** flaw   **C** defect   **D** disorder

6 Honesty and sincerity are the personal ............ I value most in a good friend.
   **A** points   **B** attributes   **C** aspects   **D** facets

7 His research work over the past thirty years has steadily been pushing back the ............ of our knowledge.
   **A** limits   **B** frontiers   **C** fronts   **D** borders

8 Her new research work served to ............ her reputation further.
   **A** magnify   **B** strengthen   **C** highlight
   **D** enhance

9 The existence of life on other planets is well within the ............ of possibility.
   **A** realms   **B** areas   **C** fields   **D** limits

10 Professor Arthur's claims ............ in the face of all the available evidence.
   **A** go   **B** jump   **C** fly   **D** move

## Grammar: reflexive verbs

> **Watch Out!** *problem areas*

- **reflexive verbs followed by *to***
  Several reflexive verbs take the dependent preposition *to*. This means that they are followed either by a noun or by the *-ing* form of a verb.
  She has *dedicated herself to* (fight**ing** for) the rights of animals. ✔
  This book doesn't *lend itself to* (be**ing** adapted for) television. ✔

- **nouns which become reflexive verbs**
  When a noun becomes a reflexive verb, there is usually also a change of preposition.
  I maintained a certain distance *between* myself and my mother. = I distanced myself *from* my mother. ✔
  She takes pride *in* her cooking. = She prides herself *on* her cooking. ✔

- ***suit yourself/please yourself***
  These two expressions are synonymous and are used rather sarcastically in spoken English, normally in the imperative.
  'I don't want to come to the party with you tonight.' '*Suit yourself.*' ✔

- ***enjoy* and *entertain***
  These verbs always need an object.
  I *enjoyed* the film very much. ✔
  I didn't *enjoy myself* very much at the party last night. ✔
  A magician *entertained* the children for over an hour. ✔
  I'm afraid I have to go out on urgent business. Can you *entertain yourselves*? ✔

- ***occupy***
  If something occupies you (or your mind or time), you are busy doing it or thinking about it.
  Dealing with the day-to-day running of the business *occupies* all his time. ✔
  How do you *occupy yourself* when you are on your own? ✔

**1   Use of English:** guided key word transformations
For each of the following sentences, write a new sentence as similar as possible in meaning to the original sentence, but using the word given. **This word must not be altered in any way**. In this exercise, all the questions test **reflexive verbs**.

1   Anne is proud of her ability to speak five languages fluently. **prides**
.......................................................................

2   Please pour yourself a drink while I'm getting ready. **yourself**
.......................................................................

3   You shouldn't feel that what happened was your fault. **for**
.......................................................................

4   She does not want to be involved in the scandal caused by her husband's remarks. **distance**
.......................................................................

5   It would be easy to make a film adaptation of Danielle Steel's latest novel. **itself**
.......................................................................

6   Raising the standard of living of the poor is all he spends his time on. **himself**
.......................................................................

7   He reluctantly accepted that he would have to spend the evening on his own. **spending**
.......................................................................

8   You need not make a final decision now about whether or not to support the proposal. **commit**
.......................................................................

9   Were the children good while the baby-sitter was here? **themselves**
...................................................................?

10   She knew she couldn't cope with the temptation to eat the bar of chocolate. **trust**
.......................................................................

**2   Use of English:** gapped sentences
Fill each of the gaps in the following sentences with a suitable word or short phrase. In this exercise some, but not all, of the questions require a **reflexive verb**.

1   I know you're nervous about the exam, but you really ......................... together before it starts!

2   Take a rest! You'll ......................... out if you continue to work as hard as this.

3   I was distracted by the noise outside to such an extent that I ......................... on what I was doing.

4   Unless you ......................... a bit more, the boss will treat you like a doormat, you know.

5   Shall ......................... us something to eat?

6   This little car ......................... to the ground. It's exactly what I need.

7   He didn't mean to steal the money. He just ......................... himself.

8   I'm resigning ......................... job – I just don't want to work here any more!

# Use of English: comprehension and summary

**Paper 3, Section B**

### Exam Strategy

Look out for comprehension questions which:

*   require you to find a **word or phrase** from the passage. Don't waste time writing out whole sentences!

*   have more than one part e.g. 'find ... **and explain**' or 'find **two** phrases which ...'

*   ask what is **suggested or implied** by the writer, or by a phrase in the passage. This means that you are not looking for the exact words of your answer in the passage itself, but have to think about whether the choice of language has negative or positive associations, or suggests a link between one idea and another: what the writer was thinking when he/she chose the words.

*   require you to find out how one word or phrase **refers to, or is echoed by** another. This is asking you to find extended metaphors in the passage e.g. if the author talks about 'floods of complaints' then later about 'drowning in the criticism'.

*   require you to 'explain **in your own words**'. This means that you should show you understand a word or phrase, and that you **must not** use the words of the passage in your answer.

### Exam Tip!

The summary is worth a lot of marks. For this reason, you should not get stuck on the comprehension questions. Always leave yourself about **25 to 30 minutes** to write the summary. You can go back to those questions you were unsure about when you have completed the second draft of your summary.

**1** Read the following passage about voice-controlled computers. Does the writer believe that natural conversation with a computer is a real possibility for the future?

# TALKING TO COMPUTERS

One of the shared assumptions in computer research is that talking to computers is a really great idea. Such a good idea that speech is regarded as the natural interface between human and computer.

5 Each company with enough money to spare and enough egotism to believe that it can shape everyone's future now has a 'natural language' research group. Films and TV series set in the future use computers with voice interfaces to show how far technology has 10 advanced from our own primitive day and age. The unwritten assumption is that talking to your house will in the end be as natural as shouting at your relatives.

The roots of this shared delusion lie in the genuine 15 naturalness of spoken communication between humans. Meaning is transferred from person to person so effortlessly that it must be the best way of transferring information from a human to another object.

20 This view is misguided on many different levels. First people are so good at talking and at understanding what others say because they share a common genetic heritage. Children's brains are hard-wired with a general language structure that they then apply to the 25 surrounding spoken-word environment. The old view that language is learned by copying parents and other adults has been discredited in recent years, to be replaced by the theory that words are attached to a pre-existing structure in the child's mind in such a 30 way that grammar 'emerges', as it were, rather than is taught.

This view of human language, added to shared human experience, shows how people understand each other precisely in a conversation where a 35 transcript would make little sense. Unfinished sentences, in-jokes, catchphrases, hesitation markers like 'er' and 'you know', and words whose meaning is only clear in the context of that one conversation are no bar to human understanding, but baffled early 40 attempts at computer speech recognition.

Recent advances in artificial intelligence address the problem – but only in part.

Pioneering linguistic research by scientists has revealed much of the underlying structure of human 45 language, so much so that programmers can now mimic that structure in their software and use statistical and other techniques to make up for the lack of shared experience between operator and machine.

50 Some of the obvious drawbacks of universal voice control have already been countered. The dreadful prospect of an office full of people talking to their machines has brought about the headset and the throat microphone; these also address the fact that 55 people feel ridiculous talking to something which is non-human. The increasing sophistication of voice-processing and linguistic-analysis tools cuts out the dangers of inaccurate responses to input, preventing the computer from having to respond to every single 60 word uttered, no matter how nonsensical in the overall context.

The fundamental objection to natural language interfaces is that they're about as unnatural as you can get. You might be able to order a computer about 65 in its limited sphere of action, but it'll never laugh at your jokes, make sarcastic comments, volunteer irrelevant but interesting information or do any of the other things that make real human conversation so fascinating. If interaction is limited to didactic 70 instruction from human to computer, why use up valuable processing time performing the immensely difficult task of decoding language correctly? To keep your hands free? For what, precisely?

There's another psychological reason why language 75 control is difficult: the decline in domestic service throughout this century, the absence of military experience from the lives of the last two generations, and the flattening out of business management have all combined to produce a population that's not 80 accustomed to giving crisp orders and expecting them to be obeyed.

Controlling a computer by word power works best if you imitate a drill sergeant, avoiding all 'could you's' and 'would you mind's' that most of us use when 85 trying to coerce someone into doing something they'd rather not do. This modern variant of the servant problem opens up the chance of ambiguity and error when interacting with a machine.

It could be said, though, that it's just as well we've 90 forgotten how to give orders. Slaves always have had a reputation for conspiring against their master's backs.

**2**   Answer the following questions about the passage.

1   Which word suggests that the writer disapproves of the aims and attitudes of large companies?

.................................................................

.................................................................

2   What does the writer suggest by using the phrases 'shared assumptions' (line 1) and 'the unwritten assumption' (line 11) when describing how computer researchers view natural language?

.................................................................

.................................................................

3   Explain in your own words what has caused the 'shared delusion' (line 14) of researchers.

.................................................................

.................................................................

4   Explain in your own words why people have no difficulty understanding one another.

.................................................................

.................................................................

5   Explain in your own words what has happened to the view that children acquire language via a process of imitation.

.................................................................

.................................................................

6   What point is the writer making when he mentions 'in-jokes, catchphrases, hesitation markers' and other features of language? (line 36)

.................................................................

.................................................................

7   Which phrase summarises the fundamental problem faced by programmers, which 'pioneering linguistic research' has partly helped to solve? (line 43)

.................................................................

.................................................................

8   Explain in your own words why increasingly sophisticated voice-processing and linguistic-analysis tools have been developed.

.................................................................

.................................................................

9   Explain in your own words how the writer feels that communication with computers will always be limited.

.................................................................

.................................................................

10   Explain how business management has changed, according to the writer.

.................................................................

.................................................................

11   What does the writer imply about the attitudes of drill sergeants?

.................................................................

.................................................................

12   According to the writer, what is essential if 'ambiguity and error' are to be avoided? (line 87)

.................................................................

.................................................................

**3**

1   Read the following summary question.

> In a paragraph of 70–90 words, summarise the problems involved in using computers to react to human orders.

2   Look through the whole passage and write a list of the points you need for this summary. For example, which problems might relate to people, and which to the efficiency of the computer system?

3   Write the first draft of your summary.

4   Check and edit your summary using the checklist in Unit 2, page 21 to help you.

### About the exam

The mark you are given for your summary depends on two things.

**1   Identification of points**
The examiner is looking for a selection of points from the passage which are relevant to the summary title. Normally, the number of points is four or five. You will be given a **maximum of four marks** for your identification of these points.

**2   Use of language**
The examiner awards marks for:
*   well-written, concise paragraphs
*   using your own words
*   good organisation of points
*   use of connectors.
You may be given up to **eight marks** for your use of language.
**Note that this is twice as much as for the selection of the points.**

# Use of English: guided sentence transformations

### About the exam

You will have to rewrite **eight** sentences in **Paper 3, Section A, Question 2**, keeping the meaning of the sentences you write as close as possible to the meaning of the sentences you are given. For each sentence you write, you may need to make changes both to vocabulary and grammatical structures.

### Exam Strategy

- Try to work out the structure which is being tested.
- When you write your sentence, don't leave out or change any important information.
- Pay particular attention to verb forms. For example, if a continuous form of a verb is used in the original sentence, you are likely to need a continuous form in the sentence you write.
- Very often you will need to change the form of a word (e.g. adjective to noun). In many cases, this change means you will also need to add a new dependent preposition, or use a different one from that in the prompt sentence.
- When you finish, check your work carefully for spelling or punctuation mistakes.

### 1

1  Read the following sentence transformation. What types of change will you have to make to transform it?

This government will only survive if unemployment goes down sharply.
Unless there ...................................................................................

2  Now compare your thoughts with the answer below. Were you right about the types of change necessary?

Unless there *is a sharp drop in unemployment, this government will not survive.*

Changes:
1  will only survive if ➜ unless ... will not survive (*if* + positive verb form ➜ *unless* + negative verb form)
2  goes down sharply ➜ there is a sharp drop in (verb + adverb ➜ *there is* + noun + adjective + preposition)

### 2

In this exercise, you have been given the **form** of the missing words to help you, although you will get no extra help in the exam.

1  If sales decreased dramatically, the company might go bust.
Were there (*infinitive*) a ............. (*adjective + noun*) ............. (*preposition + noun + unchanged rest of sentence*).

2  They have recently been attacking this intolerant government.
This government ............. (*adverb + passive form*) ............. (*dependent preposition + noun*) ............. (*dependent preposition + possessive + noun*).

3  Whatever happens, you are not to alter the settings of this instrument.
Under ............. (*fixed expression*) ............. (*inverted verb form + subject*) ............. (*infinitive + unchanged rest of sentence*).

4  You could be instantly dismissed for refusing to obey the regulations.
Your ............. (*noun*) ............. (*unchanged part of sentence*) ............. (*unchanged modal verb + verb + dependent preposition*) ............. (*adjective + noun*).

### Exam Tip!

Notice how many transformations have a phrase which **doesn't change at all**. When you first read the transformation, try to identify what is going to change in your new sentence, and what will stay the same. When you check your work, look again at the changes you have made, and try to decide if they were really necessary.

### 3

In this exercise, the answers provided for each transformation are only 'half right': they would get **some** marks in the exam, **but not full marks**. Correct each answer to make it perfect.

1  He's going to the barber's tomorrow for a haircut.
He's *having his haircut tomorrow.*

2  I stayed up far too late last night, and feel awful this morning.
Had*n't I stayed up so late last night, I wouldn't feel so bad this morning.*

3  He didn't learn how to read until he was eight years old.
It was *at the age eight that Peter learned to read.*

4  I hate the really untidy way you leave your socks around!
I wish *you wouldn't leave your socks around untidily!*

5  It looks to me as if someone has stolen all of the jewellery.
  All of the jewellery *looked to have been stolen.*

6  They are unlikely to allow him to continue with his experiments.
  There is little *likelihood of his allowing to continue with his experiments.*

**4**  In the following exercise, as in the exam, you have been give no extra help in identifying or making the necessary changes to transform each sentence.

1  His research is only comprehensible for those with a knowledge of nuclear physics.
  People who ...........................................................

2  I can't understand why you are so loathe to use a computer in your work.
  What beats ...........................................................

3  His behaviour may occasionally be unpredictable.
  There ...........................................................

4  Didn't you ever realise that he was a criminal?
  Did it ...........................................................

5  Her participation in the experiments was entirely voluntary.
  She was under ...........................................................

6  This is the tallest building in the city by far.
  No other ...........................................................

7  The inaccuracy of this machine is due to a small defect in the timing device.
  Were it ...........................................................

8  The outcome of the mission was never in any doubt.
  At no ...........................................................

9  This is a perfect book to be adapted on film.
  This book lends ...........................................................

10 If our fuel supply continues, we'll be fine.
  Unless we run ...........................................................

11 On the announcement of the news, the public's reaction was so violent that several politicians resigned.
  There ...........................................................

12 The fact that you contributed enabled me to complete my research.
  Had it ...........................................................

13 They are not very likely to pick him for the team.
  There is ...........................................................

14 The crime rate this year is much higher than last year's.
  There has ...........................................................

# Writing: discursive composition (2)

> **Paper 2**

### About the exam

In the discursive composition in **Paper 2** you may be asked to present only one side of an argument.

### Exam Strategy

- You should not discuss alternative points of view, but instead you should provide evidence which either supports or disproves the statement given in the writing task.
- You may want to evaluate the statement briefly in your introduction or conclusion, but be relevant and concise. Try to echo or mirror the words of the title or introduction in your conclusion.

**1**

1  Read the following paragraph, which is from a discursive composition about the Internet. Ignore the underlining for the moment. Is the tone of the paragraph:

1  too indecisive?
2  too blunt and direct?
3  more appropriate for a report than a discursive composition?

Large numbers of people use the Internet these days at home and in the office. (1) <u>This trend will continue</u> as people become aware of the ease with which they can send and receive information in any format and communicate with others around the world by means of e-mail. Although the benefits of this new technology are apparent, the negative aspects of the Internet (2) <u>have been ignored</u>. (3) <u>People dismiss</u> any view that is even mildly critical as being alarmist or perhaps uninformed. (4) <u>It is unfortunate</u>, for example, that many parents (5) <u>do not worry</u> about the amount of time their children spend 'surfing the net'. Even though doctors and psychologists have warned about the possibility of Internet addiction, few parents take these warnings seriously.

**2** The writer has been rather blunt in tone. We often use expressions which 'tone down' statements, to avoid appearing aggressive. Rewrite the underlined parts of the introduction on page 93, using the words or phrases from the box below. More than one answer is possible.

> to a large extent/largely    to some extent/rather
> in all probability/there is every likelihood/
> it is likely that    seem to/appear to
> is/are apt to/tend to    there is a tendency for

## 2

**1** Read the following task. How many parts are there to the question?

> Improvements in communications technology increasingly mean that people are becoming isolated from one another. Explain how you think this might be true and what could be done to deal with the problem. (About 350 words.)

**2** Read the following list of features which could be included in the introduction of a discursive composition. Which would you include if you were writing an introduction to a composition answering the task above?

1 A sentence quoting the words of a famous person.
2 A brief outline of the situation today.
3 An explanation of the meaning of the title.
4 The aspects of technology which will be discussed.
5 A detailed discussion of the benefits of improved communications technology.
6 A sentence which echoes the negative aspect of technology mentioned in the question.

**3** Now read the following introduction, which was written in answer to the task. Which of the features from the list above does it contain?

> *Recent technological advances have meant that people nowadays are generally able to communicate much more easily and effectively than ever before. This may, of course, have benefited many people, but it has also resulted in a situation where people have perhaps become more isolated from their immediate surroundings. Two good examples of this negative trend can be seen in the way large numbers of people seem to have become dependent on mobile telephones and the Internet as means of communication.*

**3** Read the three following supporting paragraphs, which make up the body of the composition. The numbered gaps indicate places where ideas or connecting phrases have been omitted. Choose the phrase or sentence, a), b) or c) below and opposite, which best fills each of these gaps. Remember that you need to consider the passage **as a whole**, to do this effectively.

> *Increasing numbers of people are using mobile telephones to communicate with friends, family and colleagues. Wherever they may be, (1) ............ . To a large extent, this has resulted in less meaningful face-to-face contact between people. It has also brought about a situation where meal times, social occasions and even (2) ............ , are apt to be interrupted by the bleeping of a mobile phone. Needless to say, (3) ............ .*
>
> *The Internet has likewise (4) ............ . Since it is possible to send and to receive almost any information you want over the Internet, the need to actually interact socially simply does not exist for some people anymore. In fact, the appeal of the Internet for many may be that they can work and play from home (5) ............ .*
>
> *Clearly, we need to be rather more aware of the effect this new technology is having on our lives and find ways to limit the damage. Mobile telephones, of course, can be turned off or left at home. It is unlikely to prove disastrous (6) ............ , and messages can always be left on an answerphone. Similarly, the use of the Internet can, and possibly should, be regulated. Parents in particular need to keep an eye on their children in order to prevent 'Internet addiction' from developing. As with most things, common sense is what is needed most.*

1 a) they can contact whoever they want easily and reasonably cheaply
   b) mobile telephones are both cheap and easy to use
   c) it will be possible to talk to whoever they want to
2 a) other important occasions
   b) when driving to work
   c) the Christmas dinner

3 a)  it has been known for people to be woken up in the middle of the night
   b)  this is both annoying and has a detrimental effect on relationships
   c)  people nowadays are simply not allowed to be 'unavailable'
4 a)  affected people's social skills
   b)  had a more disastrous effect on our relationships
   c)  grown over the past few years
5 a)  and spend very little money in the process
   b)  without ever having to get involved in human relationships
   c)  and make many new friends in the process
6 a)  unless a call is answered
   b)  if a call is left unanswered
   c)  provided a call is left unanswered

**4**   Which of these conclusions is more appropriate for the composition?

**A**

*In summing up, I feel that it would be wrong to pretend that the advantages of improved communications technology are insignificant. Nevertheless, it is true to say that there are negative aspects of this new technology and increased social isolation is perhaps the most important of these. This is something which most definitely should not be ignored.*

**B**

*In conclusion, it is obvious that this new technology is slowly destroying the fabric of society. It may even be detrimental to our health. There have been reports, for example, that mobile telephones cause cancer. We should take action now - before it is too late.*

**5**   The following two methods of organising the information would both be acceptable for the task we have been examining. Which method was used to write the composition above?

**A**

*Para. 1 – introduction*
*Para. 2 – mobile telephones – how they cause isolation*
            *– what could be done to deal with the problem*
*Para. 3 – Internet – how it causes isolation*
            *– what could be done to deal with the problem*
*Para. 4 – conclusion*

**B**

*Para. 1 – introduction*
*Para. 2 – mobile telephones – how they cause isolation*
*Para. 3 – Internet – how it causes isolation*
*Para. 4 – what could be done to deal with these problems*
*Para. 5 – conclusion*

**6**

1   Now write a discursive composition in answer to the following task.

> Some scientists believe that more money should be spent on space exploration. Discuss some of the ways in which this might benefit mankind.
> (About 350 words.)

2   Use the work you have done in Exercises 2 and 4 to write a relevant introduction and conclusion, and the language in Exercises 1 and 3 to help you express your ideas clearly, but not too bluntly.

**7**   Exchange your composition with another student if you can. Evaluate each other's work and suggest improvements.

## Reading: non-fiction

Paper 1, Section B

**1**  Which parts of your country are particularly affected by tourism? Make a list in your notebook of the positive and negative effects of tourism in these places.

**2**  The writer of the following text lives in a small town in Wales which receives large numbers of tourists every year. Read the passage and identify the extended metaphor used by the writer to refer to the effects of tourism. Underline the words which helped you decide.

The tourists are coming! Bar the gates, lock up your daughters! Here at my home in Wales just now, like many another honest citizen across half of Europe, I am standing to arms as the annual migratory horde spills once again out of the mountains to the sea. With its vast convoys of family cars, its terrible encampments of caravans, its generic concomitants of mess, wine and ugliness, it really does suggest to me, every summer, the arrival of a scavenging medieval army out of some ghastly hinterland.

As you perhaps detect, I hate mass tourism and almost everything to do with it. It is a sterile industry. It creates nothing. It degrades all it touches. It encourages pretence and phoney traditionalism. It brings out the worst in its practitioners and it reduces the mighty works of art and architecture, fateful processes of history, the noblest expressions of faith, the most magnificent scenes of nature, to the level of commercial gimmicks.

One of the miseries of tourism is that, almost by definition, it attacks everywhere most beautiful. The Côte d'Azur, Yellowstone, the Italian lakes, the Barrier Reef, the Greek islands, Venice and Sausalito, Prague and Cordoba – during the time of the mass migrations all such prodigies are as overwhelmed by the onslaught of the barbarians as is our own lovely corner of Cardigan Bay.

Of course they are not all barbarians, not all 'monsters of the sea', as a Venetian monk characterised the crowds thronging the Piazza San Marco in the Middle Ages. Of course they aren't. Some of my best friends are tourists.

But such is the scale of the modern holiday industry, so violent are its assaults and so relentlessly distributed across the face of the whole planet – even into Antarctica or the dread Sahara – that for me (and perhaps for you?) the very word 'tourist' has become a kind of shorthand for all things unlovely.

Many tourists these days don't even particularly care what country they are in – if indeed they know. Many more have long been acclimatised to the tourist version of travel. 'If today is Thursday', as an American movie title had it long ago, 'we must be in Belgium'.

I must not, however, be entirely negative. There are useful spin-offs from tourism. There are opportunities for local employment, though not half as many as the planning applications pretend. Shopkeepers or hoteliers who dislike tourism about as much as I do nevertheless get custom from the horde.

Many people in far-away places would never have tasted fish-and-chips were it not for tourism, and here at home I admit that satisfying the needs of tourists has sometimes provided happy advantages for local people – concerts, plays, amusements of one sort or another which otherwise would never have happened in a month of Sundays.

It can be said for tourism, too, that at least it draws the nations together, and tells them the truth about one another. Most inhibitions are shed when a citizen becomes a tourist, and I can imagine that if mass holidays had been happening on the present scale in 1939, there might not have been a Second World War. Surely the peoples of Europe would have been too familiar with each other's pot-bellies to take very seriously the idea of a war against a neighbour!

**3**   Read the following questions and unfinished statements about the passage. In each case, choose the answer, **A**, **B**, **C** or **D**, which fits best according to the passage.

Look again at Unit 3, page 26 and Unit 6, page 49 for guidance on the best way to approach this task.

1   Why does the writer compare the arrival of tourists to a medieval army?
   A   Tourists are often aggressive and behave violently.
   B   Like soldiers, tourists live in caravans and camps.
   C   Tourists migrate annually from the mountains to the sea.
   D   Tourists arrive in large numbers and do not respect the lives of the locals.

2   The writer hates mass tourism because
   A   tourists degrade themselves with their behaviour.
   B   tourists behave in ways which are deceitful and dishonest.
   C   it exploits the local attractions of a place solely for financial gain.
   D   it permanently alters areas of great natural beauty.

3   According to the writer, what has one result of the modern holiday industry been?
   A   The word 'tourist' has acquired a negative meaning.
   B   Local people in many places are violently opposed to it.
   C   There are hotels even in Antarctica and the Sahara.
   D   Local people in many places have become very greedy.

4   What does the writer imply about the way many tourists travel?
   A   They have no time to enjoy themselves.
   B   They have to follow a strict timetable.
   C   They are given no information about the countries they visit.
   D   They are more aware of changes in climate than changes in country.

5   According to the writer, how have the local people in Wales benefited from tourism?
   A   Cultural and entertainment opportunities have improved.
   B   Opportunities for local employment have increased considerably.
   C   Restaurants now offer their customers a wider choice.
   D   Concert halls and theatres are no longer closed on Sundays.

6   According to the writer, why does tourism bring the nations together?
   A   People tend to be more truthful when they are on holiday.
   B   People see one another for what they really are.
   C   People who are on holiday are friendlier than they normally are.
   D   People find it difficult to take one another too seriously.

# Vocabulary review: multiple-choice

### Paper 1, Section A

Choose the word or phrase, **A**, **B**, **C** or **D**, which best completes each sentence.

1   We spent at least five hours on board the yacht waiting for the wind to .............. .
   A pick up   B bring up   C start up   D blow up

2   Sales of 'Alpha' suntan cream increased last year, .............. other brands.
   A comparing   B at the expense of
   C with regard to   D opposite

3   .............. from the odd few exceptions, most tourists to the island respect the local customs and traditions.
   A apart   B except   C excepting   D bar

4   I wondered how the authorities would .............. the promotion of tourism with the need to protect the local wildlife.
   A recompense   B reconsider   C reconcile
   D reconstitute

5   He seems .............. on spoiling the holiday for us.
   A determined   B resolved   C serious   D bent

6   We always like to go somewhere off the beaten .............. for our holidays.
   A path   B road   C way   D track

7   We eventually arrived at the hotel, only to find everything .............. in darkness.
   A embraced   B shrouded   C smothered
   D enfolded

8   Most hotels agreed to .............. by the decision not to discriminate against guests wanting single rooms.
   A abide   B adhere   C observe   D obey

9   The manager of the restaurant laughed when we pointed out that the silver cutlery was .............. .
   A tarnished   B tainted   C marred   D disfigured

10   Strict guidelines have been .............. for the development of tourism in the area.
   A settled down   B taken down   C put down
   D drawn up

# Grammar: indirect speech

**1** **Use of English:** guided sentence transformations
Finish each of the following sentences in such a way that it is as similar as possible in meaning to the sentence printed before it. Choose an appropriate reporting verb in each case from the box below. Make sure you use the correct form of the verb for the context. There are some verbs you don't need to use.

> order   demand   accuse   recommend   promise
> warn   thank   plead   deny   enquire   direct
> blame   urge   threaten   compliment   advise

1 'It's your fault that we missed the train, Sandra!' said her mother.
Sandra's mother ..............................................................

2 'If I were you, I wouldn't say anything about this to the manager,' she said.
She ..............................................................

3 'Will you have finished the paper work by the time we come back, John?' she asked.
She ..............................................................

4 'If you don't behave yourselves, I won't give you back your pocket money!' our mother told us.
Our mother ..............................................................

5 'I won't ever tell anyone about the money you've given me,' she said.
She ..............................................................

6 'I didn't steal the money,' he said.
He ..............................................................

7 'Please don't pay any attention to their silly comments,' she said.
She ..............................................................

8 'You've done an excellent job here,' he told us.
He ..............................................................

**2** **Use of English:** gapped sentences
Fill each of the gaps in the following sentences with a suitable word or short phrase.

1 Although I hadn't been in his room, he accused ........................ his wallet.

2 They warned ........................ trying to make contact with her mother.

3 The misunderstanding was your fault! Don't try to put ........................ me!

4 She admitted that the plane ........................ off by the time they arrived at the airport.

5 We suggested ........................ an eye on their luggage while waiting for their train.

6 When we told them we had nowhere to stay, they offered ........................ up for the night.

## Grammar: impersonal passive constructions

> **Watch Out!** *problem areas*
>
> - **use of continuous/passive/perfect infinitives**
>   He is thought to ~~make~~ *be making* his way to the coast at this moment.
>   This painting is believed to be stolen. ✔
>   She was reported to ~~steal~~ *have stolen* the money yesterday.
>   Five terrorists were said to ~~be arrested~~ *have been arrested* by the police yesterday.
> - **negative sentences**
>   It is thought that he didn't commit the crime.
>   = He is thought not to have committed the crime. ✔
>   = He is not thought to have committed the crime. ✔
>   It is feared that he hasn't responded to treatment.
>   = He is ~~not feared~~ *feared not* to have responded to treatment.

### Use of English: sentence transformations

Finish each of the following sentences in such a way that it is as similar as possible in meaning to the sentence printed before it.

1 It is alleged that he had no knowledge of the situation.
He ...................................................................

2 It is thought that he will be arriving later in the day.
He ...................................................................

3 According to reports, the police have already arrested a man.
The police .......................................................

4 She was believed to have been using a false passport to enter the country.
It .......................................................................

5 She is not thought to have been involved in the scandal.
It .......................................................................

6 It was said that he hadn't been aware of the gravity of the situation.
He ...................................................................

## Listening: multiple-choice

> **Paper 4**

 You will hear a radio talk in which a young woman describes her experiences on the Inca Trail in Peru. Her destination was the Inca city of Machu Picchu. For each of the following questions, tick which of the alternatives, **A**, **B**, **C** or **D**, is the most appropriate response. Listen to the recording twice.

1 What made climbing particularly difficult for the speaker as she approached Dead Woman's Pass?
   A  A wall had been built across the path.
   B  She felt physically sick.
   C  The steps she was climbing up were very steep.
   D  the lack of oxygen in the air

2 On the group's first night in tents in this part of the holiday
   A  the temperature was not excessively low.
   B  the water froze in their water bottles.
   C  all their belongings were covered in a layer of ice.
   D  their sleeping bags did not keep out the cold.

3 On the second day of the journey
   A  the group made more rapid progress.
   B  some members of the group got lost in the woods.
   C  everyone walked as quickly as they could manage.
   D  some members of the climbing group travelled in the truck.

4 The speaker didn't want to sit down until
   A  she had taken photographs of Conrad.
   B  she felt sure she could relax.
   C  the whole of the group was reunited.
   D  the lunch was prepared.

5 How did the speaker feel when she arrived at Machu Picchu?
   A  disappointed
   B  delighted
   C  confused
   D  nostalgic

6 According to the speaker, the climbing group
   A  contained real professional explorers.
   B  took a very professional approach to the challenge of the climb.
   C  was exactly the right size.
   D  contained very adventurous people.

# Use of English: guided gapped sentences

### About the exam

You have to complete six gapped sentences in this part of the exam, usually using between two and five words. Some gaps may include more than one grammatical structure.

### Exam Strategy

- Read the whole sentence carefully, paying particular attention to the words which come immediately **before and after** the gap. You may be able to recognise a particular structure, collocation or expression you need to use when you fill the gap.
- Try to work out what structure (or structures) is being tested before you write anything.

For Exercises 1–3, you can use the checklist at the end of this section either to help you before starting, or to check your answers once you have finished.

**1** Fill the gaps in the following sentences with a suitable word or phrase. Key words, which will help you work out what is missing, are in italics, and you have been given hints to help you.

1 You will ........................ leave the airport *until* all your passports have been checked.
   (**HINT**: *Use a negative verb form.*)
2 Why *on* ........................ *you have told* me what you were planning to do?
   (**HINT**: *Use a fixed phrase + a modal verb.*)
3 You will need ........................ your report *by the time* we go home.
   (**HINT**: *Use a perfect verb form.*)
4 I *wish* I ........................ a better *impression* at the interview this morning.
   (**HINT**: *Use a past verb form + a collocating verb.*)
5 *He is believed* ........................ *off* on the journey yesterday morning.
   (**HINT**: *Use an impersonal passive construction + a phrasal verb.*)

**2** Complete each of the following sentences with a suitable word or phrase. In this exercise, key words are in italics to help you.

1 He *takes great pride* ........................ to speak five languages fluently.
2 If you do that, you *run* ........................ arrested by the police.
3 *Despite* ........................ *attention* to what was said, *she understood* perfectly what she had to do.
4 Exhausted ........................ , he *still* managed to keep on going.
5 It's *high* ........................ *an effort* to understand his point of view.

**3**

1 Complete each of the following sentences with a suitable word or phrase. As in the exam, you have been given no extra help.

1 It's amazing that ........................ to her, she always misunderstands him.
2 Had ........................ help they gave us, we wouldn't have been able to manage.
3 On no ........................ go on your own to the disused mine.
4 When you talk to her, you ........................ mind that she is still in a state of shock.
5 Try as she might, she was ........................ to terms with the terrible news.
6 Why is he so tired? It's not as ........................ particularly hard recently.
7 There ........................ whatsoever why you shouldn't apply for a place at that university.
8 If we'd bought a map, we ........................ that ridiculous predicament last night.
9 I am terribly sorry to ........................ much embarrassment yesterday.
10 How dare you suggest that I am to ........................ the accident on the ski-slope!
11 You'd ........................ anybody this secret or it will cause terrible trouble.
12 You need ........................ to all this trouble to cook for me – I've already eaten.

**2** Use this checklist to improve your gapped sentences. Look out for:

- a word requiring a collocating adjective, adverb, noun or verb
- a word – adjective, noun or verb – requiring a preposition before or after it (Remember that prepositions are followed by either a noun or an *-ing* form.)
- a word which is part of a fixed expression
- a preposition which could be part of a phrasal verb
- a word or phrase requiring a particular grammatical structure or verb form
- a word – such as a connector – which signals a change in meaning
- a verb form which tells you that a modal verb is required
- a word or phrase which is negative in meaning.

## Vocabulary: prepositions and prepositional phrases

For each of the sentences below, write a new sentence as similar as possible in meaning to the original sentence, but using the word given. In this exercise, you need to use either a preposition or a prepositional phrase in each new sentence.

1  How do you regard people who exploit the vulnerability of tourists? **attitude**

..................................................................

2  At least they'll look after her well at the clinic. **hands**

..................................................................

3  This building urgently needs to be renovated. **need**

..................................................................

4  Dr Jenkins no longer knows much about recent advances in medicine. **touch**

..................................................................

5  I don't mind a bit of hard work now and then. **averse**

..................................................................

6  Her homework hasn't been of the required standard recently. **scratch**

..................................................................

7  In the future, there'll be problems with this scheme. **run**

..................................................................

8  The police still haven't caught the escaped prisoner. **large**

..................................................................

## Grammar review: future forms with modal verbs

> **Watch Out!** *problem areas*
>
> - **the importance of context**
>   Sometimes only the context (and not the verb form itself) tells us that a sentence refers to the future.
>   In the future, robots *might be used* to do a number of household chores. ✔
>   If the weather doesn't improve, we *could be spending* next week sheltering from the rain. ✔
> - **modal perfects**
>   Modal verb + *have* + past participle can be used to refer to the future *or* the past. Check the context.
>   By the year 2050, we *might have reached* Mars.
>   = *perhaps we will have reached …* (= *future*) ✔
>   The plane *should have landed* by eight o'clock.
>   = *I expect it will have landed …* (= *future*) ✔
>   The robber *might have cut* his hand when he broke the window. = *perhaps he cut* his hand …
>   (= *past*) ✔

**Use of English:** guided key word transformations
For each of the following sentences, write a new sentence as similar as possible in meaning to the original sentence, but using the word given. Use a modal verb – but not *will* – in the sentence you write.

1  It's possible that plastic will be used for the bodies of cars in the future. **made**

..................................................................

2  I don't expect you to be working on that report any more tomorrow. **finished**

..................................................................

3  In all probability you'll know the results of the test by Friday. **given**

..................................................................

4  Your involvement in this would be unwise. **get**

..................................................................

5  It's possible that there will be Moon colonies in fifty years' time. **living**

..................................................................

6  There's a chance that a snake will bite you in that long grass. **bitten**

..................................................................

7  We expect your friend to arrive at the station some time before you do. **already**

..................................................................

8  There's a possibility the meeting will still be on when you arrive. **have**

..................................................................

# Writing: descriptive composition (3) (places)

Paper 2

## About the exam

In **Paper 2** you may have to write a description of a situation or a place and say how it has affected you.

## Exam Strategy

- Read the question carefully. Make sure you understand clearly what you have to describe and explain. You will lose marks if you only answer one part of the question! Plan your answer before you start writing.
- Use a range of descriptive verbs, adjectives and adverbs.
- Use direct speech where appropriate – but don't over-use it.

**1** Read the following task. Note down the place you would write about, and two other things you would try to include in your introduction.

Write a descriptive account of a visit to a place which made a great impression on you. Explain why it affected you so much. (About 350 words.)

**2**

1 Now read the following two introductions, which were written in answer to the task. Tick the one which has a more appropriate style for a descriptive composition, and makes more of an impact on the reader.

**1** ☐

*Cracow, the ancient capital of Poland. Just the name of the place is enough to bring back a flood of happy memories. It was around Christmas time, a few years back, when I first visited this city with a group of friends.*

**2** ☐

*The architecture of a city is of supreme importance. So many of our cities today have been ruined by poorly-designed buildings and a lack of planning. It is a sad fact, however, that many people do not appear to recognise the role the urban environment plays in our lives. Cracow is a city I visited a few years ago with some friends. It shows clearly what a great city should be like.*

2 Read the rest of the composition, ignoring the gaps and underlining for the moment. Has it answered the task fully?

*We arrived in Cracow at around midnight. I remember that it was <u>very cold</u> and there was a lot of snow about. Our hotel <u>had no lights on</u> when we arrived, but fortunately the receptionist was still on duty. (1) ............ .*

*Our first few days in Cracow were spent looking around, exploring <u>the streets</u> and Castle, and <u>looking at</u> the statues and monuments which seemed <u>to be in</u> every public square we came across. <u>The old buildings lining the streets were mysterious</u> and (2) ............ .*

*The snow continued to fall constantly, (3) ............ . Everywhere was covered in <u>a layer of snow</u>, which had the effect of softening the sound of cars and passing trams. (4) ............ . <u>I will never forget New Year's Eve</u>. An enormous crowd had gathered in the main square of the city, and most people were dancing. (5) ............ .*

*My time in Cracow was a truly unforgettable experience.*

**3** Use the words in the box to rewrite the parts of the composition which are underlined.

> narrow, cobbled    to grace    gazing up in awe
> shrouded in darkness    thick blanket
> was particularly memorable    bitterly
> there was an air of mystery about    muffling

**3** The composition fails to deal with how the place has affected the writer. Match one of the sentences or phrases from the following list a)–g) to each of the numbered gaps in the composition, adding any necessary punctuation. There are two letters you don't need to use.

a) throughout our stay in the city, we were frequently overwhelmed by the sense that we had somehow walked back into a magical kingdom belonging to another age

b) what amazed us was how friendly and hospitable she was, even though it was late and she was obviously tired

c) the fact that everyone seemed so happy and well-behaved – and intent on enjoying themselves – made an enormous impression on us

d) which made me feel small and insignificant

e) reminding me of scenes from novels I had read by Tolstoy and other Russian and Polish writers

f) it also made us feel like travellers in some mysterious, silent land, far away from the noise and bustle of modern city life

g) what struck me was how incredibly beautiful it all was

**4** The conclusion of the composition is very weak. The writer does not **reflect** at all on his experiences in Cracow or say what overall effect it had on him. Write a more appropriate conclusion from the following notes.

- *will never forget week in Cracow*
- *have been back several times since*
- *each time - struck by friendliness/openness of inhabitants*
- *Cracow - one of those places which reminds us of splendour lost/destroyed in many cities today*

**5** Now plan and write a descriptive composition in answer to the following question.

> Write an account of a journey where everything seemed to go wrong, describing your reactions to the problems you encountered. (About 350 words.)

Remember to include in your composition:

- an introduction with impact
- vivid language
- a reflective conclusion.

Use the phrases in the box below to help you incorporate your personal reactions into your description.

> **Phrases to introduce personal reactions**
>
> I was overwhelmed by …
> I was amazed at how/what amazed me was how …
> the fact that … made a great impression on me
> it made me feel …
> what struck me was how …
> it reminded me of …
> I felt as if …

**6** Exchange your composition with another student if you can. Evaluate each other's work and suggest improvements.

> **Study Tip**
>
> Group vocabulary for descriptive compositions together in your vocabulary notebook. You could, for example, group words and phrases:
>
> - according to the type of thing described, e.g.
>   old buildings ➡ dilapidated, haunted, tumbledown, austere, cosy …
>   facial expressions ➡ (positive) beaming, glowing … (negative) gloomy, downcast …
>
> - according to the feelings associated with them, e.g.
>
>   sealed in, trapped, enclosed (spaces)
>   narrow, cramped, squashed
>   a wave of panic (colloc.)    claustrophobia
>   to break out in a cold sweat (fixed phrase)
>   oppressive, stifling, thick/heavy (atmosphere)

# The price of success

## Vocabulary review: multiple-choice

Choose the word or phrase, **A**, **B**, **C** or **D**, which best completes each sentence.

1 The father of Mozart ruthlessly exploited the fact that his son was a musical .............
A protégé  B prodigy  C progeny
D prophecy

2 ............. fabrics should never be washed in a washing machine.
A dainty  B refined  C delicate  D sensitive

3 Throughout the investigation the behaviour of the police officers was ............. reproach.
A under  B over  C beyond  D past

4 Do stop .............! You haven't said a word to me all day!
A sulking  B grumbling  C moaning
D complaining

5 The road was blocked in several places by snow ............. .
A piles  B heaps  C stacks  D drifts

6 After having shuffled the cards, he placed the ............., face down, in the middle of the table.
A deck  B group  C packet  D set

7 She picked up the baking tin and ............. butter all around the inside with her fingers.
A scratched  B smudged  C smothered
D smeared

8 She ............. at me to let me know that I shouldn't take what she was saying seriously.
A blinked  B winked  C twitched
D jerked

9 When I told him the news he simply ............. with laughter.
A shouted  B yelled  C wailed
D bellowed

10 My little mirror wouldn't stay upright on the dressing table, so I ............. it up with a book.
A propped  B supported  C maintained
D shored

## Grammar: continuous aspect

**Watch Out!** *problem areas*

The continuous aspect refers to **temporary** states or actions which are **unfinished**. It is usually used when we are especially interested in the nature of the activity, its duration or the experience of the person performing it, rather than its results or consequences.

- **Past continuous**
  The Past continuous is used to refer to an activity or repeated action continuing up to or around a time in the past. It is *not* used to refer a past habit or state.
  When I was a child, I ~~was going~~ ‸*used to go* fishing with my grandfather every weekend.
  We ~~were living~~ ‸*used to live* in a large house in the country.

- **stative verbs**
  Stative verbs are not usually used in the continuous form. If they are used, a change in meaning is often involved.
  I ~~think~~ ‸*am thinking* of changing my job.
  You aren't ‸*being* very honest with him about this matter.
  Why ~~do you smell~~ ‸*are you smelling* the milk? It can't have gone off already!
  You can't have seen Jack yesterday – you must ~~imagine~~ ‸*be imagining* things.

- ***always/constantly/forever* + Present (or Past) continuous**
  This structure is used to refer to the frequency of people's habits, often ones which we find irritating. It can also be used to refer to things which happen frequently, and probably unexpectedly or by accident. (*Never* cannot be used in the same way!)
  ~~He's never tidying up his room!~~ *He's forever leaving his room in a terrible mess!*
  He *is always turning up* with a bottle of wine under his arm. ✔

- **prepositional phrases**
  Prepositional phrases are sometimes used instead of verbs in the continuous aspect, to avoid clumsy complex sentences.
  The lift will be ~~being repaired~~ ‸*under repair* all week.

**1**   Read the following pairs of sentences and answer the questions below. The first one has been done for you.

1  1  I've come to see Dr Hawkins.
   2  I've been coming to see Dr Hawkins for weeks.
   Which sentence:
   a) focuses on the purpose of the visit? ...*1*...
   b) focuses on the frequency of the visits? .......

2  1  He's chopped up the wood for the fire.
   2  He's been chopping up wood for the fire all morning.
   Which sentence:
   a) suggests that he may now be feeling tired? .......
   b) suggests that the wood is now ready for use? .......
   c) makes it clear that he still hasn't finished? .......

3  1  He's been working on the car all day to fix the ignition.
   2  He was working on the car to fix the ignition until five o'clock.
   Which sentence:
   a) suggests that he is now doing something different? .......
   b) suggests that the work may or may not be finished? .......

4  1  She'll probably be studying for her exams all afternoon.
   2  She'll probably study medicine at university.
   Which sentence:
   a) focuses on how busy she is? .......
   b) focuses on her future plans? .......

5  1  I'll go to the post office later, if that letter needs posting.
   2  I'll be going to the post office later, if that letter needs posting.
   Which sentence:
   a) suggests I was already planning this? .......
   b) is a spontaneous offer of help? .......
   c) is the more indirect way of making an offer? .......

6  1  I saw her slap him.
   2  I saw her slapping him.
   Which sentence:
   a) suggests that she slapped him several times? .......
   b) suggests that the slapping started before I arrived? .......

**2**   **Use of English:** sentence transformations
Finish each of the following sentences in such a way that it is as similar as possible in meaning to the sentence printed before it.

1  Negotiations for a settlement have been in progress for over two months now.
   They ......................................................................

2  Journalists have attacked the minister's policies several times.
   The minister's policies have ..........................................

3  His sarcasm was plainly obvious to all but a few people in the room.
   The fact that ..........................................................

4  Political talks are already underway to bring peace to the region.
   Politicians have ......................................................

5  Shortly before his eighteenth birthday he left home to go to university.
   By the ................................................................

6  That house has been up for sale for over a year now.
   They ..................................................................

**3**   **Use of English:** gapped sentences
Fill each of the gaps in the following sentences with a suitable word or phrase.

1  I know I should trust him, but I can't ........................ he's cheating us.

2  From these inconsistencies, I'd say your accountant ........................ records up to date lately.

3  He thinks ........................ point by arriving late, but everyone in the office just thinks he's lazy.

4  I've ........................ over, and I'm afraid I'll have to reject your offer.

5  They were drinking lots of champagne, so they ........................ a celebration.

6  Is it midday yet? I can't believe I've spent the whole ........................ dishes.

7  I'm afraid he ........................ up debts of over £20,000 already this year!

8  I can't believe she ........................ me lies all this time!

# Use of English: comprehension and summary

**1** Do you think school and university exams indicate how successful someone will be in later life? Why/Why not? Write down your ideas briefly in your notebook.

Now read the following passage and see if any of your thoughts are mentioned by the writer.

# The place of exams in British life

Every year fresh cohorts of young people pour out of the trenches to do battle with school and university examinations. The emotional casualty rate is grievously high. It is no exaggeration to say that the great majority
5 of us emerge from this ordeal feeling like failures, with lowered self-esteem. And just as the generals in the First World War failed to question the purpose of the carnage, so it is with modern-day educationists. They will not ask themselves the fundamental question: what is the point
10 of exams?

Of course, all children need to emerge from school knowing how to read and write, and it is a definite advantage nowadays for children to know a second language. But this does not justify the fiercely
15 competitive exams we see throughout British schools at ever younger ages.

Schoolchildren are cudgelled into studying by the threat that exams are critical to their occupational future. In reality, the evidence clearly shows that teachers and
20 parents who scare children with the idea that exams are essential for success are perpetuating a myth.

There are now only a few, mostly technical, occupations in Britain in which good school or university exam results are an important determinant, even of initial
25 acceptance. Many large retail companies now rely on their own assessment systems and regard exam results as an unhelpful guide.

If it is a fable that good exam results help most survivors of the educational system to get a job immediately on
30 leaving, the idea that exams predict long-term educational success is a downright lie. While that old saying 'First in School, Last in Life' may not be true, doing well at school certainly does not determine success later on. When I surveyed captains of industry,
35 they were unanimous in declaring university degrees irrelevant to ultimate success. Studies show that among top business people, school failure is actually the norm.

It is staggering, then, when you consider that parents and teachers consistently exhort children to 'do well at
40 school for your future', that there is no scientific evidence that school or university exam results predict success throughout life. There is even evidence suggesting the opposite. In the 1970s Professor Liam Hudson published a number of studies showing that
45 high level researchers with the highest grades at university were actually less successful than those with lower grades.

Given what it takes to get a first class degree at university, this should not be surprising. You need to
50 please your teachers, enjoy being supervised closely and, ultimately, please the examiners. You must ignore what you think and concentrate on what they want. To do important scientific research you need the opposite: to think originally and be highly self-motivated rather
55 than craving constant praise, and to be able to work alone for long periods.

I suspect that it is a myth that those who achieve the best grades are of superior originality. They work hard and they are ambitious to do well in exams, but that does
60 not prepare them for success in their subsequent careers. In many cases they peak too early, exhausting their supplies of competitiveness and adaptability, and their university success is their last outstanding achievement. If so, we need to question the
65 underpinning of a system the crowning glory of which is getting the highest possible mark.

Indeed, success at any stage in the process is probably more a measure of motivation and the desire to please than of talent or intelligence. Good exam results at
70 school do not tell us that someone is able to think, only that they are able to identify what examiners want and comply with it. Exams do not test knowledge or scholarship so much as memory and eagerness to succeed.

**2**   Answer the following questions about the passage.

1   What does the phrase 'cohorts of young people pour out of the trenches' suggest about students taking exams? (line 1)

   ........................................................................

2   Which phrase is echoed by the word 'carnage' in line 7?

   ........................................................................

3   Explain in your own words how the writer considers modern educationists to be like the generals of the First World War.

   ........................................................................

4   What does the phrase 'cudgelled into studying' imply about the students taking exams? (line 17)

   ........................................................................

5   What does the writer suggest about students with good exam results who apply for jobs in retail companies?

   ........................................................................

6   Explain in your own words how parents and teachers are 'perpetuating a myth'. (line 21)

   ........................................................................

7   Explain in your own words why the opinions of captains of industry might be sought.

   ........................................................................

8   What does 'this' refer to in line 49?

   ........................................................................

9   Explain in your own words why the highest grades from a British university do not automatically indicate that someone will be successful in the field of scientific research.

   ........................................................................

10   Explain in your own words what is meant in this context by the phrase 'they peak too early'. (line 61)

   ........................................................................

11   Explain in your own words what it is we 'need to question'. (line 64)

   ........................................................................

12   In 70–90 words summarise what the writer considers to be the negative aspects of school and university examinations in the British educational system.

   ........................................................................
   ........................................................................
   ........................................................................
   ........................................................................
   ........................................................................
   ........................................................................
   ........................................................................
   ........................................................................
   ........................................................................

## Vocabulary: phrasal verbs and expressions: *stand*

**1**   Rewrite each of the following sentences using a phrasal verb with *stand*, and making any other necessary changes. Use a dictionary to help you if necessary.

1   Whatever the outcome of the trial, we must be supportive and remain loyal to him.
   We must ......................... the outcome of the trial.
2   What do the letters REM represent in this sentence?
   What do the letters ......................... sentence?
3   We find such behaviour quite unacceptable!
   We won't ......................... behaviour!
4   It will be easier for people to see the sign at night if we use neon lights.
   Neon lights will ......................... at night.
5   It's a pity nobody defended him when they started making their accusations.
   I wish somebody ......................... their accusations.
6   Make it clear you don't accept his unfair treatment of you, otherwise he'll never change.
   He'll continue to treat ......................... him.
7   Of all the singers, Carol is by far the best.
   Carol ......................... the singers.
8   Would you mind doing Robin's job while he's away?
   Would you mind ......................... he's away?

**2**   **Use of English:** guided key word transformations
For each of the sentences below, write a new sentence as similar as possible in meaning to the original sentence but using the word given. **This word must not be altered in any way.** Use an expression with *stand* in the sentence you write.

1   They will try Abrams for murder at the High Court next week. **trial**

   ........................................................................

2   After such a long time together they are still happily married. **test**

   ........................................................................

3   How do our sales compare with those of other firms? **relation**

   ........................................................................

4   He is unlikely to win the competition. **chance**

   ........................................................................

5   I'm not going to prevent you from leaving, if that's what you really want. **way**

   ........................................................................

6   It's obvious that hard work and determination lead to success. **reason**

   ........................................................................

# Vocabulary: verb + noun collocation

Complete the following sentences with a verb in the correct form from the box below. You may need to use some of the verbs more than once.

| take | set | seize | handle | achieve |
| get | jump | make | | |

1 I know it's difficult to know what to do, but I think you should ............ a chance and apply for the position.
2 You've certainly ............ your mark as director of the company. Things are running much more smoothly now than they ever have before.
3 She seems to have ............ the crisis very well. She should be congratulated.
4 Let's not ............ to conclusions – we don't know for sure that Robert is responsible for this mistake.
5 We need to ............ a more realistic target. How about aiming for a 30% increase in production by the end of the year?
6 When he was given the new position, he ............ the opportunity to make a number of radical changes.
7 He may be an unpleasant man to deal with, but he does ............ results.
8 In order for us to ............ our aim, we all need to work a lot harder.
9 The organisation is expanding too quickly. We ought to ............ certain limits to growth, I think.
10 I can't believe I ............ such a mess of that interview!

# Vocabulary: dependent prepositions and prepositional phrases

Fill the gaps in the following sentences with one or more suitable prepositions.

1 Mrs Summers is unable to attend the meeting, so I'm going to speak ............ her behalf.
2 He's currently ............ threat of legal action.
3 ............ my knowledge, there have been two break-ins already there this year.
4 This building is being converted ............ a restaurant soon.
5 He stared at her intently, but could say nothing ............ response to her offer.
6 He scanned the morning paper quickly ............ stories of interest.

# Listening: three-way choice

Paper 4

**About the exam**

In **Paper 4** you may have to listen to a conversation or discussion between two speakers. You have to say whether the statements reflect the opinions of one or other of the speakers, or of both of them. You will hear the recording twice.

**Exam Strategy**

- Listen carefully for the stated facts, the attitudes and opinions of the speakers.
- Try to determine which points they agree or disagree on.
- There may be some colloquial language you don't understand. Try to work out the meaning from the context or from the tone of voice of the speaker.

 You will hear part of a radio show in which two people, Angela Simpson and Rita Gilbert, talk about the secrets of success in a job interview. As you listen, decide whether each of the opinions listed below is reflected in what is said by Angela (A), Rita (R) or both of them (B), and write the correct letter in the space provided. Listen to the recording twice.

1 It is important to check up on an employer before the interview. .......
2 Many candidates need to believe in themselves more. .......
3 Some candidates are too arrogant to prepare properly. .......
4 Candidates should emphasise useful skills to the employer. .......
5 It is best to be truthful about areas of weakness. .......
6 It is important not to be too general when talking about achievements. .......
7 Many interviewers may try to catch candidates out with unexpected questions. .......
8 Candidates should keep their answers to questions brief and relevant. .......
9 A candidate may come across as a threat to the interviewer. .......
10 An informal dinner is still part of the interview. .......

## Vocabulary: dependent prepositions and prepositional phrases

**Read the following passage and fill the gaps with appropriate prepositions.**

The writing is on the wall for the brilliant but bullying boss. Driving ambition and a high IQ might give you a head start in the race for the top, but a lack of 'emotional intelligence' will be a hindrance (1) ............. achieving medium to long-term success.

Senior managers have long been convinced (2) ............. the value of interpersonal skills in the workplace. The concept that emotional intelligence can account (3) ............. the difference (4) ............. outstanding and average performance, however, is comparatively new. But what exactly is emotional intelligence? One psychologist defined it (5) ............. the ability to regulate your behaviour so that there is a balance (6) ............. personal feelings, emotions and drives, and the feelings and needs of others. It is about being able to resolve the conflict that may arise (7) ............. high motivation and conscientiousness and integrity. People with low emotional intelligence don't get promoted because others object (8) ............. working with them.

In the workplace, there is a great need (9) ............. sensitivity in relationships, and people in managerial jobs should focus more (10) ............. understanding people's feelings (11) ............. change and their fears (12) ............. redundancy. An organisation which attaches importance (13) ............. the emotions of the employees is more likely to be an effective organisation. If a manager regularly compliments his staff (14) ............. their work, and sympathises (15) ............. them when they have problems, the profits of the company will increase (16) ............. a greater rate. And people will enjoy working with each other.

Getting in touch with your own feelings has benefits which extend (17) ............. the workplace. If you are only working with your brain, you won't see the emotional cost to yourself. Making a move that is beneficial (18) ............. your career but means travelling all the time could result (19) ............. the destruction of your relationship with your partner and children. Without emotional intelligence, (20) ............. the medium to long-term, you will have a less balanced personal life and make a lot of enemies.

## Writing: magazine article

**Paper 2**

### About the exam

In **Paper 2** you may have to write an article for a magazine. As with other types of task-directed writing (letters and reports), you only have to write 300 words. This is because the examiner will expect to see evidence of appropriate register, suitability for the intended reader of your writing, and thorough coverage of all the requirements set out in the task. **This means that extra time needs to be spent on planning and careful organisation** in order to gain a good mark.

### Exam Strategy

When planning your article, focus on these questions.

**What is the purpose of the article?**
- An indication of why the article is being written, and who for, should appear in the task.
- Think about the tone (e.g. light, persuasive, friendly, angry) you should adopt, and how formal your language needs to be.

**What do I need to include?**
- You may be given some points to include. If so, good marks depend on including them all appropriately. Look carefully to see if the task also tells you to incorporate your own ideas.
- An article needs an eye-catching title, and an introduction with impact. Try to conclude your piece too with a reflective comment which reinforces your purpose for writing.
- Many articles include reported speech or ideas. Use a variety of methods of reporting, to maintain interest, and show your own views of the opinions expressed.

## 1

1 Reported speech is often used in magazine articles. A careful choice of reporting expressions can convey your own feelings, as well as those of the person whose ideas are being reported. Read the following statements. Are there any differences in **tone** between them?

1 I inferred from what he said that business was booming. .......
2 He implied that business was booming. .......
3 I was given to understand that business would soon be booming. .......
4 He claimed that business was booming. .......
5 He acknowledged that business was booming. .......
6 I detected in him a sense of pride that business was booming. .......

2 Now match each of the statements above with one of the 'attitudes', a)–f), below.

a) The manager admitted that this was true.
b) The manager said that this was true, but the writer has his doubts.
c) The manager didn't actually say this, but it was the opinion formed by the writer.
d) This was the impression which the writer got, but we can't be sure how he came to believe this.
e) The manager found this quite hard to conceal.
f) The manager suggested this, without actually saying so.

## 2

As in all writing tasks for the exam, the vocabulary you use in a magazine article should be varied and rich. Rewrite the following sentences, which come from an article reviewing a restaurant. Use the words given in brackets and start your sentences with the words provided.

1 You won't believe how amazing the place is if you don't go and see for yourself. (seen)
The place has to ...............................................................

2 The first thing that makes an impression on you as you enter is the sheer size of the place. (strikes)
The first ...............................................................

3 The restaurant is more like a warehouse than a place for eating and drinking in style. (wining)
The restaurant is ...............................................................

4 It extends in all directions for a very long distance. (eye)
The restaurant extends as far ...............................................................

5 The place is now making a lot of money. (handsome)
The place is ...............................................................

## 3

Read the following task and the article which has been written in answer to it. Ignore the numbered gaps for the moment. Check your answers to Exercise 2.

You have been asked to write an article for a local magazine about a new restaurant in your town, giving your personal perspective and recommending it to the readers of the magazine. (About 300 words.)

### Eating under the sea !

When I visited the new seafood restaurant 'Taste of the Atlantic' last week I wasn't expecting any surprises. But surprised I was – for the place has to be seen to be believed.

The first thing that strikes you as you enter is the sheer size of the place. The restaurant is more like a warehouse than a place for wining and dining, covering three floors and extending in all directions as far as the eye can see. In fact, first impressions are not so misleading, for the 'Taste of the Atlantic' is housed in an old fabrics warehouse. (1) ............. was just what he had been looking for.

Mr Childes, who showed me around, (2) ............. of the old warehouse and (3) ............. he had been willing to pay any price for a place with 'real atmosphere'. (4) ............. money spent on restoring the warehouse and transforming it into a restaurant has already been recovered, and the place is now making a handsome profit.

On every floor of the restaurant there must be at least twenty to thirty small tables, some hidden away in snug alcoves, and the only lighting comes from the hundreds of candles fixed into the stone walls. Waiters rush from table to table, taking orders or bringing food, and the pleasant buzz of conversation is accompanied by the tinkling of a fountain on the ground floor.

I spoke to one or two of the customers at the restaurant, and (5) ............. . (6) ............. as delightful as the surroundings. Why not go there and see for yourself?

**4** Now choose the phrase, a) b) or c), which best fills each of the gaps in the article. Think carefully about the writer's **attitude** and what suits the **style** of the article best.

1 a) According to the manager, Mr Frank Childes, this
  b) I inferred from the manager, Mr Frank Childes, that this
  c) The manager, Mr Frank Childes, acknowledged that this
2 a) lamented the 'discovery'
  b) enthused over the 'discovery'
  c) decried the 'discovery'
3 a) gave me to understand that
  b) denied that
  c) claimed that
4 a) If Mr Childes is to be believed, the
  b) I was somewhat hesitant to believe his claim that the
  c) I was rather cynical about Mr Childes assertion that the
5 a) they were all highly favourable
  b) they were all very positive
  c) they all spoke with relish
6 a) The food, it seems, is
  b) The food, I was made to understand, is
  c) The food, I detected, is

**5** The conclusion of the article is rather abrupt. Which two additional sentences **A** or **B**, 'round off' the article in a more appropriate way? Remember that the conclusion of such an article should:

• take the reader back to the writer's sentiments or comments in the introduction
• clarify the purpose of the whole article
• suit the style of the article (in this case, quite personal and light-hearted).

**A**

*I'm going this weekend, at the invitation of the manager. Since I'll know what to expect this time, I won't be distracted from what's most important – eating!*

**B**

*You are bound to like the food and the décor. In all probability you will want to take your friends there in the future too.*

**6** Now write an article in answer to the following task.

> You have been asked to write an article for a student magazine about a sports centre which has just opened in your town and is proving to be a great success. Mention the factors which have contributed to the success of the sports centre, and detail the reasons why you recommend it to all local students.
> (About 300 words.)

Don't forget to give your article an eye-catching **title**. Use the Exam Strategy box and exercises on these pages to help you plan your article, to use appropriate language, and to write an introduction and conclusion which create impact.

**7** Exchange your article with another student if you can. Evaluate each other's work and suggest improvements.

**Study Tip**

**Style** and **tone of voice** are particularly important in newspaper and magazine articles. Collect and keep as many articles as you can from English newspapers and magazines and compare them:

• with each other – can you find any differences in style, vocabulary, structures or layout?

• with newspapers and magazines in your own language – look for features which are typical, and check how these differ in English publications.

Try rewriting a variety of articles from your own language into English, and vice versa, to help you discover the types of expressions you need to learn.

# 14 Revision unit

This unit contains strategy advice to help you approach the various tasks in the Proficiency exam in a structured and confident way. The practice tasks revise much of the language you have studied throughout the course. The revision checklists prompt you to analyse **what each task tests**, and how you can learn from mistakes you have made in the past to **maximise your exam success**.

## Vocabulary: multiple-choice revision

### Paper 1, Section A

---

### Exam Strategy

- Read the options carefully and eliminate any words which you are sure are not correct. When deciding, think about:
  - the grammar of the sentence, and any patterns associated with the words in the options (e.g. dependent prepositions, verbs followed by an infinitive/-*ing* form, (un)countable nouns)
  - the connotations of the words (e.g. positive/negative)
  - collocations and fixed phrases.
- If you're not sure, always guess, as you lose no marks for incorrect guesses. Multiple-choice questions are designed to test **passive vocabulary** (the words you recognise and understand, but might not be able to use), and so very often your instincts about the answer may be correct.

---

Choose the word or phrase, **A, B, C** or **D**, which best completes each sentence.

1 Dr Roberts has a(n) ............ knowledge of early nineteenth century French poetry.
   **A** extensive  **B** total  **C** absolute  **D** keen

2 This stretch of coast is slowly being ............ by the sea.
   **A** eroded  **B** corroded  **C** erased
   **D** dissolved

3 ............ so much opposition, it would be unwise to continue with our plans.
   **A** With regard to  **B** With respect to
   **C** On the grounds of  **D** In the face of

4 We gave the children some crayons and paper and then left them to their own ............ .
   **A** tricks  **B** devices  **C** thoughts  **D** abilities

5 ............ the embargo, some countries have been supplying the breakaway state with oil.
   **A** Contrary to  **B** In defiance of  **C** As against
   **D** As opposed to

6 One problem we haven't ............ so far is what to do with all the waste from the factory.
   **A** addressed  **B** invoked  **C** regarded  **D** directed

7 Asking me to return that watch she'd given me was really adding insult to ............ , don't you think?
   **A** pain  **B** injustice  **C** suffering  **D** injury

8 In such circumstances, I am not ............ to working long hours.
   **A** capable  **B** obliged  **C** averse  **D** reluctant

9 If your signature is not on the document, then legally you don't have a leg to ............ on.
   **A** stand  **B** jump  **C** hop  **D** walk

10 We spent the night listening to the rain ............ on the roof of the caravan.
   **A** jangling  **B** pattering  **C** knocking
   **D** thumping

11 It is ............ obvious to us that you have no idea what you are talking about.
   **A** woefully  **B** greatly  **C** painfully  **D** profoundly

12 It almost seems as if some dentists enjoy ............ pain on their patients.
   **A** imposing  **B** bringing  **C** subjecting
   **D** inflicting

13 The cat jumped onto the chair, ............ up and went to sleep.
   **A** wound  **B** twisted  **C** rounded  **D** curled

14 The prospect of bankruptcy loomed ............ in his mind.
   **A** large  **B** heavy  **C** enormous  **D** hard

15 When he returned to his car, he found that someone had ............ his tyres.
   **A** hacked  **B** ripped  **C** chopped  **D** slashed

# Reading: multiple-choice revision

*Paper 1, Section B*

### Exam Strategy

- Read the text for a general understanding of its content and the author's attitude or tone. Don't worry about unknown words.
- Look at each question or stem and try to find the information you need in the text without reading the four options.
- Then consider the options and choose the one which most closely resembles your answer from the text. Watch out for options which:
  - contain words which appear to be similar to those in the text
  - have negative expressions in them
  - only answer half the question
  - seem to answer the question logically, but are not actually what is said in the text
  - look very similar to each other. Try to distinguish the difference between them, and go back to the text to double-check.
- If there are unknown words in the text, first decide if these are essential to answer the question successfully. If they are, try to deduce the meaning of necessary words from the form of the word itself or from the context.
- Remember that the questions follow the order of the text. The last question may ask about the text as a whole, often focusing on the attitude of the writer.
- Look again at Unit 3, page 26 and Unit 6, page 49 for guidance on how to deal with distractors.

# Vocabulary: phrasal verb revision

Choose the correct phrasal verb, **A**, **B**, **C** or **D**, to complete the following sentences.

1 I can't understand why you didn't ............. the agreement we had made.
   **A** keep to  **B** stand for  **C** stay over
   **D** bring about

2 Thieves broke into the gallery and ............. paintings worth £50,000.
   **A** ran out of  **B** made off with  **C** got off with
   **D** came in for

3 The children are very quiet, aren't they? What do you think they are ............. to?
   **A** putting up  **B** doing up  **C** getting up
   **D** playing up

4 The publicity his novels received ............. a change in the way people viewed his work.
   **A** made up  **B** brought about  **C** got across
   **D** set out

5 I want you to leave. I'm not prepared to ............. your bad behaviour any longer.
   **A** take out on  **B** stand up to  **C** look out for
   **D** put up with

6 I was ............. by his opposition to the changes.
   **A** put over  **B** pushed over  **C** brought up
   **D** taken aback

7 During the interview he ............. as being rather arrogant and rude.
   **A** gave off  **B** got over  **C** came across  **D** put out

8 You'll have to cut back on spending – you're ............. huge debts.
   **A** running up  **B** making up  **C** setting up
   **D** putting up

9 Are you implying that I'm incompetent? I don't understand what you are ............. .
   **A** getting at  **B** getting across  **C** getting over
   **D** getting through

10 It's clear they are short-changing their customers. I don't know how they've ............. it for so long.
   **A** run away with  **B** made away with
   **C** done away with  **D** got away with

11 The comedian's jokes were perceived as racist and didn't ............. very well with the audience.
   **A** bring down  **B** go down  **C** go through
   **D** get across

12 Don't ............. with the idea that because I don't say much, I don't know what's going on here.
   **A** take away  **B** bring off  **C** bring up
   **D** run away

13 So far, they've rejected all the proposals we've ............. to increase the turnover of the business.
   **A** made up  **B** put forward  **C** got across
   **D** put through

14 Roger has ............. a brilliant idea for the new advertising campaign.
   **A** come up with  **B** thought over  **C** called up
   **D** started up with

15 'Shall I ............. the cheque to you or to your company?' she asked.
   **A** make out  **B** write up  **C** write down
   **D** put down

# Use of English: cloze

**Paper 3, Section A, Question 1**

### Exam Strategy

- Read the passage quickly for general understanding. Remember that some of the gaps in the cloze are designed to test your understanding of the passage **as a whole**, so it's essential to pay attention to the whole passage, especially the sentences before and after each gap.
- Go through the passage again. Write in those words you are sure about and make a note of the **form** of other missing words (e.g. verb, adjective, preposition).
- Never put two alternative answers or leave any gaps. Also avoid using the same word twice, as the gaps in the test are designed to have different answers.
- Always read the whole passage once you have filled the gaps, to make sure that what you have written is logical. Check your spelling and punctuation, as you lose marks for this type of mistake on **Paper 3**.

Fill each of the gaps in the passage with one suitable word. Refer to the checklist below to help you before you start or when you've finished.

## The artist's perspective

It is the job of the artist to encourage people to look at the world afresh. In a great (1) ............ of art, colours and forms may (2) ............ from those people are used to. For this (3) ............ , many people, some of (4) ............ consider themselves to be experts on art, (5) ............ with indignation when they see that an artist has painted the sky red or made (6) ............ a person from geometrical shapes. The artist is somehow (7) ............ to be incapable of representing reality 'correctly'.

(8) ............ these people do not understand, (9) ............ , is that their prejudices are (10) ............ them from seeing the world in a new and exciting (11) ............ . Unless we approach a painting with an open mind, we will be (12) ............ to discover anything of value in ourselves or in the world (13) ............ us. We will remain in the darkness of our pre-conceived (14) ............ and opinions (15) ............ the time when we are prepared to open our minds as well as our eyes.

People of (16) ............ ages, it would seem, want the things around them to be familiar. However, hardly (17) ............ claiming to be a 'real' artist would subscribe to (18) ............ comfortable an outlook on life. Artists can be (19) ............ to beings from (20) ............ planet, seeing things from a different perspective and attempting to convey this freshness in the pictures they paint.

 Use this checklist to help you when doing cloze tests.
Look out for:

- verb tenses or patterns (e.g. passives, *-ing* forms, modals)
- prepositions (if these are followed by a verb form, it should be an *-ing* form) and prepositional phrases
- collocations and dependent prepositions
- punctuation (commas often indicate that there is a relative clause, for example)
- articles and determiners (you often need to look at the passage as a whole to spot when these are needed)
- connectors which help you to make sense of the general meaning (e.g. *however, whilst, meanwhile, although*)
- vocabulary items such as phrasal verbs and fixed phrases.

# Use of English: sentence transformations

**Paper 3, Section A, Question 2**

Look again at Unit 11, pages 92–93 for guidance on the best way to approach this kind of task.

Finish each of the following sentences in such a way that it is as similar as possible in meaning to the sentence printed before it. Refer to the checklist below to help you before you start or when you've finished.

1 'Well done, Mark! They've finally accepted you on the course!' said his father.
   Mark's father .......................................................

2 They allege that someone has been giving her large bribes.
   She is .......................................................

3 The only reason he stayed at home was to watch the football match which was on television.
   Had .......................................................

4 Many people criticised the government over its plans to privatise the railways.
   The government came .......................................................

5 People who haven't seen his paintings are in no position to be critical.
   Nobody .......................................................

6 Our reason for calling this meeting was to acquaint people with the facts.
   It was with .......................................................

7 It's a pity they refuse to even talk about their plans.
   I wish .......................................................

8 Geoffrey Richmond's inability to write another novel dates from the time of his riding accident.
   Ever .......................................................

9 You can shout at me as much as you like, but I won't change my mind.
   No matter .......................................................

10 I don't want to get involved in all the rumours that are circulating.
   I want to distance .......................................................

When you check sentence transformation tasks, look out for places where you need to:

- change the verb form (e.g. active to passive, Past simple to modal perfect)
- change the part of speech of a word (e.g. verb to noun)
- change the word order
- change negative to positive (e.g. from *un-* + adjective to *not/don't* + verb)
- change a comparative form, or a comparative to a superlative (e.g. *far better than* to *not nearly as good as*)
- change a word/phrase to a synonym or antonym (e.g. *there are few* to *there aren't many*)
- add, change or omit a word, phrase or preposition (e.g. *on* fire to *in* flames)
- change an adjective/adverb/verb to a noun or *-ing* form because it follows a preposition (e.g. *happy to be here* to *delight in being here*)
- use a verb/noun/adjective/adverb which collocates with a particular word (e.g. a *round* of applause, *gratuitous* violence).

# Use of English: gapped sentences

**Paper 3, Section A, Question 3**

Look again at Unit 12, page 100 for guidance on the best way to approach this task.

Fill each of the gaps in the following sentences with a suitable word or phrase. Refer to the checklist below to help you before you start or when you've finished.

1 You ........................ mad to have invested so much money in one company!

2 Rather surprisingly, Franklin and Richards, ........................ is particularly renowned for his research, have been jointly awarded the science prize.

3 Although Peter is an excellent artist, he ........................ means the best I have ever taught.

4 I've never met such a slow reader – I bet you ........................ that book in six months' time!

5 They'll never persuade me to work for them, ........................ money they offer me.

6 These days, CDs are so good that hardly ........................ to music on tape any more.

7 Very little ........................ paid so far to the role of memory in language learning.

8 I don't know what he did in the end, but when I saw him, he didn't seem ........................ his mind whether to buy it or not.

9 The fire spread so quickly through the zoo that all efforts to save the ........................ vain.

10 His alibi was so convincing that he is now thought ........................ part in the robbery.

11 You are under ........................ whatsoever to sit here and answer their questions!

12 Were ........................ the money, I would have stopped working here years ago.

When you check gapped sentences, look out for a word or phrase which:

- requires a particular grammatical structure or verb form (e.g. adjective + infinitive)
- tells you that the sentence is negative in meaning (e.g. *hardly, scarcely, any* and *(n)ever*)
- tells you a modal verb is required (e.g. an infinitive without *to*)
- tells you what is being referred to (e.g. *this/these, one* or a relative pronoun)
- tells you that an uncountable noun might be needed (e.g. *little*)
- requires a collocating adjective, adverb, noun or verb (e.g. deepest *sympathy, sigh* of relief)
- requires a preposition before or after it (e.g. *on* reflection, responsible *for*)
- suggests that the -*ing* form of a verb is necessary (e.g. after a preposition, starting a sentence with a verb form)
- is part of a fixed expression or phrasal verb
- suggests that a comparative form is necessary (e.g. *than, as*)
- signals a change in meaning (e.g. *however, despite*).

## Use of English: key word transformations

*Paper 3, Section A, Question 4*

### Exam Strategy

- Read the prompt sentence carefully to be sure of its meaning.
- Look at the key word you are given – do you recognise it as part of a pattern, phrase or idiom?
- Decide what kinds of change you need to make to fit the key word into your new sentence. When you have thought about the key word itself, read the rest of the sentence carefully. Normally, you have to change **more than one thing** in this task.
- Include all the information from the original sentence, unless you are sure that a word or expression you have used contains this information.

For each of the sentences below, write a new sentence as similar as possible in meaning to the original sentence, but using the word given. **This word must not be altered in any way**.

Refer to the checklist opposite to help you before you start or when you've finished.

1 Staying on late at work is becoming less of a problem for me. **used**

.................................................................

2 She won't allow you to leave the building, will she? **intent**

.................................................................

3 The new regulations will begin to apply on June 1st. **effect**

.................................................................

4 Being a film star involves making sacrifices in your personal life. **parcel**

.................................................................

5 It doesn't seem likely that they'll make him resign. **likelihood**

.................................................................

6 I'm sure Charles bought them a lovely present for their wedding. **bound**

.................................................................

7 She won't settle for anything less than the first prize. **heart**

.................................................................

8 Although I assured him it wasn't true, he still believed that I had betrayed him. **contrary**

.................................................................

9 She didn't try very hard to get to know the others on the course. **little**

.................................................................

10 Our experiments cannot continue because of the serious problems we have encountered. **against**

.................................................................

11 It's difficult not to smile when he tells us off. **keep**

.................................................................

12 It's impossible for us to agree to their terms. **question**

.................................................................

 When you check key word transformations, look out for these changes that you may have to make:

- a word/phrase to a set phrase or expression (e.g. *it's a good idea* to *you'd better*)
- a word/phrase to a phrasal verb (e.g. *they have a good relationship* to *they get on well*)
- a word/phrase to a synonym or antonym
- the word order
- the verb form
- an adjective/adverb/verb to a noun or -*ing* form because it follows a preposition
- a verb in a particular tense to the appropriate infinitive form (including passive, continuous and perfect)
- adding a verb/noun/adjective/adverb which collocates with a particular word.

# Use of English: summary writing and editing

Paper 3, Section B

In Paper 3, Section B you have to answer comprehension questions on a non-fiction text and summarise certain aspects of the writer's argument in a set number of words.

Look again at Unit 11, page 89 for guidance on the best way to approach the comprehension questions.

## Exam Strategy

- Read the summary question carefully, underlining key words. Decide what information is required for the summary.
- Find and underline the relevant points in the text. There are usually **four to six points** for a Proficiency summary.
- Note down these points. Expand them into a paragraph, **using your own words** as far as possible.
- When you have finished, count the number of words you have used. If the paragraph is too long, decide how you can shorten it, using the techniques outlined below. Look back at the question – are all your points relevant?
- **Rewrite** your summary. Your final summary should be well organised and sentences should be linked together clearly and logically.

Read the following summary task and the notes below.

> Summarise in 70–90 words the advantages of ordering books from an Internet bookshop.

Notes

1  books – less expensive than from traditional bookshop

2  find almost any book in print

3  ordering – quick and easy

4  many Internet bookshops – information about other books/same author, related subject

5  reviews by other readers

6  books which are ordered over the Internet – sent airmail, arrive quickly

Now read the first draft of the summary made from these points. What's wrong with it?

........................................................................

summary – first draft

It is very often much less expensive to buy books from an Internet bookshop than to buy them from a conventional bookshop. For example, some Internet bookshops sell books at half the price they would be in a normal bookshop. In addition to this, it is possible to find almost any book which is in print and to order it over the Internet both quickly and easily. As well as providing a lot of useful and interesting information about books by the same author or books on a related subject, a large number of Internet bookshops encourage readers to send in reviews of books they have read and would recommend to other readers. These reviews enable readers to order books they know are good. Finally, when books are ordered over the Internet, the bookshop usually sends them by airmail, which means they arrive in much less than a week. (149 words)

Use this checklist to guide you in editing the first draft of the summary to the correct length. Always remember to:

- check that every sentence makes a new point or points
- check that you haven't made the same point twice in different ways
- remove supporting examples
- remove unnecessary adjectives and adverbs
- replace phrases with single words
- replace full clauses with participle clauses.

# Writing: all tasks

### Exam Strategy

- Read the question carefully to see **what** you have to write – and, for the task-directed, **why** and **to whom**. Make sure you are confident what type of composition is required (e.g. narrative, description, report, etc.) and how many parts there are to the question. Underline them in the composition task to remind you, and always keep the title where you can see it while you plan and write your composition.
- Note down a few ideas to start you thinking, making sure you only include details which are **relevant** and which **support** the main points you want to make.
- Plan your writing. Think about what you will put in each of the paragraphs, and how you will organise the information. Look again at Unit 1, page 15, for guidance on useful methods of organising your paragraphs.
- Make notes of the structures and vocabulary you would like to use, **before you start writing**. It is essential to have an appropriate tone and register for your purpose and your reader.
- Pay particular attention to how you write the introduction of your composition. Think of the reader, and his/her expectations.
- Make sure each of your paragraphs covers a particular point and that you include a **topic sentence** to make clear to the reader what this point is.
- Try to make the conclusion of your composition as strong and effective as you can – this may involve echoing the title or introduction, or adding an element of reflection.
- Spend time checking for grammar, punctuation or spelling mistakes when you finish, as these create a poor impression. If something is incorrect, cross it out neatly and write your correction above.

In this section, there is further practice for each type of writing task.

Use the checklists on these two pages for guidance on the particular characteristics of the different types of composition, and the titles in each section to give you further practice in writing each one.

**1** Description

> Describe what you like most about your home town or village and explain how you feel about any changes which might be occurring at present. (About 350 words.)

 Whenever you write a description, make sure you:

- include details which tell the reader your reflections and reactions, with reasons
- use a range of descriptive adjectives, verbs and adverbs
- make comparisons using *like* (+ noun) and *as if* (+ clause)
- use direct speech if appropriate, but use it *only* for dramatic effect.

**2** Narrative

> Write a story beginning or ending with the words: *Her heart sank when she saw the letter waiting for her on the kitchen table.* (About 350 words.)

 Whenever you write a narrative, make sure you:

- make the story 'focused' – don't include too many details or make the plot too complicated
- write a dramatic or interesting beginning and a clear, strong ending (e.g. end on a note of suspense or mystery)
- include details which show how the main characters feel and react. Using direct speech is one good way of doing this
- use a range of descriptive adjectives, verbs and adverbs
- use flashback to tell the reader about background events or to explain the way characters feel or react.

### 3   Discursive

Violence at sports events is becoming increasingly common in many countries. Discuss the ways in which this trend can be combatted, and suggest which may be the most successful. (About 350 words.)

Whenever you write a discursive composition, make sure you:

- write an introduction which does not simply repeat the question. Outline the situation as it is today, or has been recently. Perhaps use a rhetorical question to lead into the main body of the composition
- divide the composition into clear paragraphs, each paragraph covering a particular point in your argument or a particular aspect of the subject
- identify whether the task demands a 'balanced' or a 'one-sided' argument. If the composition is 'one-sided', don't develop points which contradict the statement you are given; mention the alternative view briefly in the introduction or conclusion
- support your ideas with brief examples
- use connectors and adverbs to join your sentences and ideas together
- write a conclusion which 'echoes' the words of the introduction or title.

### 4   Formal letter

You were recently one of a group of delegates at a student conference, and found the arrangements for lectures, accommodation, and travel to be inadequate. Write a letter of complaint to the conference organiser, detailing how you expect arrangements to improve before next year's conference, which you are also planning to attend. (About 300 words.)

Whenever you write a formal letter, make sure you:

- think carefully about what the reader of your letter already knows about the situation, what he/she needs to know, and what sort of register is required
- organise your letter clearly. A standard method of paragraphing is:
  1   your reason for writing
  2   detailing your concerns
  3   expanding on why you feel this way
  4   any action you want taken/suggestions/requests
- only include details which are strictly relevant.

### 5   Report

As the local tourist officer, you have been asked by your regional manager to prepare a report on the standard of facilities for visitors to your town. Comment on the reactions of visitors to these facilities, and suggest ways in which they could be improved. (About 300 words.)

Whenever you write a report, make sure you:

- organise it for your reader. Use headings for each of the sections, and group your ideas together very clearly. A standard organisation of a report is:
  1   introduction/background information
  2   main body of the report in headed sections
  3   comments/recommendations
- use a formal, impersonal style and tone
- only include details which are strictly relevant.

### 6   Magazine article

You have been asked to write an article for your school or college magazine about a teacher or lecturer who has recently retired. In your article, you should include any biographical details you think important or interesting, as well as the reactions of other members of staff and students to his/her departure. (About 300 words.)

Look again at Unit 13, pages 109–111 for guidance on the best way to approach this type of writing task.

#### Exam Tip!

Keeping to an appropriate length is important for all the composition types. An examiner will ignore any material beyond the length specified in the task, and will mark only what remains. You could lose marks with overlong compositions.

Use the techniques outlined for summary editing on page 117 to help you to shorten your composition if necessary.

# Practice exam

## PAPER I    READING COMPREHENSION    (I hour)

There are **forty** questions in this paper. Attempt **all** questions. For each question there are four possible answers **A**, **B**, **C** and **D**. Choose the **one** you consider correct and record your choice in **soft pencil** on the separate answer sheet.

### Section A

In this section you must choose the word or phrase which best completes each sentence. Indicate the letter **A**, **B**, **C** or **D** against the number of each item **1** to **25** for the word or phrase you choose. Give **one answer only** to each question.

1    After the prize-giving .......... most students posed for photographs with their families.

    **A**   rite           **B**   ceremony         **C**   ritual         **D**   liturgy

2    Nobody was able to .......... her when she was made redundant last week.

    **A**   relieve        **B**   brighten         **C**   console       **D**   alleviate

3    She .......... out with her best friend last week and hasn't spoken to her since.

    **A**   fell           **B**   took          **C**   split         **D**   broke

4    I'm .......... aware of the lack of support you have received from the authorities.

    **A**   sharply        **B**   utterly          **C**   acutely       **D**   powerfully

5    An offer of £1,000 for your old car is not to be .......... at, you know.

    **A**   coughed       **B**   glanced         **C**   slapped       **D**   sneezed

6    Although he is a wonderful poet and playwright, he is not .......... with Shakespeare.

    **A**   compared      **B**   in league        **C**   on a par      **D**   consistent

7    Despite his common sense, he is occasionally susceptible to .......... of fancy when talking about the future.

    **A**   trips           **B**   journeys         **C**   voyages       **D**   flights

8    She's such a close friend that she's always been .......... as a member of the family.

    **A**   considered to      **B**   thought about      **C**   considered being      **D**   thought of

9    Before putting the pie into the oven, sprinkle a little .......... cheese on top.

    **A**   sliced          **B**   grated          **C**   mashed       **D**   minced

10    On a number of occasions, the doctor has .......... him to give up smoking.

    **A**   suggested      **B**   urged          **C**   insisted       **D**   pleaded

**11** She gained access to the documents .......... her relationship with the boss.

    **A** in view of         **B** with regard to         **C** in recognition of         **D** by virtue of

**12** Looking round that factory has .......... me off hamburgers for life!

    **A** got         **B** taken         **C** put         **D** set

**13** Many students do .......... jobs in hotels over the summer to earn extra money.

    **A** inferior         **B** low         **C** poor         **D** menial

**14** You're too critical of yourself – that performance was virtually ............... .

    **A** marvellous         **B** excellent         **C** perfect         **D** complete

**15** It was so .......... on the plane that I couldn't stretch out my legs.

    **A** restricted         **B** narrow         **C** limited         **D** cramped

**16** It is believed that many coral .......... off the coast of Australia are dying.

    **A** colonies         **B** orchards         **C** fields         **D** reefs

**17** By behaving so carelessly, you have put the whole operation at .......... .

    **A** danger         **B** risk         **C** hazard         **D** peril

**18** The ............... of lethal gases from nearby factories has caused a lot of local protests.

    **A** emulsion         **B** emanation         **C** emission         **D** emergence

**19** On leaving university Andrew did a two-year .......... in the navy.

    **A** patch         **B** stint         **C** period         **D** segment

**20** She .......... me a nervous look before going into the manager's office.

    **A** threw         **B** pitched         **C** hurled         **D** tossed

**21** How did it come .......... that he was found in a restricted area of the laboratory?

    **A** about         **B** off         **C** over         **D** around

**22** I consider your demand to look at my letters to be an ............ of privacy.

    **A** intrusion         **B** trespass         **C** invasion         **D** assault

**23** To the .......... amusement of the audience, the comedian began to imitate the Prime Minister.

    **A** high         **B** total         **C** vast         **D** wild

**24** On receiving the bomb threat the police .......... the whole building immediately.

    **A** evicted         **B** exiled         **C** expelled         **D** evacuated

**25** She .......... to have solved the problem we've been working on for the last two years.

    **A** claims         **B** confesses         **C** admits         **D** announces

## Section B

In this section you will find after each of the passages a number of questions or unfinished statements about the passage, each with four suggested answers or ways of finishing. You must choose the one which you think fits best. Indicate the letter **A**, **B**, **C** or **D** against the number of each item **26** to **40** for the answer you choose. Give **one answer only** to each question.

### FIRST PASSAGE

There seems little doubt that the majority of people in many wealthier nations would like the idea of wildlife surviving to share the planet with them. They have a basic sympathy with animals that is by no means shared in all the countries of the world. This regard for animals may only manifest itself in keeping a pet. Nevertheless, it is a short step from enjoying the company of a dog, cat or even a budgie to feeling a pang of regret if their pets' wild relatives are in danger of disappearing from the face of the Earth. For the cause of conservation, it is fortunate that these feelings exist in so many wealthy nations, who are able to afford and support 'saving' operations.

There are deeper reasons why so many people feel an empathy with wild animals struggling to exist in an ever-contracting world. Between wildlife and humanity, there is a subconscious connection that stretches back to the origins of man. Many people sense that wildlife and humans are all part of the same living scene and that man should therefore strive to see that the other actors have at least a walk-on part.

For the majority, conservation was initially thought of as only relevant to creatures. Their plight could be readily understood and saving them was the focus point for both moral and material public support. Now it is recognised that conservation must also be applied to the environment in which both wildlife and humans live. There is little doubt that this enlargement of public awareness would never have come about, had the original emphasis not been on protecting the panda, the rhino, the whale, the elephant and many more species beleaguered in the wild. It is scarcely an exaggeration to say that the 'Green Movement' itself owes its origins to public concern for vanishing wildlife. The realisation that it is as important to protect the entire environment, including the atmosphere and the oceans, as it is to conserve our flora and fauna, now affects many people's entire lifestyle. It influences what they eat and drink, what they buy and wear, and for whom they vote.

Having said all that, and having acknowledged the scope and power of the 'Green Movement', let us return to the bedrock of conservation – protecting wildlife. Common to each operation aimed at saving wildlife is the fact that man's requirements have clashed with, and taken precedence over, those of wild animals and places. All too often, this means that he either slaughters the animals or destroys the habitat in which they live.

Sometimes such a clash of interests is justifiable from a human standpoint. Under-privileged people often have to make a precarious living from land that is occupied by wildlife. If those people's welfare, let alone their survival, is at stake, then obviously these must take priority. Occasionally a compromise can be found, but in a world in which over-population is a major cause of starvation and 'land hunger', this is increasingly hard to bring about.

Conservation itself has many problems yet to solve. Scientists will readily admit that too little is yet known about the ecology of some threatened species. Scientific knowledge often lags behind the operation that is being mounted to save an endangered animal. Perhaps the most profound dilemma is one of education, not only of the general public, but also of industry and governments. These latter, of course, have it in their power to do the most damage, as well as the most good.

26  Conservation benefits from the fact that many wealthier nations

    **A**    have a tradition of keeping animals as pets.

    **B**    are choosing to save a number of animals.

    **C**    are worried about the relationship of wild and domestic animals.

    **D**    are financially equipped to fund conservation projects.

27  Awareness of conservation issues has

    **A**    historically been man's responsibility.

    **B**    changed the entire lifestyle of the majority of people.

    **C**    expanded from initially focusing primarily on animals.

    **D**    gained general moral and material support.

28  What is responsible for the disappearance of wildlife in every case?

    **A**    The desire of some people to make money.

    **B**    A conflict of interests between animals and people.

    **C**    The destruction of the habitat in which animals live.

    **D**    People's need for more land.

29  The wish to protect wild animals cannot be justified if

    **A**    people's lives are therefore imperilled.

    **B**    some people continue to starve.

    **C**    impoverished people hunt the animals to live.

    **D**    the population of the world continues to grow.

30  The key factor affecting conservation nowadays is

    **A**    accurate scientific knowledge of species under threat.

    **B**    availability of funds for conservation projects.

    **C**    educating the general public about environmental issues.

    **D**    the knowledge and attitude of those in industry and government.

## SECOND PASSAGE

Preceding the use of astronomy and mathematics for navigation and calendar reckoning, there must have been centuries during which men, filled with instinctive wonder and an awe of nature, with irrepressible philosophical drives, patiently observed the movement of the Sun, Moon and stars. These seers, obsessed by the mystery of nature, overcame such handicaps as the lack of instruments and woefully inadequate mathematics to distil from their observations the patterns which are described by the heavenly bodies.

The early farmer learned to watch the face of the sky. He hunted, fished, sowed, reaped, danced and performed ceremonies at the times the heavens dictated. Soon particular constellations received the names of the activities their appearance sanctioned. Sagittarius, the hunter, and Pisces, the fish, are still in the sky.

The heavens decided the time of events. But such imperious masters would tolerate no delay in compliance with their orders. The farmer in many hotter countries, who made his living by tilling the soil which the river covered with rich silt during its annual overflow of the fields, had to be well-prepared for the flood. His home, equipment and cattle had to be temporarily removed from the area, and arrangements made for sowing immediately afterwards. Hence the coming of the flood had to be predicted. Not only in hotter countries, but in all lands, it was necessary to know beforehand the time for planting and the coming of holidays and days of sacrifice.

Prediction was not possible, however, by merely keeping a count of the passing days and nights. For the calendar year of 365 days soon lost all relation to the seasons, just because it was short by a quarter of a day. Prediction of a holiday or a river flood even a few days in advance required the accurate knowledge of mathematics and the motions of the heavenly bodies which was possessed only by priests. These holy people, knowing the importance of the calendar for the regulation of daily life, exploited this knowledge to retain dominance over the uninformed masses. In fact, it is believed that many early priests knew the solar year, that is, the year of the seasons, to be 365.3 days in length but deliberately withheld this knowledge from the people. Knowing also when a flood was due, priests could pretend to bring it about with their rites, while making the poor farmer pay for the performance.

Wonder about the heavens led, via astrology's more respectable partner, the science of astronomy, finally to mathematics. Religious mysticism, meanwhile, itself an expression of wonder about life, death, wind, rain and the panorama of nature, eventually became concerned with mathematics, as a means of understanding astrology. Of course, the importance of astrology in ancient religions must not be judged by its current discredited position in most cultures. In almost all these ancient religions, the heavenly bodies, the Sun especially, had personalities and cosmic influence over events on Earth. The wills and plans of these bodies might be fathomed by studying their activities, their regular comings and goings, the sudden visitations of meteors, and the occasional eclipses of the Sun and Moon. It was as natural for the ancient priests to work out a formula for the divination of the future based on the motions of the planets and star constellations as it is for the modern scientist to study and master nature with his techniques.

**31**  What was the initial urge which prompted man to study the stars and planets?

**A**    the need to develop methods of navigation

**B**    the need for life to be regulated by an accurate calendar

**C**    a desire to improve the woefully inadequate mathematics of the time

**D**    the desire to unravel the wonder of nature

**32**    Primitive farmers made a careful watch of the sky

    **A**    to see when certain activities should be performed.

    **B**    to receive the blessing of particular constellations.

    **C**    to receive comfort in times of hardship.

    **D**    for guidance in their religious rituals and ceremonies.

**33**    Farmers in hotter countries needed to know when the rivers would flood because

    **A**    the results could potentially be disastrous.

    **B**    various rituals had to be prepared.

    **C**    their prosperity was dependent on it.

    **D**    their cattle needed to be moved elsewhere.

**34**    What was the principal benefit to priests of possessing an accurate calendar?

    **A**    It enabled them to maintain their power over ordinary people.

    **B**    They knew when they had to perform religious rites.

    **C**    They could pretend to cause the annual flood of rivers.

    **D**    They received payment from farmers.

**35**    In ancient times, astrology was

    **A**    scorned by astronomers and mathematicians.

    **B**    held in similar esteem to the standing of science today.

    **C**    discredited, in comparison with astronomy.

    **D**    primarily used to try to divine the future.

**THIRD PASSAGE**

John Hobday sat on the edge of the desk and swung his left leg with characteristic boyishness. He waited for the staff to get settled in their seats and then spoke with careful informality.

'I know how frightfully busy you are. As a matter of fact, I am myself,' he said with the half-humorous urchin smile that he used for such jokes. Only his secretary, Veronica, gave the helpful laugh he expected. It was not going to be an easy meeting, he decided. 'So I'm not going to waste your time with a lot of talk,' he went on. 'I just thought …' He paused and beat with his pencil against the desk while Mrs Scrutton moved her chair fussily out of the sunlight. 'Ready?' he asked with an over-elaborate smile. 'Right. Then we'll start again. As I was saying, we're all very busy, but all the same I thought it was time we had a little meeting. I've been here a week now and although I've had some very helpful chats with each of you in turn, we've never had a chance to get together and outline our plans.' None of the three who formed his audience made any response. Veronica thought, he hasn't got the tone right, he doesn't realise that he's coming up against deeper loyalties with these people, loyalties to scholarship and ideas. She almost felt like letting him fend for himself, but old habits were too strong.

'I'm sure it's what everybody's been wanting,' she said in her deep voice. She had gauged rightly, his moment of uncertainty had gone, her faithful bark had guided him at the crucial moment. Mrs Scrutton tried to discomfit him. She rustled the papers on her lap and whispered audibly to Major Sarson, 'Our plans. His plans for us would be more honest.' But it was too late, she had missed her chance. John merely frowned at the interruption and it was Mrs Scrutton who was left with burning cheeks, hiding her embarrassment by lighting a fresh cigarette.

'As you know,' John went on, and Veronica could tell by the loud trumpeting, rhetorical note of his voice that he was once more the confident salesman lost in the dream world of the grandiose schemes he was putting before them, 'I've got some very big ideas for the Gallery. I'm not an expert in any way as you people are, but I think that's possibly why Sir Harold's executors chose me for the job. They felt the Gallery had already got its full weight of scholars and experts, what it needed was a man with administrative experience, whose training had led him to take an overall view of things, to think, shall I say, widely rather than deeply. That's why they got me in. But I'm going to be absolutely frank with you,' tossing back a lock of brown, wavy hair from his forehead, he stared at his audience with a wide-eyed appeal, 'I need your help. Without my staff I can get nowhere.'

Major Sarson winced slightly. All this theatricality and the loud pitch of John's voice got on his nerves.

**36** What manner did John Hobday adopt to address the staff of the Gallery?

    **A** He attempted to put them at their ease.

    **B** He spoke slowly and carefully.

    **C** He interspersed his talk with jokes.

    **D** He was deliberately patronising.

**37** How did John Hobday respond when Mrs Scrutton moved her chair?

    **A** He concealed his displeasure.

    **B** He took no notice of it.

    **C** He displayed his annoyance.

    **D** He encouraged her with a smile.

**38** Why did Veronica help him out when she saw he was having difficulties?

    **A** She liked him and wanted to help.

    **B** She felt it was her duty to support him.

    **C** She felt sorry for him.

    **D** She believed in what he was trying to do.

**39** How did Veronica view the schemes John Hobday was proposing?

    **A** They were necessary for the survival of the Gallery.

    **B** They were too ambitious and unrealistic.

    **C** They would make the Gallery a lot of money.

    **D** They represented a long-held dream of his.

**40** Which of the following statements correctly describes the feelings of the staff?

    **A** They disliked everything that John Hobday stood for.

    **B** They resented John Hobday's arrival in a position of authority.

    **C** They were indifferent to anything John Hobday had to say.

    **D** They felt that John Hobday was not an expert.

# PAPER 2 COMPOSITION (2 hours)

Answer any **two** questions.
Your answers must follow exactly the instructions given.
Write your answers on the separate answer paper provided.
Write clearly in pen, not pencil. You may make alterations but make sure that your work is **easy to read**. Write both question numbers clearly in the left-hand margin at the beginning of your answers.

1   Describe a visit to a restaurant which was memorable in some way, explaining what happened and how you felt. (About 350 words.)

2   'Crime is the direct result of parents' unwillingness to teach their children right from wrong.' Discuss. (About 350 words.)

3   Write a short story beginning or ending with the words: *Sonia picked up the telephone and listened for a short while without saying a word. When she put it down again she knew exactly what she had to do.* (About 350 words.)

4   Your recent holiday was ruined by the poor customer service of the airline you chose to fly with. Unhelpful airline personnel, a severely delayed flight and mislaid luggage were just some of the problems you encountered. Write to the airline, outlining your experiences and the compensation which you feel would be appropriate. (About 300 words.)

5   Based on your reading of one of these books, write on **one** of the following. (About 350 words.)

   **(a)**   Set book 1
         What part does the relationship between ___ and ___ play in the story?

   **(b)**   Set book 2
         What effect did ___ have on the main characters in the novel?

   **(c)**   Set book 3
         Do you think that '___' is an appropriate title for the novel? Give your reasons.

# PAPER 3  USE OF ENGLISH   (2 hours)

## Section A

1   Fill each of the numbered blanks in the passage with **one** suitable word.

### Herbs

During the last hundred years, much of the art of using herbs in cooking, as medicines, or for cosmetics, has been lost, (1).......... in industrialized societies. Until recently, (2).......... people in crowded cities had space to grow anything and gardens were a luxury to be (3).......... by the minority. In the (4).......... , however, knowledge of their uses lingered on. (5).......... the advent of refrigeration, however, (6).......... meant that the strong (7).......... of old meat no (8).......... had to be disguised, and equally that of full time work for women (9).......... the home, and finally the appearance of readily prepared packaged food, not to (10).......... medicines and beauty preparations, the growing of herbs declined rapidly, until recently.

Today, (11).......... we will admit it or not, most people have far more leisure time, and there is (12).......... anyone who does not have at least a small patch of garden or a (13).......... sill or balcony large (14).......... for a pot or two of herbs. These facts, coupled with the beginnings of a revolt (15).......... standardized foods, and perhaps also a (16).......... of the side-effects of some of today's medicines, mean that herbs have taken (17).......... a new popularity.

The culinary uses of herbs are endless and they can be used to good (18).......... , all year round, (19).......... in dried form or cut fresh. As aids to beauty and for medicinal (20).......... , to combat hundreds of ailments, there is now a vast range of herbs available. They are multi-purpose plants, for all occasions and all seasons.

**2** Finish each of the following sentences in such a way that it is **as similar as possible in meaning to the sentence printed before it**.

EXAMPLE: There was a terrible crash inside the room almost immediately after Henry left it.

ANSWER: *No sooner had Henry left the room than there was a terrible crash inside.*

**(a)** His efforts to find a solution didn't deserve such savage criticism.

He shouldn't ..................................................................................................................................

**(b)** The number of road accidents has soared in recent months.

There ......................................................................................................................................

**(c)** She is now leading a normal life as a result of all the support she received from social workers.

If she .....................................................................................................................................

**(d)** A work permit will only be issued on receipt of the correct documents.

Not .........................................................................................................................................

**(e)** Didn't you realise that he was only pretending?

Didn't it ...............................................................................................................................?

**(f)** The completion of the work was scheduled for last week.

The work was to .....................................................................................................................

**(g)** They'll soon find out what she's been doing.

It won't ...................................................................................................................................

**(h)** Most newsagents these days have ice-cream available all summer.

Ice-cream can ........................................................................................................................

**3** Fill each of the blanks with a suitable word or phrase.

EXAMPLE: It looks as if *he'll do* well in his exams next summer.

**(a)** Hadn't you ..................... a call? I'm sure she's been waiting by the phone all afternoon.

**(b)** Why on ..................... waited until the police arrived before going into the building?

**(c)** By the end of today steps ..................... to deal with this situation.

**(d)** The tigers were thought ..................... free from the zoo by an animal rights group.

**(e)** Don't let him know you have given me this information, ..................... do – he'd never forgive me if he found out!

**(f)** I couldn't reconcile ..................... to give up playing my drums, although the noise made all the neighbours complain.

**4**  For each of the sentences below, write a new sentence **as similar as possible in meaning to the original sentence**, but using the word given. This word **must not be altered in any way**.

EXAMPLE:   They don't get on well with their neighbours.
           **terms**

ANSWER:   *They are not on good terms with their neighbours.*

**(a)**   Whatever happens, we must avoid adverse publicity.
          **costs**

          ......................................................................................................................................................................

**(b)**   I worry far less about trivial matters these days than I used to.
          **nearly**

          ......................................................................................................................................................................

**(c)**   This is the first time I've seen her in my life!
          **set**

          ......................................................................................................................................................................

**(d)**   Since my arrival, you have criticised me constantly.
          **nothing**

          ......................................................................................................................................................................

**(e)**   It's unlikely he'll be picked for the Olympic swimming team.
          **chances**

          ......................................................................................................................................................................

**(f)**   If you go there without a map, you might get lost.
          **run**

          ......................................................................................................................................................................

**(g)**   I know I can convince Dave that I'm right about this matter.
          **bring**

          ......................................................................................................................................................................

**(h)**   He is different from his brother in almost all respects.
          **bears**

          ......................................................................................................................................................................

**Section B**

5    Read this passage, then answer the questions which follow it.

## The magic and the misery of science

What does the job of a research scientist have to offer the young, the bright and the ambitious? The pay is poor, the hours are long and the job security is virtually non-existent. But picture yourself in a quiet room, holding a piece of knowledge in your hand that no one else in the world yet knows or has ever known. For three minutes, three hours, three days, that piece of knowledge is yours and yours alone, until you choose to share it with the world. You have stepped from the calm of the boat and into uncharted territory. This is the   5
moment that every scientist dreams and hopes for.

What a scientist has to endure on the journey into the unknown will often be long days of despair: experiments that won't work, funding that disappears before you've even got off the ground, or a competitor who appears from nowhere and pips you at the post. In the shadow of defeat, you disconsolately shuffle back to the lab and begin seriously rethinking your career options. Because if you can't publish even a part of your journey   10
to the unknown, for the benefit of your colleagues and those who fund you, then you don't stand much chance of being given another ticket off terra firma.

But the journey itself can be fun, even if the outcome or the final destination turns out to be not quite what you had expected. The challenge of pitting yourself against nature's myriad complexities can be endlessly rewarding, and of course endlessly frustrating. Why would anyone want to find out how the internal organs   15
of a worm develop? Why would anyone want to devote their life to the reproduction of yeast, the substance used in the making of bread? Because we are not as distant from our fellow organisms as we would like to think.

What seems obscure under the scrutiny of science becomes less so in a wider context. Unless you're a devotee of home-baked cottage loaves, there's not been much in the humble yeast plant to get really excited   20
about. But there is now. Yeasts are organisms and so are we. Understanding how yeasts grow and divide helps us understand how our own cells replicate. Since a number of serious illnesses are caused by cells that are unable to control their growth or replication, you can see how understanding the lacklustre existence of a yeast could eventually lead us to new methods of treatment for some of them. This is just one example of how many apparently obscure facts can come together to give scientists the 'discovery rush' that they are   25
all working for.

Scientific research is personal – it is not abstract or remote for those who live it and breathe it every day. It bugs you, it ruins your weekends and evenings, it hangs over you like a bad conscience. It can make your bank manager disagreeable, and your nearest and dearest bewildered and confused. Every morning you are faced with your own personal nemesis. Every day you take small steps towards your goal, doing your best   30
to avoid the pitfalls and traps that nature delights in setting. On a good day you are puzzled, thrilled and amazed by what your work produces. Most days you grit your teeth in stubborn determination not to let the disappointment and frustration drive you into the arms of local accountancy firms offering on-the-spot training, for a far more stable and lucrative, if less challenging, career. So why do it, why not take up a profession that offers a modicum of job security and decent financial rewards?   35

Science is not a vocation. Funding is very hard to come by, university research posts are awarded on short term contracts and teaching tenure prospects are bleak for the young and capable. Each time you triumph over bafflement, however, each time you experience the sense of discovery, each time you learn something new, the buzz comes back. The battle, for the day, seems worthwhile.

**(a)** What do the words 'you have stepped from the calm of the boat' in line 5 suggest about sharing a scientific discovery with the world?

.......................................................................................................................................................
.......................................................................................................................................................

**(b)** What does the writer mean when she says that another scientist 'pips you at the post'? (line 9)

.......................................................................................................................................................
.......................................................................................................................................................

**(c)** What phrase in paragraph 2 suggests that a scientist may occasionally feel fed up or depressed?

.......................................................................................................................................................

**(d)** Which phrase in paragraph 1 is echoed in lines 10–11 by the words 'journey to the unknown'?

.......................................................................................................................................................

**(e)** In your own words, explain how a scientist may lose his/her chance 'of being given another ticket off terra firma'. (line 12)

.......................................................................................................................................................
.......................................................................................................................................................

**(f)** Describe in your own words how natural phenomena are portrayed in paragraph 3.

.......................................................................................................................................................
.......................................................................................................................................................

**(g)** According to the writer, how would the study of a worm's anatomy or the reproduction of yeast be viewed by non-scientists?

.......................................................................................................................................................
.......................................................................................................................................................

**(h)** What general point is the writer making about science when she mentions yeast and cells which are unable to control their growth? (line 22)

.......................................................................................................................................................
.......................................................................................................................................................

**(i)** What does the writer imply about the public view of scientific research when she says it is 'personal'? (line 26)

.......................................................................................................................................................
.......................................................................................................................................................

**(j)** In your own words, explain two ways in which scientific research can be personal.

.......................................................................................................................................................
.......................................................................................................................................................

**(k)** Explain in general terms what the 'disappointment and frustration' mentioned in line 32 might cause a scientist to do?

..............................................................................................................................................................

..............................................................................................................................................................

**(l)** Which word in the last paragraph echoes the 'discovery rush' mentioned earlier in the passage? (line 24)

..............................................................................................................................................................

..............................................................................................................................................................

**(m)** In a paragraph of **70–90** words, summarise what makes a career in scientific research both pressurised, and particularly worthwhile.

..............................................................................................................................................................

..............................................................................................................................................................

..............................................................................................................................................................

..............................................................................................................................................................

..............................................................................................................................................................

..............................................................................................................................................................

..............................................................................................................................................................

..............................................................................................................................................................

..............................................................................................................................................................

..............................................................................................................................................................

# PAPER 4   LISTENING COMPREHENSION   (about 40 minutes)

**PART ONE**

You will hear an interview with the presenter of a popular radio series about food and cooking.
For questions **1–5**, indicate the most appropriate response **A**, **B**, **C** or **D**.

**1**   What has made 'Just a Taste' so popular?

   **A**   It gives advice about how to cook traditional dishes.

   **B**   It features interviews with professional chefs.

   **C**   It presents food and cooking in a more personal light.

   **D**   It takes a humorous approach.

**2**   The presenter of the series believes that smells

   **A**   will one day be made available to listeners.

   **B**   can never be part of a radio cookery programme.

   **C**   are more important than sounds in the kitchen.

   **D**   cannot be successfully imagined by listeners.

**3**   What makes describing a dish particularly difficult?

   **A**   There are too many ingredients to describe.

   **B**   Listeners are mainly interested in what they should be aiming for.

   **C**   Each stage of the cooking process needs to be described.

   **D**   There is a lack of appropriate vocabulary.

**4**   The presenter of the series mentions Iceland because

   **A**   it has a particularly unusual cuisine.

   **B**   fish-based dishes are particularly popular there.

   **C**   it has turned natural features to its advantage.

   **D**   it produces large quantities of fruit and vegetables.

**5**   The spices asafoetida and turmeric are used in South Indian cooking

   **A**   mainly for their taste.

   **B**   mainly for their therapeutic properties.

   **C**   by filtering them into the food.

   **D**   for traditional reasons only.

You will hear part of an interview where Dr Heather Clark is talking about her job as a doctor and her passion for dancing. For questions **6–17**, fill the gaps in the sentences with a word or short phrase.

Dr Heather Clark hit the headlines when she performed [_____ **6**]

in a London pub.

She travels [_____ **7**] to get to people who need her help.

When travelling to [_____ **8**] she never knows what awaits her.

She likes her job because people can be saved [_____ **9**] by the doctor.

Although she carries [_____ **10**] she often has to run to get to patients.

When young she wanted to become a ballerina, but she was [_____ **11**]

She now stays fit by dancing [_____ **12**] a week.

Dancing also helps her [_____ **13**] off when she is under stress.

The rehearsals she attends with a [_____ **14**] sometimes don't finish until

the small hours of the morning.

She often [_____ **15**] hospital to discuss cases with colleagues.

As a junior doctor she once suffered from a kidney infection because she was so

[_____ **16**]

In the future she intends to do an MSc in [_____ **17**] and work for

the Royal Ballet.

## PART THREE

You will hear two speakers, Andy and Joe, talking about possible reasons for the increase in crime in recent years. For questions **18–25**, indicate which of the opinions listed are given by each speaker.

In each box, write either:

    **A** (Andy)

or  **J** (Joe)

or  **B** (both Andy and Joe)


**18**   Fewer crimes are reported to the police nowadays.                   ☐ **18**

**19**   People used to be shocked by even minor offences.              ☐ **19**

**20**   Crime increases as people become richer.                        ☐ **20**

**21**   When people were poorer, they had more reason to steal.       ☐ **21**

**22**   Sentences were much heavier in the past.                        ☐ **22**

**23**   Convicted criminals serve less of their sentence nowadays.     ☐ **23**

**24**   Many criminals are not convicted by courts these days.        ☐ **24**

**25**   The police catch fewer criminals than they used to.           ☐ **25**

# PAPER 5   SPEAKING

**Note**: In the actual examination, instead of reading printed instructions for each part of the interview you will be told what to do by the examiner. Discussion of various themes or communicative activities will also, of course, involve the examiner and/or another candidate.

The timing for each part of the interview (indicated in brackets) is given for **each individual candidate**. For example, in **Part 1**, where you talk about one or more photographs, each candidate speaks for about five minutes.

**Consumerism**

**Photographs**   (about 5 minutes)

Compare and contrast these three photographs, saying where and when you think they were taken. When you have done this, discuss how you think shopping today might be different from shopping a hundred years ago.

1.

3.

2.

| **Passages** | (about 2 minutes) |

Read one of the passages below and say where you think it comes from (and why) and how it relates to the general theme of consumerism.

1.  I just adore supermarkets. I get a real buzz every time I walk into one. I don't know why I feel this way – maybe it's the fluorescent lighting, maybe it's that dreamy kind of music they always have playing in the background, or maybe it's just the sight of all those shelves packed with things waiting to be bought. Whatever it is, it certainly has quite an effect on me! I must be the ideal consumer. I can't resist going round with my trolley and grabbing anything – absolutely anything – that takes my fancy. It doesn't matter whether I actually need it or not. That's not the point. If it's a special offer, or a new product, or attractively wrapped – I've just *got* to put it in my trolley!

2.  In Britain the emergence of a relatively large, literate middle class in the early eighteenth century created the preconditions for advertising in its modern sense. Advertisements from that period were directed at frequenters of coffee houses, where magazines and newspapers were read, and significantly, the products advertised were such 'luxuries' as coffee, tea, books, wigs, patent medicines, cosmetics, plays and concerts, and lottery tickets.

3.  **IMPORTANT NOTICE – PRODUCT RECALL –** *Solar Haze 420*
    A small batch of these heaters has been found to suffer from an electrical fault which, while not dangerous to the user, may affect the performance and operating life-span of the product. Anyone who purchased one of our *Solar Haze 420* heaters during June or July of this year is requested to examine the serial number on the back of the appliance. Those models bearing a number within the range *AZ 1346* to *AZ 1520* may not meet the high standards you rightly expect from all *'Solar Range'* heaters, and should be returned immediately to the place of purchase, to receive an exchange or a full refund. The fault has now been rectified, and no other *'Solar Range'* heaters are affected. Anyone with further questions or concerns can contact our freephone *Cosy Customer 24-hour Helpline* on 1044 854 236.

Choose one of the following communicative activities.

1.   | **Discussion** |

Look at these **two** statements. Comment on them with reference to what you consider to be role of advertising.

> Advertising is the single most important factor contributing to the success of a new product.

> It's the product which is most important. If the product fails to please, no amount of advertising can disguise that.

**Suggested prompts**:
- different types of product
- other factors (price, packaging, etc.)
- brand names and brand loyalty

- the influence of advertising
- what consumers expect from a product
- target consumers

2.   | **Selection** |

Look at the following factors. Which are most important for you when you are shopping for clothes?

- price
- opinions of friends/parents
- size and comfort
- fashion
- colour and fabric
- shop brand or designer label

3.   | **Selection** |

**Role play** the following situation.
You are going to open a clothes shop with a friend. You want to attract as many customers to the shop as you can in the first week, and are thinking of different ways to do this.
Look at the suggestions below and discuss what you should do. A limited budget means that you must agree on **three** of the suggestions only.

**Ways of attracting customers in the first week**
- advertisements in local newspapers and on the radio
- fashion shows every day outside the shop
- leaflets distributed to people in the town centre
- hiring an expert to design attractive window displays
- sale of all clothes at 'cost price' for one week
- food and wine to be served to customers
- loud music in the shop

In the Proficiency exam, you will transfer your answers
for **papers 1 and 4** to answer sheets like those below.

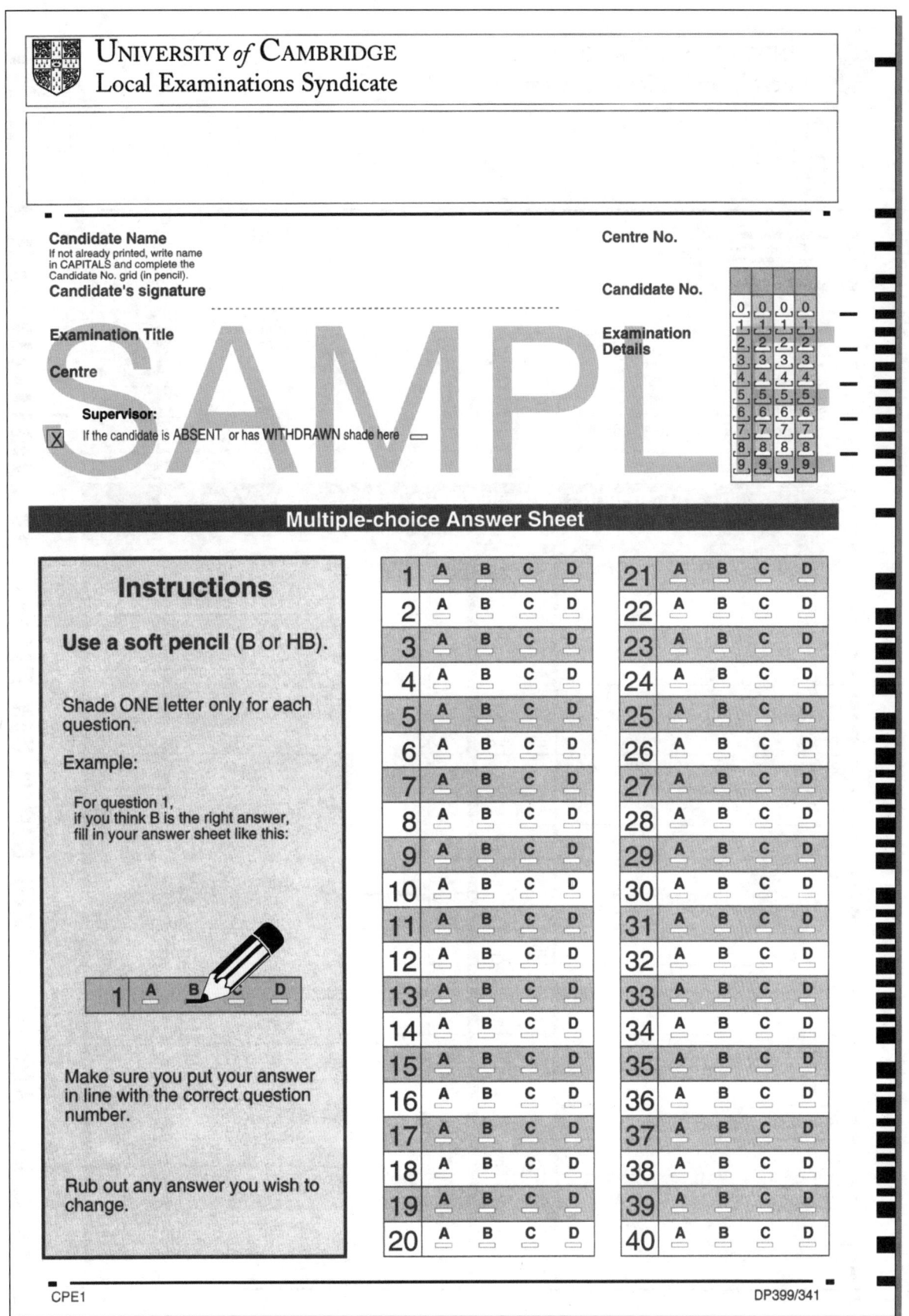

# UNIVERSITY *of* CAMBRIDGE
## Local Examinations Syndicate

**Candidate Name**
If not already printed, write name in CAPITALS and complete the Candidate No. grid (in pencil).
**Candidate's signature**

**Examination Title**

**Centre**

**Supervisor:**
[X] If the candidate is ABSENT or has WITHDRAWN shade here ▭

**Centre No.**

**Candidate No.**

**Examination Details**

SAMPLE

Candidate No. grid:
```
0 0 0 0
1 1 1 1
2 2 2 2
3 3 3 3
4 4 4 4
5 5 5 5
6 6 6 6
7 7 7 7
8 8 8 8
9 9 9 9
```

## Listening Comprehension Answer Sheet

| Enter the test number here ▭▭▭ | | For office use only | CPE ⊏3⊐ CAE ⊏5⊐ ⊏0⊐⊏1⊐⊏2⊐⊏3⊐⊏4⊐⊏5⊐⊏6⊐⊏7⊐⊏8⊐⊏9⊐ ⊏0⊐⊏1⊐⊏2⊐⊏3⊐⊏4⊐⊏5⊐⊏6⊐⊏7⊐⊏8⊐⊏9⊐ | |
|---|---|---|---|

| **Write your answers below** | Do not write here | **Continue here** | Do not write here |
|---|---|---|---|
| 1 | ▭ 1 ▭ | 21 | ▭ 21 ▭ |
| 2 | ▭ 2 ▭ | 22 | ▭ 22 ▭ |
| 3 | ▭ 3 ▭ | 23 | ▭ 23 ▭ |
| 4 | ▭ 4 ▭ | 24 | ▭ 24 ▭ |
| 5 | ▭ 5 ▭ | 25 | ▭ 25 ▭ |
| 6 | ▭ 6 ▭ | 26 | ▭ 26 ▭ |
| 7 | ▭ 7 ▭ | 27 | ▭ 27 ▭ |
| 8 | ▭ 8 ▭ | 28 | ▭ 28 ▭ |
| 9 | ▭ 9 ▭ | 29 | ▭ 29 ▭ |
| 10 | ▭ 10 ▭ | 30 | ▭ 30 ▭ |
| 11 | ▭ 11 ▭ | 31 | ▭ 31 ▭ |
| 12 | ▭ 12 ▭ | 32 | ▭ 32 ▭ |
| 13 | ▭ 13 ▭ | 33 | ▭ 33 ▭ |
| 14 | ▭ 14 ▭ | 34 | ▭ 34 ▭ |
| 15 | ▭ 15 ▭ | 35 | ▭ 35 ▭ |
| 16 | ▭ 16 ▭ | 36 | ▭ 36 ▭ |
| 17 | ▭ 17 ▭ | 37 | ▭ 37 ▭ |
| 18 | ▭ 18 ▭ | 38 | ▭ 38 ▭ |
| 19 | ▭ 19 ▭ | 39 | ▭ 39 ▭ |
| 20 | ▭ 20 ▭ | 40 | ▭ 40 ▭ |

EFL 4

DP308/82

# Answer key

## UNIT *1*

### Vocabulary: what's in a word?  p.8

**2**

**1**

1 exam (*inf.*); passed; take; examined on
2 examined; for; detailed
3 under (*being examined*)   4 cross-examination (*legal term*)

**2**   1b)   2c)   3a)   4d)

**3**   1 F (*scientific examination is normally uncountable*)
2 F (*not in **fixed phrases** and **collocs.** like 'under examination'
or 'cross-examination'*)   3 T   4 F (*you examine sb **on** specific
information which they have learned – e.g. 'We're going
to be examined on the reign of Elizabeth I tomorrow'*)
5 F (*'I've passed...'*)   6 T

**4**   1 **vast** majority   2 **do well**   3 information
(*uncountable*)   4 meaning(s) **of**   5 pronunciation
6 insight **into**   7 *no prep. is needed*   8 **phonetic**
transcriptions   9 make room **for**   10 **on** a regular basis

### Grammar: past tenses and Present perfect  p.10

**1**

1 When the mistake **was discovered** yesterday, she denied
all knowledge of it.
2 By the time I finally **won** the lottery, I **had been playing**
it for thirty years
3 Once she **had overcome** her initial reservations, she
actually **enjoyed** the concert
4 He **was covered** in splashes of paint at lunchtime,
because he **had been decorating** the kitchen all
morning.
5 He **thought** briefly about the question before he **replied**.
6 The police **were called** to the scene of the accident, as
soon as there **was** absolute certainty of its location.

7 By the time his latest novel **was published** last week,
tens of thousands of pounds **had been spent** on
promoting it.
8 She **didn't go** to bed until she **had checked** all the safety
catches on the windows.

**2**   When I **was** a little girl... **used to go / went** every
New Year (*repeated action – you don't need Past continuous*) ...
it **was** rumoured to be haunted (*Past simple passive*) ... **had
seen** the ghost (*on several occasions*) ... **used to like / liked**
(would *can only be used for habitual **actions***) ... **had been**
snowing (*until that point*) ... **were** sitting (*this was interrupted
by the crash*) ... **had** galloped (*when it was finished*) ... **had**
snapped (*before the moment we arrived*) ... **have never been**
so scared (*she was talking about all of her life, an unfinished
period of time*).

**3**

**1**
1 Vienna is **the loveliest** city **I've** ever visited.
2 I hadn't expected them to **get on so** well together.
3 Ever **since** Anna was a little girl she **has been afraid of**
the dark.
4 It's ages **since I've spoken** / I **last** spoke to Alex.
5 By the **time** the police arrived, the robber had **already**
escaped.
6 They have **been** negotia**ting** the terms of the contract for
over a week now.
7 They staff used **to have to** file everything by hand before
computers **were** installed.
8 There **has been** a sharp rise **in** the level of atmospheric
pollution this year.
9 Heather did**n't learn** to swim **until** she was eighteen / the
age of eighteen.
10 He has **been unemployed for** over six months.

**2**   *Watch out for this **checklist sign** after exercises. These
questions about the exercise are designed to help you to notice
**what each particular task is really testing**, to be aware of
typical mistakes, and to **learn from your own errors**
throughout your course. Keep a record of the mistakes you have
made in a separate place in your notebook, and refer to it
regularly, to help you to improve your performance in the same
type of task in the future.*

In this task, there were:
• tense changes in 2 (*Past simple* to *Past perfect*), 3 (*Present
simple* to *Present perfect*), 5 (*Past simple* to *Past perfect*),
6 (*Present perfect simple* to *Present perfect continuous*),
7 (*Present simple* to *used to* and *Past simple*) and 10 (*Past
simple* to *Present perfect*)
• prepositions to add in 3 (afraid / frightened + *of*),
4 (*since*), 8 (rise + *in*), 9 (not + *until*) and 10 (*for*)
• changes in the form of a word in 3 (*fear* to *frightened /
afraid*), 5 (*arrival* to *arrived*), and 8 (*risen sharply* to
*sharp rise*).

## Vocabulary: multiple-choice p.11

*Always use a good **monolingual** dictionary to help you check your answers when practising Paper 1, Vocabulary multiple-choice questions. It will help you identify precise meanings for words, as well as the collocations and contexts they are typically used with.*

1B   2C   3A   4C   5C   6B   7C   8A   9A   10C

## Vocabulary: phrasal verbs *keep* p.12

**1**  2 b) *Sentence two is wrong because of word order. The position of the object can vary with phrasal verbs, and a good dictionary shows you this information. This verb appears as* keep s.b. on, *(not* keep on s.b.*), and this means the verb is **separable**:*
– *I'm afraid we can't afford to* **keep on you.** ✗
– *I'm afraid we can't afford to* **keep you on.** ✔
*Always record whether a phrasal verb is separable or not, when you make a note of it in your vocabulary notebook.*

**2**  1 keep in with (*insep.*)   2 Keep out of (*insep.*)
3 keep to (*insep.*)   4 kept them up (*sep.*)   5 keep up (*sep.*)
6 keeping back (*sep.*)

**3**  *Fixed phrases really are **fixed** – you have to learn the articles, pronouns, word order, etc. which are used with them, if you want to use them accurately.*

1 keep track of   2 keep our heads   3 keep me company
4 keep your / an eye on   5 keep a straight face

## Use of English: guided cloze p.12

*Don't forget to give the gapped word a **capital letter** if it starts a sentence (like 7 below), and make sure your **spelling** is correct, as you lose marks for mistakes in this part of the exam.*

1 people   2 place   3 contrary   4 life   5 great   6 food
7 There   8 grew   9 as   10 life   11 up   12 addition
13 regarded / seen   14 used   15 such   16 of   17 played
18 lose   19 quality   20 their

## Writing: paragraph organisation p.14

**1**  1 c) – a) *too general*, b) *too specific*   2 c) – a) *too general*, b) *too specific*   3 a) – b) *too specific*, c) *too general*

**2**  *Sample answers*
4   The government could do a lot more to improve the lives of the elderly. (*Note the critical tone of the paragraph*).
5   The leisure centre has a wide range of facilities for the disabled. (*The paragraph goes on to examine these in detail, and has a very positive tone*).

**3**  Change is a part of life … for the worse (*this is more appropriate to a discursive composition*)   I've always longed … approve of long hair (*this is not relevant to her sister*)   … and there were plenty of those, I can tell you! (*this doesn't add anything to the description of the sister, and is a rather distracting detail*).

**4**  para. 1D   para. 2A   para. 3C   para. 4C   para. 5B

## UNIT 2

## Vocabulary review: multiple-choice p.16

1B (completely / hopelessly + inadequate *are also used*)
2D   3A (well-intentioned = *thoughtful actions*; well-built = *physically strong or heavy*; well-informed = *knowledgeable about a particular situation*)   4C   5B   6A (*you* have time to kill *if you arrive too early, and then have nothing to do for a period of time*)   7B   8D (*she shows what she's really good at*)   9C (immediate family = *your father, mother and siblings*; the nuclear family = *the institution or idea of the family as a social unit*)   10D (close / intimate / strong + relationship *are also used*; unshakable = *commitment, faith or trust*; firm = *belief, idea or agreement*)

## Grammar: conditional forms, *wish / if only* p.16

**1**
1   If I hadn't been **so** nervous in the exam, I would / might **have been able to** write better.
2   If there **is no improvement in** the weather, we'll have to …
3   I wish they **would** reconsider their plans.
4   If I **hadn't had to** revise every night throughout my exams, I wouldn't / might not have been **so** bad tempered.
5   I wish my car **would** start …
6   If we **hadn't** received **so** much money, we wouldn't **have been able to** build …
7   If you **contact / get in touch with** me, I'll **stop** my plans.
8   I might **have been able to** go to the lecture, if I **hadn't had so** much work to do.

 **2**  There was / were:
- modal verbs in 1 (*couldn't* to *been able to*) and 8 (*couldn't* to *been able to*)
- the adverb *so* in 4 (*really* to *so*), 6 (*all* to *so*) and 8 (*too* to *so*). *Notice how many different expressions can be transformed to the adverb* so *in sentence transformations.*
- will / would in 3 (*refusing* to *would*, = *volition, or willingness to do s.t.*) and 5 (*it's so annoying* to *would* = *expressing irritation*).

## Use of English: gapped sentences p.17

**2**  1 I was given   2 long as you are   3 time he took
4 better answer the   5 if he'll do (*he'll = 2 words*)
6 you didn't shout (*didn't = 2 words*)   7 rather make
8 you kept

 **3**  There was / were:
- important words not immediately around the gap in 1 (*by*); 3 (*his*); and 6 (*deaf*)
- phrasal verbs or fixed expressions in 1 (*give + feedback*); 3 (*high + time   take + responsibility*); 4 (*hadn't you better*); 5 (*do + well*); 7 (*make + arrangements*) and 8 (*keep out*)
- passive voice in 1 (with *by*)
- a change of verb form in 1 (*active* to *passive*); 3 (*high time + Past simple*); 6 (*I'd rather + Past simple*); and 8 (*It's time + Past simple*).

## Listening: sentence completion p.18

### 1

**1**  1B  2A  3D  4C

**2**  1 practically everything  2 contributions  3 easy
4 achievements

**3**  different register – sentence 1; different forms of words –
sentences 1 and 4; different word order – sentences 1 and 4

**2**  1 translation  2 source of the Nile  3 forty languages
4 was nothing  5 systematic  6 persistent  7 long periods
of time  8 abroad  9 play with children  10 adolescence

### Tapescript

#### Extracts for Exercise 1.1

A  *It would be wrong to claim that his contributions to mankind
were on a par with those of a Darwin or an Einstein, both of
whom chose to concentrate …*
B  *Burton's achievements were on a far broader front. He
excelled at practically everything.*
C  *Is there any key that can help account for Burton's amazing
achievements? I think motivation provides such as key, at
least to his success at mastering foreign languages.*
D  *Burton did not hit upon any particular method or technique
for language learning that might have made the task
especially easy for him, or given him a special advantage.*

#### Exercise 1.2

*My talk tonight will be the last in the current series of talks
about famous artists, scientists and scholars in history. If a
competition were to take place to decide on the person in recent
history whose achievements at learning have been the most
stunning, my vote would go to the nineteenth-century
Englishman, Sir Richard Burton. It would be wrong to claim that
his contributions to mankind are on a par with those of a
Darwin or an Einstein, both of whom chose to concentrate their
energies in particular directions, maximizing the impact of their
work. But Burton's achievements were on a broader front. He
excelled at practically everything.*

*A list of Burton's feats gives a fair indication of the man's
phenomenal powers. He is best known for his translation into
English of sixteen volumes of the stories known as the Arabian
Nights. He also translated large quantities of Portuguese
literature, the folklore of many countries and Latin poetry. His
own poems were published in two volumes. What's more, in an
age of Victorian heroes, he was an outstanding explorer and
traveller. He journeyed in search of the origins of the Nile, and he
made a number of dangerous expeditions of discovery in
northern Africa and the Near East.*

*Perhaps the most impressive of all Burton's achievements,
though, was his mastery, to a high level of proficiency, of no less
than forty separate languages, plus a huge number of related
dialects.*

*Is there any key that can help account for Burton's amazing
achievements? I think motivation provides such a key, at least to
his success at mastering foreign languages.*

*Burton did not hit upon any particular method or technique
for language learning that might have made the task especially
easy for him, or given him a special advantage. He has left an
interesting account of the methods and study habits he followed
when he was learning a new language, and there seems to have*

*been nothing extraordinary about his techniques for studying.
Undoubtedly he was very systematic in his approach to learning
unfamiliar languages and he went about the task with
extraordinary persistence. But he reported that he did not find
acquiring foreign languages at all easy, and he wrote with feeling
about the difficult and time-consuming nature of the learning
tasks he set for himself.*

*What did set Burton apart as a learner was his remarkable
energy, determination and his refusal to give up. To learn a new
language, Burton would devote long periods of time to study and
he refused to be put off. He worked and worked, and he kept at
the task, persevering in the face of all the discouragement,
boredom, frustration and fatigue that wears down any normal
student.*

*The young Richard Burton was a bright lad, although
definitely no infant prodigy. His early life gives us few hints of
future intellectual excellence, but it's in his childhood that we
find the key to the determination which made his efforts to learn
so persistent, and eventually so successful. An unusual feature of
his childhood is that it was mostly spent abroad. His father had
a limited income and no paid profession, so it was financially
necessary for the family to spend quite a bit of their time away
from Britain, in various parts of continental Europe. So if the
high-spirited Burton children wanted to play with local children
of the same age, they had to learn the relevant language .
Richard Burton, then, was repeatedly placed in a position in
which the effort of learning a new language was amply justified
and quickly rewarded.*

*By the time he reached adolescence he had gained
considerable language skills, in addition to a good deal of
general experience in acquiring new languages. Language-
acquisition tasks that might have appeared daunting and
excruciatingly tedious to others looked very different to Burton.
He knew that he could succeed because he had reaped the
rewards of his own efforts in the past.*

*In later life, Burton often said that …*

## Vocabulary: descriptive verbs p.19

### 1

ways of speaking – shriek, mutter, yell, groan, moan, whine
ways of walking – stagger, stride, stroll, amble, trudge
ways of looking – glare, frown, gaze, glance, peer, stare
ways of taking or holding – clutch, hug, grasp, snatch, grip

**2**  1 snatched  2 yelled  3 trudged  4 glaring  5 peered
6 muttering  7 staggered  8 gazed

## Use of English: writing a summary p.19

### 1

**3** The omitted information is either irrelevant to the
summary question, or is repetitive, and does not add
anything to the underlined parts of the text.

**2**  The student still needs to edit the summary to the
correct length (30–40 words).

**3**  extremely important = *vital*; spend their time only on
things which are important = *prioritise*; things they need to
do by certain times = *deadlines*; notes which are organised
and cover all points = *thorough notes*; preparing for exams =
*revising*

*Sample answer*

It is vital for students to prioritise, making lists of deadlines. They should also develop effective reading habits and keep thorough notes. Finally, when revising for exams, it is essential for students to leave themselves enough time. (*37 words*)

**5** The 'key' words in the summary task are *educational benefits* (*not problems, or other types of benefits*) and *according to the writer* (*this reminds you to look only in the text, and not to add your own opinions about the topic*).

**6** 1 concentration and memory   2 motivation with / attitude to school work; them to   3 in parallel; quickly and effectively   4 computer graphics; future careers 5 pre-school children; to read and write / reading and writing skills.

*Sample answer*

Computer games may increase children's powers of concentration and memory. They may also have a positive effect on children's school work by encouraging them to look for greater challenges when they complete tasks successfully. It is believed that game players think differently and learn to deal with problems more quickly and effectively, and familiarity with computer graphics may help children in their future careers. Finally, computer games can even be used to help pre-school children to learn to read and write. (*81 words*)

## Writing: descriptive composition (1) (experiences) p.22

**1**   introduction – examinations are very important in our lives – 3 reasons
**1st supporting para.** – school in modern building – over 1,000 students there – good reputation
**2nd para.** – head teacher only been at school for six months – everyone likes him
**3rd para.** – known my friends for many years – holiday together previous year
**closing para.** – watched TV – favourite soap opera

**3**   1E   2B   3F   4C   5A   6D

**4** 1 The task has three parts: *1 what happened   2 how you felt   3 why you felt this way.* This composition answers parts 1 and 2 excellently, and 3 **only moderately well**. 2 The composition uses method D for organising the paragraphs (from the box in Unit 1, page 15) – (*putting details in chronological order, to give a strong sense of story, and to create a sense of suspense and immediacy when describing feelings*).

# UNIT 3

## Vocabulary review: multiple-choice p.24

1B  2C  3A  4C  5D  6C  7B  8A  9C  10D (*questions 5, 8 and 10 illustrate collocations. Record them in your notebook and try to use them in your writing when you can.*)

## Grammar: emphasis (1) (inversion) p.24

**1** 1 At no time **did it seem** ...   2 **Only when / after** our visas had been double-checked **were we allowed** ... 3 Under no circumstances **are you to** visit ...   4 Never before **has television played** ...   5 Seldom **do you come** across ... 6 **Had he not** been listening to the radio ... (Hadn't he been *is impossible, because the* not *is stressed, and so can't be contracted*)   7 **No sooner** had we sat down **than** ...   8 Never **will I** ...   9 Little **did she realise** what ...   10 So well **does he act** that ...   11 Not **for** another six months **did Sally meet** ...   12 **Rarely does he do** his fair share of the work.

**2**   There was / were:
- extra auxiliary verbs in 1 (*did*); 8 (*will, to indicate volition, or willingness to do s.t.*); 10 (*does*) and 12 (*does – this verb, when the verb of action is also* do, *is very commonly forgotten. Make a special note, if you made this mistake. You can see that the most common auxiliary verb which has to be added is a form of* do).
- a negative added or removed in 2 (*were we allowed*); 3 (*are you to visit*); 5 (*do you come across*) 9 (*did she realise*) and 12 (*does he do*). *This happens a lot in inversions, because so many expressions with negative meanings are used, such as* rarely, never, little, *etc.*
- an inverted subject and verb in every question
- a change in the order of information in the sentence in 2 (*only after our visas ...*); 3 (*under no circumstances ...*); and 6 (*had he not been ...*).

**2** 1 1 anyone had   2 did he congratulate   3 account are 4 having read   5 pleased / impressed were they   6 the worst

**2**   There were:
- no inversions in 1, 4 or 6
- words with dep. preps. in 2 (congratulate + *on*) and 5 (impressed / pleased + *with*).

## Reading: literary text p.26

**1**   d) romantic, or e) detective

**3**   The parts of the text which give you the answers are included here to help you.   1B (*... in whether the employer would satisfy hers*)   2D (*regarded a secretary as a status symbol*)   3C (*... was convenient both for the City and for the towering offices of Docklands. Neither had so far produced much in the way of business*)   4C (*while other agencies had foundered in the waves of recession, Mrs Creasley's small ... ship ... was still afloat*)   5C (*she occasionally spent the night in defiance of the terms of the lease*)   6D (*... which represented all Mandy had ever known of the comfort and security of home*)   7B (*a father* *whose idea of parenthood had gone little beyond ...)*   8B (*in acrimonious camaraderie ... the main cause of dispute being ...*) 9C (this is not directly stated, but is implied by the embarrassment she felt about her feelings about the cosy, and the general picture we get of Mandy as an apparently tough character).

**4**   a)4   b)1   c)3 and 6   d)2 and 9

## Use of English: guided key word transformations p.28

1 She didn't want to leave the room **for fear of** missing ... 2 What I'm telling you know is **in confidence.**   3 We must avoid a scandal **at all costs.**   4 **To the best of my knowledge** ...   5 I wanted to find a new job because **I was in (a bit of) a rut.**   6 They **are not on good terms with** their neighbours.   7 I had something particular **in mind.** 8 There's **no question of our** sell**ing** this painting.

## Grammar: participle clauses p.28

**1**   1b)   2a)   3c)   4c)   5d)   6a)   7b)   8c)   9e)   10c)

**2**   **Sitting** under a palm tree, **sipping** his cocktail, Tom Sloane kept his eye on the exceptionally fat man who was moving ponderously towards him. Something about him was not quite right. Maybe it was the slightly insane grin which made him feel uneasy. **Not having brought** his gun with him to the beach, Sloane naturally felt vulnerable. What should he do? **Putting** his glass down, he stood up and strolled towards the man, **whistling nonchalantly** as he went. Even though **exhausted** from his previous mission, he understood that a moment's carelessness could cost him his life. **Having been attacked** by a knife-wielding nun the previous week, Sloane was ready for anything. Especially a fat man wearing a black bowler hat ..... The hat!  Why hadn't he noticed it before? **Seeing** the man reach for the weapon on his head, Sloane dived for cover. Zzzzzz! The bullet just missed him, **burying** itself in the sand beside him. **Unperturbed**, the fat man continued to grin at Sloane. 'Good afternoon, Mr Sloane. How nice to see you,' he muttered, **clenching** his teeth.

## Writing: descriptive composition (2) (people) p.29

**1**   Introduction 2 is inappropriate because:
- the style and register are more appropriate for a discursive composition
- there is no clear topic sentence, and certainly no obvious topic which is relevant to the task
- the sentences are not organised in a clear way which makes it easy to follow the writer's argument.

**3**   First supporting paragraph:
d) and f) = 1st hobby   c) and g) = 2nd hobby   e) = 3rd and most important hobby. *Notice how hobbies 1 and 2 are each introduced with an* **extra detail** *which tells the reader about Peter's* **personality**. *The emphatic order of this paragraph means that the most important hobby comes last, and is then described in more detail in the paragraph which follows.*

Second supporting paragraph:
a), h) and i). *This paragraph shows how serious Peter's main hobby is, and illustrates this with points which show both negative and positive aspects of his personality.*

Closing paragraph:
b) *closes the composition nicely by suggesting how Peter's hobbies may shape his future.*

**5**
- the topic statement in para. 1 = *A particularly good example ...*
- the topic sentence in para. 2 = *Peter likes to pursue ...*
- the topic sentence in para. 3 = *Ever since he was a little boy ...*
- the summing up phrase in the final para. = *Generally speaking, ...*

# UNIT 4

## Vocabulary: multiple-choice p.32

1B (commercials = *television advertising*;   propaganda *and* manifestos *are generally used in political contexts*) 2C (*advertising / marketing / political / military* + campaign *are also used*)   3C (produce = *fruit and vegetables*   products *would fit here*)   4D   5A   6C   7A   8C (*this is a colloc. to* record and learn)   9B   10C (*this is a standard prep. phrase*)

## Use of English: guided key word transformations p.32

**1**

**2**
1 **The** cost **of** a university education is very **high** these days. (*This transformation requires you to supply the adjective* high *to collocate with the noun* cost.)
2 Over the past five years **there has** been **a considerable** increase **in** the number of people buying mobile phones. (*Here you need to change the form of the adverb* considerably *and transform the verb* rise *to the noun* increase, *plus its correct dep. prep.* in.)
3 The discovery of the theft led **to his / Mike's** immediate **dismissal.** (*As well as supplying the correct dep. prep. for the verb* lead, *you need to change the verb* dismiss *to a noun*).
4 We **were** unaware **of** what had been happening **until** after the accident. (*The transformation of* only + when / only + after *to* not / *negative form* + until *is very common in key word or sentence transformations.*)

**3**
1 I think you should **keep out of** this argument
2 He was (rather) **reluctant to go** on the climb.
3 She can be **relied on / upon** to help. (*Notice that a modal verb and a passive are necessary here, as the supplied form of* rely *is the past participle*).
4 The manager's inefficiency **contributed to** the failure of the enterprise. (*Here, it was also necessary to change the form of the adjective* inefficient *and the verb* failed, *to fit the new sentence*).

**4** 1 **Quite a few** people seem to be shopping at the new supermarket.   2 I **don't** spend **nearly as much** money on groceries as she does.   3 Of all the stereo systems we have seen, this one is **by far** the best.   4 There is **hardly any difference between** these two brands of ketchup.

**5** 1 I decided **on the spur of the moment** to take the bus home.   2 The pickpocket appeared and **in a flash** my wallet was gone.   3 I've **set my heart on** an exotic foreign holiday. (*This expression normally appears in Present or Past perfect tenses*)   4 When he was lecturing us on our bad behaviour, I found it difficult to **keep a straight face**. (*This expression remains the same even when the number of people is plural, e.g. we found it hard to keep a straight face – **not** straight faces*).

**6** 1 Petrol is **highly inflammable**, so ... (*This is an adverb + adjective colloc.*).   2 Would **it put you out** if I brought a friend ...?   3 It was **virtually impossible for me to** understand ...   4 When times are hard, we ought to **spare a thought for** ...   5 I cannot understand her **craving for** popularity.   6 When we later returned to the shop, **there was no sign of** the manager ...   7 **Over the past** ten years, this shop's profit **has doubled**.   8 Can you **keep an eye on** my children ....?   9 **No sooner had** the match started **than** ...   10 She **had your safety at heart** when ...

 **2**   There was / were:
- changes of tense in 1.3, 3 (*active* to *passive*)   1.5, 3 (*I won't ...* to *I've set my heart on ...*) and 1.6, 7 (*Past simple* to *Present perfect*) and 1.6, 9 (*Past simple* to *Past perfect*)
- key words which could have been more than one form (*noun / verb / adjective, etc*) in 1.2, 1 (*cost*)   1.2, 2 (*increase*)   1.4, 1 (*few*)   1.5, 1 (*spur*)   1.5, 2 (*flash*)   1.5, 3 (*set*)   1.5, 4 (*face*)   1.6, 4 (*spare*)   1.6, 5 (*craving*) and 1.6, 6 (*sign*). You can see that it is extremely common for the key word to be a word which can be a noun or verb / adjective or verb **with no change in spelling**. Watch out especially for this when attempting this type of task.
- A necessary dep. prep. in 1.2, 1 (*cost + of*)   1.2, 2 (*increase + in*)   1.2, 3 (*led + to*)   1.2, 4 (*unaware + of*)   1.3, 3 (*relied + on / upon*)   1.3, 4 (*contributed + to*)   1.4, 3 (*by +far*)   1.6, 5 (*craving +for*)   1.6, 6 (*sign + of*) and 1.6, 12 (*at + heart*). These are also **very commonly tested** in this task.
- negatives or opposites in 1.3, 1 (*don't think* to *keep out of*)   1.3, 2 (*didn't fancy* to *reluctant to go*)   1.4, 2 (*spend much less* to *don't spend nearly as much*)   1.5, 3 (*I won't* to *I've set my heart*)   1.5, 4 (*difficult not to* to *difficult to keep*) and 1.6, 3 (*only with the greatest difficulty* to *virtually impossible*). Watch out especially for **key words which mean the opposite** of a word in the original sentence, and for **adverbs with negative meanings** like hardly or rarely.
- a change of the form of a word in 1.2, 2   1.2, 3   1.3, 2   1.3, 4 and 1.6, 5. *See notes on individual answers above for more details.*
- fixed expressions or phrasal verbs in 1.3, 1   all of Exercise 1.5   1.6, 2   1.6, 4   1.6, 8   and 1.6, 12. *See notes on individual answers above for more details.*

## Grammar review: determiners and substitution p.34

**1**   1 neither   2 none   3 do   4 all   5 did   6 each   7 did so   8 so

**2**   1 the   2 it   3 these (*refers to the* factors *of the previous sentence*)   4 a   5 faced / confronted (*note the verb* is *before this gap, suggesting a passive form*)   6 that   7 might / could / may (*the gap is followed by a bare infin., suggesting a modal verb*)   8 there   9 a   10 It   11 considers (*this verb is followed by an infin., while the verbs* view *or* regard *are followed by the dep. prep.* as)   12 this   13 it   14 It (*fixed phrase*)   15 play (*collocating verb with* role)   16 for (*dep. prep. after* opt)   17 those   18 this   19 market   20 launch (*colloc. with* product – *meaning to create and try to sell a new product*).

## Listening: note-taking p.35

1 (a blast of) cool air / that the air is cool   2 large open space   3 casually dressed   4 folded   5 (the) race track   6 fashion black   7 escalator(s)   8 slimmer   9 to make us feel positive / confident   10 to keep us alert / awake.

**Tapescript**

*Interviewer: In America and in many parts of Europe big fashion stores are employing psychologists to help them boost their profits. Sandra Adams – a psychologist herself, from the University of Essex – explains how the modern clothes shop may have more tricks in store for us than we might have imagined. Sandra?*

*Sandra Adams: Thanks, Stella. If you're lucky ... or perhaps unlucky enough ... to have such a shop near you, many of the things I'm going to say will already be familiar to you. Um ... for example, every little thing in a shop like this is thought out in minute detail to coax the money out of your pocket. On entering, for example , you – the unsuspecting customer – are met by a blast of cool air. Now, this relaxes you and refreshes you, of course ... puts you in the right frame of mind from the very start and ... and ... you'll also notice that there's a large open space in front of you ... with absolutely no clutter anywhere. This gives you a corresponding sense of luxury ... makes you feel good ...*

*I: So ... right from the very moment you enter the shop ... right from the first breath you take, in fact ... the retailer is working on your senses?*

*SA: Yes, that's right ... from the very second you step into the shop everything is against you ... although you probably wouldn't see it that way! Anyway .... you've entered the shop. So, what happens now? Well, from here you turn right – the Invariant Right, researchers call it ... most of us do it instinctively ...you turn right and you usually find three things. You find the best and most expensive fashions here ... there's also a casually dressed assistant who smiles and greets you .... asks how you are ... you know ... and ... then you'll see the tables. On these tables are fashion's latest 'must-haves' – you know, embroidered tops, suede skirts, ponchos – all folded casually, even sloppily, so that you the shopper don't feel bad about opening them up and holding them up for closer examination ... and all at 'buy-now' prices ...*

*I: Now hold on, Sandra ...  what you're saying then, is that the shop makes a point of arranging the clothes carelessly or*

*untidily ... so that customers will be encouraged to pick them up and look at them? That's amazing! And then?*

*SA: Well, then angled tables coax you further into the shop and mirrors in the aisles keep you moving slowly but carefully along a pre-determined route ... known rather cynically in the trade as the 'Race Track'... and there are accessories and rotating displays with reflective surfaces used to lure you into places you had no intention of going ... but generally speaking, you keep on moving further and further into the shop. Towards the back of the shop, we find the first of what retailers call fashion black spots ... places with 'low foot traffic' as they say ... and the shop tries to draw you into these areas. One trick is to place the escalator there – apparently we can't resist going up one of those ....*

*I: Yes – but try to find an escalator which is going down when you get to the top!*

*SA: Well, that's the whole point, of course, Stella! Because apart from the escalator, another trick is to have some real bargains displayed here ... you know 'everything in the basket less than £10' or something similar. Some retailers even slip in the odd designer label among all the other clothes to make all that rummaging around seem worthwhile. And ...*

*I: What happens when you find something you actually want to buy?*

*SA: Mmm. I notice you use the word 'when' and not 'if'! That's the way the retailer sees it as well! Anyway ... you want to buy something ... you need to try it on first, of course ... so you look for the changing rooms. Now, these are traditionally a place of torture for many women as they see just how bad their bodies look in this season's clothes .... but it's not like that here – as you might expect. The mirrors in the changing room are tinted to make you look tanned ... and they use convex mirrors to make you look slimmer as well. And you also find that ... there's probably also make-up available in the changing room ... easy chairs outside it ... and of course there'll be sales staff milling around to flatter you ...would you believe they call them 'style consultants' in America?*

*I: Yes ... I think I would ... Um ...what else would a customer notice in a shop like this, Sandra?*

*SA: Well, now ... everywhere you go in the shop, of course, there's lots of space ... nothing is cramped ... fewer garments on display is seen as a sign of quality or luxury. Um ... and clever use of colour is made in many shops ... retailers use colours that psychologists say make us feel more positive and confident – orange, green, blue, yellow, red or purple, for example ... and, oh, you'll never believe this ... many retailers even make use of particular smells. Artificial coffee, citrus or lavender smells are circulated in the store ... in the air-conditioning perhaps ... to encourage alertness ... keep you awake ... because you know, by the time you get to the centre of the store you are beginning to flag ... not taking things in ...*

*I: So ... in the end ... everything .... absolutely everything ... is carefully calculated to make us spend more money ...*

*SA: Yes. I'm afraid it is. That's exactly what it's about.*

## Grammar: structures with *it* p.36

1 There **is no need for you** to work during the ... 2 I found it rather **strange that she was** reluctant to take part in the ... 3 It looked **as if the burglar had** broken in through a ... 4 It doesn't **interest me whether** you succeed or ...

5 I'll leave it **(up) to you to** decide what time you come to ... 6 It's **surprising how / so many** people still believe whatever advertisements ... 7 There seems **to be no point in your continuing** to write ... 8 Didn't it **occur to you that** he might not be **telling** ...?

## Vocabulary: phrasal verbs and expressions: set p.36

**1** 1 set off 2 set off 3 set up 4 set off 5 set up 6 setting up 7 set up 8 set off

**2** *Expressions with* set *tend to be quite emphatic in tone.* 1 never **set eyes on** him (before) 2 will I **set foot in** this ... ! 3 **set her heart on** winning ... 4 **set in his ways** to cope ... 5 **set great / a lot of store by** the attentiveness ...

## Vocabulary: connectors and adverbial phrases p.37

1 While / Even though (despite *is a prep., and can only be followed by a noun or participle clause, not a full clause*); 2 thus / consequently 3 Furthermore (also *would appear between the subject* they *and the verb* shake, besides *is rather too informal for this context, and is usually used to add reasons for a particular course of action*) 4 Owing to (since *would need to be followed by a full clause, and* due to *suggests a causal connection between the lack of legislation and companies' desire to mislead customers*) 5 As a matter of fact / Actually 6 Or rather / At least

## Use of English: guided cloze p.37

1 saying (*fixed phrase*) 2 extent (*notice the dep. prep.* to) 3 words (*fixed phrase*) 4 though (*notice the two commas around the blank.* Although *would not fit here, as it needs to be followed by a full clause*) 5 with (*fixed phrase*) 6 bounds (*fixed phrase*) 7 however (*notice the two commas around the blank*) 8 Consequently / Therefore / Indeed (*don't forget to include a capital letter in your answer when necessary*) 9 Nor (*this refers back to the previous sentence*) 10 By (*fixed phrase*) 11 more (*fixed phrase*) 12 attitudes (*this noun is preceded by the adjectives* anti-social *and* racist) 13 banned (*the auxiliary* been *suggests that a passive form is required here*) 14 advertisers (*this is part of a reduced relative clause – the pronoun* which *has been omitted*) 15 how 16 some (some ... or other *is a fixed expression*) 17 world 18 appeal (*notice the dep. prep.* to) 19 What 20 despite

## Writing: formal letter (complaint) p.38

**1** The letter is being written to the manager of a restaurant by a customer who was very dissatisfied with the standard of the food and service on a recent visit.

**2** 1f) 2b) 3a) 4g) 5d) 6e) 7c)

**3** Answers provided in the composition on p.39.

**5** 1A (*at the same time*) 2B (*immediately after he had returned*) 3A (*adding a further complaint*) 4C 5C

# UNIT 5

## Reading: non-fiction p.40

**1** para. 1=D  para. 2=B  para. 3=E  para. 4=C
para. 5=A

**2** 1 infliction = the action of making s.b. suffer s.t.
unpleasant  2 deprived = not given something (*normally
something basic or essential*)  3 rehabilitation = to help s.b.
live a healthy, useful life again, after they have been ill or in
prison  4 ambivalent = not sure whether you want or like
s.t. or not  5 parties = groups of people involved in an
action, issue or agreement  6 in lieu = in place of, or
instead of

**3** and  **4** 1A  2B  3D  4A  5B

## Grammar: modal verbs p.42

**1** 1 could you have (*you can't shorten this to* could
you've)  2 should've had more (*the verb* have *collocates with
the noun* sense, *and the comparative form* more *is suggested by*
than *after the gap*)  3 can't / couldn't have  4 didn't have to
5 must've  6 they might / may not (couldn't *can't be used
here, as it means* I'm sure they are unsafe)

 **2**

**1** 1 Although **I was supposed to** phone ...  2 We **were
obliged to** register with ...  3 You **could've had him
arrested** for...  4 You **might've / have warned** me ...
5 She **needn't have bothered** trying to help, as ...  6 **There
was no need for** the robber to use a gun ...  7 I **wasn't able
to** ask him his name before he left.  8 You **are under no
obligation to** ...

**2** There was / were:
- a passive form in 1 (*was supposed to*), 2 (*were obliged to*),
  and 3 (*had him arrested* ... This is known as *the causative
  form* of *have*)
- a verb pattern after a noun or adjective in 1 (supposed +
  *infin.*), 2 (obliged + *infin.*), 3 (bothered + *infin.* or *-ing
  form*), 6 (need + *infin.*) and 8 (obligation + *infin.*).
- dep. preps. in 6 (need + *for*) and 8 (under + *obligation*).

## Vocabulary: multiple-choice p.43

**1**

**1** 1D (convicted / accused + *of,* arrested + *for*)
2D (*the other answers would all require a full infinitive*)
3B (suggested / demanded / insisted + *that* + *clause*)

**2** 1C  2C (*of is unnecessary after* despite)  3B (= *in general*)

**2** 1C (*colloc.*)  2A  3A (= *framed by someone, who tried to
make it appear he was guilty*)  4A (*colloc.*)  5B (*this is the
only one of the four options with negative connotations*)
6D (*colloc.*)  7A (*investigating has no dep. prep.*)  8A (*fixed
phrase*)  9C (= *taking this into account*)  10C (*colloc.*)

## Use of English: comprehension and summary p.43

*Notice that you **don't need to write full sentences** to answer the
comprehension questions. Use the amount of space indicated on
the Proficiency exam question paper to help guide you about the
required length of the answer.*

**2**

1 It is often more upsetting to know that a stranger has
  been in your home, or that items of sentimental value
  have been stolen.
2 people who are worried about protecting their homes
3 because you may therefore feel safe from burglars,
  although in fact you are not
4 those who strongly recommend the purchase or use of
  alarms
5 because too many alarms were going off by mistake and
  disturbing neighbours
6 Alarms must not be too noisy, and have to switch
  themselves off automatically after 20 minutes.
7 to reduce the number of false alarms
8 They may be unreliable / go off accidentally.
9 They may be set off by changes in room temperature, and
  they may be too inflexible to allow those who live in the
  house to move freely after the alarm has been set.
10 that they are connected to a police station
11 They are more expensive.

**3** 1 Paras. 6–8 contain information about available
alarms and their disadvantages.

**4** *Sample answer*
*The essential points that should be covered have been numbered
to help you to assess how well you have answered the task.*

Most alarms on the market use (1)infra-red sensors to detect
burglars. These may be (2)unreliable, however, and can be
set off by changes in room temperature. Other alarms, which
are much more expensive, are connected to a (3)monitoring
system. Finally, there are devices which (4)create smoke or
take photographs of the burglar, but these could also be
ineffective. (5)Electric fencing can even be installed, although
this could injure both burglars and innocent people.
(*73 words*)

## Writing: narrative composition (1) p.45

**1** **2** 1E  2A  3C  4B  5D

**2** A gives the action an immediate background ...
B develops the action further ...  C involves a decision or
turning point...  D reflects on the events ...  E sets the
scene ...

**3** 1 Past simple = adding action ...  2 Past perfect =
providing background ...  3 Hypothetical structures =
reflecting on the action ...  4 Past continuous = setting the
scene ...

**4** **2** There are irrelevant details in Para. 1 (*looking
forward to party*)  Para. 2 (*remembers he must write to
grandmother*)  Para. 3 (*woman sounds very busy*)  Para. 4
(*meets friend on the way*) and Para. 5 (*goes out to celebrate*).

**5** 1 Looking to the left and right, ...   2 Not until he had reached ... Never before had he seen ...   3 Feeling unable to continue, he ...   4 Had he kept the money, he would never have been able to live with himself. (*Never would he have been able to live with himself ... is also grammatically possible, but extremely formal, and so would be unlikely to be used.*)

**6** 1 thumping   2 stuffed   3 faded   4 gasped
5 crumpled   6 over the moon   7 scrawled   8 an eternity
9 spotted   10 felt a wave of relief sweep over him.

# UNIT 6

## Vocabulary review: multiple-choice p.48

1C   2A (*= it was later evident;* ended up *has a very similar meaning, but is followed by an* -ing *form*)   3B (*fixed phrase*)
4C (apt / likely *+ infin.;* capable *+ of*)   5D (*colloc.*)
6C (*colloc.*)   7A (glitter / sparkle *= a small, moving light;* flame *= a real fire*)   8B (*colloc.*)   9D   10D

## Grammar: the passive p.48

**1**

**1** 1 The best architect **will be presented with** a prize **by** the mayor.   2 An increased **number of** drivers **have been arrested** this year **for** drunken driving.   3 The town **is slowly being covered in** chemical dust from nearby factories.   4 Smoking **is to be banned** in the city's restaurants **from** next week.   5 You **could be arrested** if you **ignore** the ...   6 He **was made to** fill in ...   7 The project was to **have been completed** (by) last month. 8 The housing problem needs **to be solved / solving** urgently.

**2** There was / were:
- dep. preps. required in 1 (*presented with ... by the mayor*) 2 (*number + of*)   3 (*covered + in*)
- the word *number + a plural countable noun* in 2
- changes in the form of words in 4 (*ban to banned*), 5 (*arrest to arrested*), 7 (*completion to completed*) and 8 (*solution to solved / solving*)
- an extra auxiliary (*a form of* be) in all of the questions.

**2** 1 was blown   2 will have been made   3 (should) be made   4 is being looked   5 has been added   6 is included.

## Reading: non-fiction p.49

**1** 2 **A** These words refer to the art which you see in exhibitions; this part of the text doesn't compare the art of architects with that of painters and musicians.

**B** The phrase *fertile imaginations* is used to describe architects, but no comparison is drawn between them and other types of artist in this part of the text.

**C** The words themselves do not appear in the text, but are paraphrased: *the art of architects is all around us, demanding a response*. The sentence about leaving an exhibition compares architecture and other forms of art by saying that the viewer can choose to ignore other forms of art if s/he wishes. People who consume other types of art are described as *a select paying few*. This is the correct answer.

**D** These words have a different meaning in the text and in this multiple-choice option. *Select* in the text is an adjective meaning a small number of (probably wealthy, important or intellectual) people.

**3** *Notice how the correct multiple-choice option* **rarely uses exactly the same words** *as those found in the text.*   1C (*to design buildings from scratch – to tear down and rebuild*) 2B (*a natural reaction to the policy of decamping people ... where the extended family patterns of support were destroyed*) 3D (*architects and planners do not necessarily have the monopoly of knowing best about taste, style and planning*) 4D (*the affinity between the buildings and the earth ... houses looked almost as though they had grown out of the earth*)   5A (*which complements [the facade of the National Gallery] and continues the concept ...*)   6B (*the other three options are either too extreme or too narrow, and do not cover the writer's feelings about architects* **in general**).

**4** 1 spearheaded   2 dwarfed   3 stump   4 organic

## Grammar plus: relative clauses p.52

**1** 1 whom   2 living (*fixed phrase*)   3 problems / difficulties (*fixed phrase*)   4 of   5 majority (*colloc.*)   6 staff / workforce / workers   7 willing / ready   8 earned (*colloc.*) 9 enabling (*notice the* to which *follows*)   10 however (*notice the commas around this blank*)   11 both (*refers back to* traffic problems *and* pollution)   12 to / for   13 but (*this often appears with* none-the-less, *between two commas*)   14 times 15 upon (*fixed phrase*) / and   16 blocks (*colloc.*)   17 built / constructed (*notice the auxiliaries* have been, *suggesting a passive form*)   18 little / scant (*colloc.*)   19 all (*fixed phrase*) 20 longer

**2**

1 People **working** in large cities often long to escape from 'the rat race'. (*Although it is impossible to omit just the relative pronoun, because it is the subject of the relative clause, you can replace the relative clause with a participle clause.*)
2 Most houses **built** more than a hundred years ago have problems with damp. (*As no. 1. Here, the participle is a past one, which has a passive meaning.*)
3 The tram starts from the castle, the oldest surviving building in the town. (*The relative clause can be omitted altogether, with no loss of meaning.*)
4 The house I lived in as a child has just been knocked down. (*This is a defining relative clause, and the relative pronoun is not the subject of the relative clause. The pronoun can therefore be omitted.*)
5 The city council, **well known** for its radical ideas, recently developed this dock area. (*As no. 3*)
6 Visitors **caught** taking photographs inside the church are usually asked to leave. (*As no. 2*)
7 The mosaic was discovered by workmen digging in the street. (*As no. 1*)
8 The square is surrounded by old buildings, now on the verge of collapse. (*As no. 3*)

9   The river **flowing** through the town centre is liable to flood in winter. (*As no. 1*)
10  The man I have been talking to used to live in this neighbourhood. (*As no. 4*)

# Listening: multiple-choice p.53

**1**   1 aggressive   2 enthusiastic   3 depressed

**2**   1D

**3**   2B   3C   4D   5B   6A   7C

## Tapescript

**1**

*Speaker 1*: What do you mean exactly? What do I think about the Council's plan to pedestrianise the centre? Why are you asking all these questions anyway? Don't you know what the majority of people feel about this scheme. Oh yes … They're really looking forward to it! All that noise and confusion, and all the building work …

*Speaker 2*: Well, I think it's a great idea! You know, there are bound to be problems … there always are with this sort of thing, aren't there? … what with all the digging and knocking down of things … I dare say it'll take them much longer than they anticipated, but still, never mind …

*Speaker 3*: Yes, I know all about it … my mother doesn't talk about anything else these days. Wonderful proposal, isn't it? Since I won't be able to use my car anymore to get into the centre of town I really don't know how I'll manage. I just don't want to think about it at the moment.

**2**

*Journalist*: Excuse me, sir. Can you spare a minute to answer a question or two about the local Council's plan for pedestrianising the centre of the town? I'm writing an article for the Herald.

*Young Man*: Sure. Go ahead.

*J*: Well … first of all … what do you think about the Council's plan?

*YM*: Yeah, well, it's one way of solving the traffic problem, I suppose … it seems to be getting worse all the time, doesn't it? It's not really the lorries … the passing traffic that's to blame – although it can get pretty awful at times – it's all the local traffic as well. People seem so unwilling to walk anywhere … they'll take the car rather than … you know, take a bus or something … but that's probably not the root of the problem … fact is, I think that people have forgotten what buses look like … there've been so many cutbacks lately – you know, things are a bit tight so let's halve the number of buses going into town and so on … that in the end things fall apart a bit. Banning cars from the centre is just the Council's way of dealing with it, isn't it?

**3**

*Journalist*: Do you think so? I mean do you think there is anything else you think the Council …

*Young Man*: Anything else? How do you think they would answer that one? I'm sure they won't feel the need to do much more than they're already planning to do. They

certainly don't see the buses – or rather the lack of them – as a problem … they might even come up with some bright idea for a tram or something, I don't know. Anyway … it goes without saying they'll have to do something about all the traffic which is diverted. A modern bypass, … the roads which already skirt the town are too narrow and unsuitable for heavy traffic … it'd be a complete nightmare.

*J*: Yes, there's a thought. Thank you very much, sir, for your time.

*YM*: Cheers mate.

*J*: Um … what about you, sir? I'm a journalist for the Herald. Could you tell me what you think about the council's plan to ban cars from the centre of town?

*Older Man*: Mmm. Interesting, isn't it? I'm all for it. It's a sign, I think, that the present Council seems to be trying to improve the quality of life for the people who live in this town … Yes, I'm sure that it would make the historic centre of the town much more attractive, less grotty, you know. I've heard there are plans to plant more trees in the centre … though there are quite a lot of them already … as well as to clean up the main square of the town, so that people can actually sit there of an afternoon and enjoy the sun – well, the little we get of it, that is. They are also talking about putting up some statues and sculptures around the town, aren't they? I've read about that a few times … not been much of that kind of thing so far, has there? … as well as commissioning local artists to brighten up some of the older buildings. Sounds OK to me.

*J*: What about problems, though? Is there anything you don't like about the Council's plans?

*OM*: Yes … as a matter of fact, there is. It would be a great shame, I think, if they pulled down the Gregory Building, just off the High Street. You know, it's the present-day Post Office. I admit it's in pretty poor shape … but surely they could renovate it? It's part of our local history, after all … dates, I think, from the early nineteenth century … put to its present use forty years ago or so, wasn't it? We've certainly been posting our letters there for … oh, I forget how many years … it's got character, and we've grown used to it. Um … is there anything else you wanted to ask, by the way?

*J*: No, thank you, Sir. I'll try and mention the Gregory Building in my article.

*OM*: Pleased to help. I'll be looking forward to reading that in the paper, son.

*J*: Thank you. Thank you again … Er … madam … have you got a minute or two? Would you mind if I asked you about your views on the plan to pedestrianise the centre of town? I'm preparing an article for the local paper.

*Older Lady*: No, not at all. And which paper's that, then?

*J*: The Herald actually.

*OL*: Oh, the Herald, oh … I never read it! Anyway. The Council's plan to pedestrianise the centre is it? Well, I'm firmly against it, of course – as are lots of other people like me. I've got a shop in the centre of town, you see … and quite frankly, it'll be bad for trade. But nobody seems to take much notice of what we think. Do you know how much money we'll lose from passing trade? Thousands upon thousands of pounds. Not to mention all the disruption and noise there'll be while they're knocking *down buildings, pulling up trees, covering everything in concrete … But, oh well, there we go … typical of this council, isn't it?*

**J:** *Yes … but won't you benefit from those who visit the town … you know … who come as tourists? There aren't many of those at the moment, are there?*

**OL:** *Who knows? Oh dear, maybe, I don't know. I'll just wait and see what happens … I can't really do much else, can I? Now, if you've got no more questions, I must be getting on. Been nice talking to you, goodbye.*

**J:** *OK, Madam. Thank you for your perspective … quite an eye-opener … I'd thought safer shopping streets might be good for traders … Um … pardon me, Miss. Can I ask you a couple of questions …*

## Writing: formal letter (2) p.54

**1**  1 F  2 N (*F would appear arrogant*)  3 I(*N would appear unfriendly*)  4 N (*F would appear arrogant*)  5 F  6 N (*F would potentially appear distant or arrogant*)  7 N (*I would probably irritate them, since you are bringing unwelcome news, F would alienate them completely, and might cause them to leave the club*)  8 F  9 I (*N would seem unfeeling*)  10 F (*in general, the more formal the letter, the more effectively it can express your anger*)

**2**  <u>1</u> and 3   <u>2</u> and 12   <u>4</u> and 10   5 and <u>7</u>   <u>6</u> and 9   8 and <u>11</u>

**3**

1  Whatever measures **are** (deemed) **necessary will be taken** to … (deemed *makes the sentence more formal*).

2  I regret that **I will / shall be unable to** see / consult … (Shall, *when both forms are grammatically appropriate, generally gives a slightly more formal impression than* will.)

3  Should you refuse to co-operate, **I will / shall have no alternative but to** …

4  I am writing to you to express **my disgust at** the action you **propose to take.**

5  This situation should **not be allowed to** continue / worsen / deteriorate further. (Deteriorate *gives the most formal impression here.*)

6  I have serious **doubts about your sincerity.** (*While remaining formal and polite, this sentence is extremely direct, and should only be used in a situation where the letter writer is very angry, and wishes to make this clear.*)

7  We should be making **every effort to** …

8  Should **you need / wish to contact me,** I will / shall be at home all weekend. (Wish *is more formal than* need *here.*)

**4**  *Further suggestions for alternatives have been added to answers to help you. Make a note of any new expressions which you consider useful.*

1  I am writing to you / contacting you to express my concern about / over …

2  as I am sure you are aware / as you may be aware

3  … would be / find themselves unable to …

4  (I feel) This should not be allowed to happen. (*Avoid addressing the reader personally when possible.*)

5  Surely we should be making every effort to … / every effort should be made to

6  I have serious doubts about whether (or not) this project would (genuinely) benefit …

7  Should you decide / see fit to … (see fit *is more formal, and can give the impression that you are annoyed, or feel s.b. is being arrogant*)

8  … we shall have no alternative / option but to …

9  … take whatever measures necessary …

## UNIT 7

## Vocabulary review: multiple-choice p.56

1 C (*this word is frequently used to describe the range of animals and plants in a particular environment*)  2 A (*colloc.*)  3 A (*colloc.*)  4 C (*colloc.*)  5 B (herds = *cows or similar;* flocks = *sheep or birds;* swarms = *very small animals, either flying or on the ground, such as bees or ants*)  6 C  7 A (*colloc.*)  8 C (*fixed phrase*)  9 B  10 C

## Grammar: mixed and open conditions p.56

**1**  1 If you **had gone** on the expedition, you **might have been killed.**  2 The disaster **could have been avoided** if the government **had taken more** action.  3 If I **hadn't visited** the Congo last year, I **wouldn't have caught** malaria.  4 If he **is guilty,** he **should've been sent** to prison.  5 Had **more people listened** to the warnings of the ecologists, some species of animals **could have been saved.**  6 Should I **be prevented from** entering the USA, I'll have to reconsider my options.  7 Were I **(to be) made to** take the exams again, I **would** probably stop doing the course.  8 Had the Minister of Agriculture **ignored** the advice of so-called 'experts', large tracts of farmland **might still be** productive.

**2**  1 **As long as** you obey the regulations, you will …  2 **Provided** you take …  3 Don't be late for the meeting, **otherwise he'll** give you the sack!  4 **Were we to** take effective action now, we …  5 **Should you refuse** to co-operate, they would **expel** you **immediately** …  6 **But for the minister's insistence**, the ban on hunting **would not have been imposed.**

**3**  1 unless the  2 have to take  3 can't you tell  4 think about / consider  5 we are to find

## Vocabulary review: multiple-choice p.57

1A (waned = *decreased in popularity or fortune;* sunk = *gone to the bottom of the sea;* descended = *physically gone down, e.g. climbed down a mountain*)  2C (*colloc.*)  3D  4C (*fixed phrase*)  5A (*colloc.*)  6 B (*fixed phrase*)  7D  8C (insisted / suggested / made + *bare infinitive*)

## Use of English: comprehension and summary p.58

**1**  to publicise (*the work of the Monkey Sanctuary*), to inform (*people about the plight of the woolly monkeys*).

## 2

1 irrepressible
2 His energy and communicative skills will have to be impressive, if he is to manage to deliver a lecture of twelve hours or more.
3 first world record; leading force
4 They are scattered around.
5 They might die, as the trees in which they live are cut down or destroyed.
6 monkeys which are already living there, and have not been brought in from elsewhere
7 They provide a sanctuary of sufficient size, where the monkeys can be protected and monitored.
8 illegal pet monkeys which have been seized by the police
9 The Cornish monkeys could teach the orphans social skills, while the orphans could show the Cornish monkeys how to live in the forest.
10 As a result of his speaking skills, Casamitjana is extremely good at raising money.
11 that he will be able to put across his ideas effectively, and that the lecture should be a success
12 He has considered everything that might happen carefully beforehand.

## 5

**1** 1 and 2 ... they ~~the monkeys would not be restricted~~ ... would be protected and could be monitored.  3 ~~known as orphans~~ ... pet monkeys seized by ...  4 and 5 ~~strongly, successfully, which have developed social skills but in cages~~ ... in the forest, while the Cornish monkeys ...

*Sample answer*
The islands of Lake Balbina are ideal as a monkey sanctuary because they are large enough for the monkeys to live on; they would also be protected and could be monitored. Illegal pet monkeys seized by the Brazilian authorities could also be sent to live with the Cornish monkeys. It is believed that the pet monkeys would teach the Cornish ones how to live in the forest, while the Cornish monkeys would teach the 'orphan' monkeys social skills they do not possess.
*(82 words)*

## Vocabulary: dependent prepositions and prepositional phrases p.60

**1** 1 with  2 to  3 for  4 in  5 at  6 under
7 on / upon  8 to  9 inside  10 in  11 as  12 to  13 with
14 with  15 on  16 at  17 on  18 in  19 in  20 in.

**2** 1 ... the police discovered (that) he **was in possession of** ...  2 ... have the situation **in hand**.  3 The trip was cancelled yesterday **on account of** ...  4 Tours of the Olympic stadium are only / strictly **by (special) arrangement**.  5 The fine he paid was **out of (all) proportion to** the offence (he had) committed.

## Vocabulary: descriptive verbs p.60

1A  2C  3D  4C  5A  6D

## Listening: multiple-choice p.61

1B (*... the most recent one ... was caused by the impact of a meteorite*)  2D (*calculations of the timings ...*)  3C (*the muons have enough energy to irradiate and kill almost every living thing in their way*)  4A (*a lethal burst of atmospheric muons would explain the massive extinctions deep underwater*)
5D (*insects can ... tolerate up to 20 times the radiation that kills most other animals*)  6D (*listen to the tone of his voice on the recording*).

### Tapescript

*Interviewer: As if you didn't have enough to worry about already, it turns out we're 100 million years overdue for a mass extinction. Keep watching the skies if you want some warning. When you see a strange blue glow, slightly bigger than a full moon, it means that you've got just a few days before the end of the world. At least – that is – if you accept the theories of Arnon Dar, a space physicist at the Israel Institute of Technology. Arnon ... can you tell us a little more about the findings of your research?*

*Arnon Dar: Yes, of course. Geological records – as you may know – show there have been five major mass extinctions in the past 500 million years. Scientists believe the most recent one ... which wiped out the dinosaurs 64 million years ago ... was caused by the impact of a meteorite. Some 300,000 tons of the element iridium was laid down in the Earth's crust at this time, and high levels of iridium have also been found in asteroids. What caused all the other extinctions, however, is still an open question. Um ....*

*I: Yes ... but haven't scientists suggested that volcanic eruptions were to blame?*

*AD: Yes they have ... and they've also suggested that supernova explosions were the cause. However ... it turns out that there is no geological evidence for coincident volcanic activity ... and supernova explosions don't occur close enough, at a sufficiently high rate. My theory is that collapsing neutron stars were the cause. Um ... calculations of the timings of nearby neutron star collapses show that – just like mass extinctions on Earth – that they seem to occur about once every 100 million years. Um ... unfortunately ... unfortunately for us, that is ... the evidence suggests that the last one probably happened 200 million years ago.*

*I: I see. Why are collapsing neutron stars so dangerous though?*

*AD: Well, when a pair of neutron stars collapses ... cosmic rays ... are produced ... and, um ... become a very serious threat. I and my colleagues have been studying the likely effects of jets of cosmic rays flung out by neutron star collapses for several years now .... um ... and ... on entering the Earth's atmosphere ... the cosmic rays create showers of high-energy particles known as muons. And ...*

*I: I'm sorry. The cosmic rays create particles – called muons, did you say?*

*AD: Yes, yes ... that's right. muons. As cosmic ray jets rain down on the Earth ... the muons have enough energy to irradiate and kill almost every living thing in their way. Um ... they would also destroy the Ozone layer, irradiate the environment, and damage vegetation ...*

*I: So muons are extremely dangerous?*

*AD*: Yes … extremely dangerous. Muon radiation can be fatal even hundreds of metres underwater … or underground. So … a lethal burst of atmospheric muons would explain the massive extinctions deep underwater. The fossil record's reported extinction of marine life – as well as continental life – begins to make sense.

*I*: Mmm. And I also believe, Arnon, that you can explain other features of previous mass extinctions that current theories leave to one side.

*AD*: Indeed I can. Muon radiation is very powerful and causes biological mutations … which would account for the fast appearance of new species after massive extinctions. Um … and examination of the fossil record also shows that there is a clear relationship between the extinction pattern of a species and its reaction to radiation.

*I*: Meaning?

*AD*: Meaning … insects, for example. Insects have been the great survivors of mass extinctions. This is not surprising as insects can, in general, tolerate up to 20 times the radiation that kills most other animals. The only time they were severely affected was in the largest mass extinction, 251 million years ago. Even then, only 30 per cent of insect species were destroyed, compared with up to 95 per cent of other orders of species. I find that very interesting.

*I*: Mmm – interesting – but also rather worrying … since we are apparently 100 million years overdue for another bout of mass extinction.

*AD*: Well … things might look bad … but being 100 million years overdue for an apocalypse doesn't make it any more likely to happen today. The chance of extinction doesn't in fact increase with passing time – the fact that you have not been killed in a car accident so far doesn't increase the chances of it happening in the next 10 years. Actually … astronomers have examined the orbits of the five pairs of neutron stars observed in our galaxy and it seems that we could have a breathing space of about 50 million years before the first one collapses. … There's just one problem, though.

*I*: What's that?

*AD*: The data they have gathered seems to indicate that our galaxy also contains other neutron star pairs that no one has yet seen. Until we see them, we can't know when they will collapse.

*I*: So nobody can actually be sure that the apocalypse is not just around the corner?

*AD*: I'm afraid that's right.

*I*: Well, thank you very much, Arnon Dar.

*AD*: Thank you.

*I*: Now to turn to …

## Vocabulary: phrasal verbs and expressions: *run* p.61

**1** 1… **ran into** someone I … 2 … **would** (have) **run out of** / **would soon run out of** … / **were running out of** … 3 … at college he **ran into** 4 … proposal **ran into** a lot of 5 … old woman **was run over**

**2** 1 … eat those mushrooms, **you run the risk of** being … 2 … as we're careful **we won't run short** … 3 … **blood ran cold** when I heard 4 … **run of the mill**

## Writing: report (1) p.62

**3** *Sample answers*

para. 1 – Background information para. 2 – Environmental benefits para. 3 – Safety para. 4 – benefits to the community para. 5 – Comments and Recommendations. Para. 3, about safety, would be better placed after the current para. 4. *This would group the positive and negative points in the report together, and would also link with the concerns about safety in the final para.*

**4** **1** to recommend the proposal to build a car factory **2** The proposal to build a car factory in the suburb of Westham (1)**has much to recommend it**. (2)**Offering** over 2000 jobs to the local population, it would **solve the problem of unemployment** and **increase the wealth of** the whole area. (3)**In addition, not only would it provide** opportunities for work, **but it would also** offer **a number** of other services, **including** baby-sitting facilities, a free health-care scheme and a company pension. (4)**The major drawback, however**, would be that the factory is **to be located** 30 miles from the town centre. This would (5)**undoubtedly** be a problem for **those who do not possess their own means of transport**, as bus and train services to Westham **are infrequent**. (6)**Should the factory management be reluctant to** provide company transport, the Town Council would have to **consider** improving existing services.

## UNIT 8

## Vocabulary review: multiple-choice p.64

1A (dissolve *s.t. into s.t. else*, disintegrate + no prep., decompose = *rot, like a dead body*) 2B (*prep. phrase*) 3C (= *the parts refused to move*) 4B (*colloc.*) 5D (*colloc.*) 6B 7C (*colloc.*) 8D (*colloc.*) 9C (*colloc.*) 10D (= *start that process, with all its potential problems*)

## Grammar: intensifiers p.64

**1** 1 The **mere thought of** climbing that mountain terrifies me. 2 I am **very grateful indeed** for … 3 I'm **not in the least** / **the least bit** surprised that you … 4 Jack Carlton is **without exception the best player** in the team 5 I've never met / Never have I met **so quick a** learner. 6 I've told you this **time and time again**. 7 **The one thing** he's (really) good at **is** long … 8 On looking around, we realised we were **well and truly** lost. 9 I'm afraid that there is **no chance** / **question whatsover** of … 10 **Such was the strength of** the opposition that we found it impossible to win / beat them.

**2** 1 was very little 2 earth didn't you tell 3 poor / bad was the 4 by no 5 whatever you 6 make a bit 7 so strong

**3** 1 the (the + *one thing*) 2 On (= *when they find. Don't forget to give your word a capital letter when appropriate.*) 3 their (their + *own*) 4 no (no + *whatsoever*)

5 merest / barest / smallest (*notice* the *before the blank,* *suggesting a superlative*)   6 Whatever (*notice* may *later in this* *sentence*)   7 least (*fixed phrase*)   8 purely (*fixed phrase*)   9 a   10 what   11 After   12 although / though   13 very (*notice* indeed *later in this sentence, indicating that* very *is necessary*)   14 so (*notice the inverted verb and subject which follow*)   15 lost (*collocates with* lives)   16 even (*This connector stresses that this loss of life is extreme or unexpected. You can only fill this blank by considering the meaning of the text as a whole*).   17 whom   18 should (*notice the bare infinitive* be *which follows, suggesting a modal verb*)   19 tiniest / smallest / slightest (*slightest is the best colloc. here, compare with no. 5*)   20 Needless (*fixed phrase*)

## Reading: literary text  p.66

**1**  *Sample answer*

The voyage will probably be rather rough, with poor weather conditions and it doesn't seem that the two people aboard the boat will get on at all well.

**2**   1A (*instead of the champagne parting ... there had only been ...*)   2C (*if the forecast held good then I couldn't hope for a better departure wind*)   3B (*I had lost count of how many times I had ...*)   4D (*I was not at all sure I wanted her on board*)   5D (*the notion of Jackie coping on the boat had energised David and Betty with a vast amusement*)   6C (There is no one part of the text which states this, but it is implied by the way he observes her reaction to his snapped comment and his lack of knowledge about her abilities.)

**3**

**1**  *Sample answers*

slipped = *moved smoothly, easily and quietly*
splash = *the noise made by water hitting a solid surface*
hiss = *a sound like 'sss', such as that made by a snake*
shift = *to move something heavy or awkward, probably rather slowly*
winked = *turned on and off*
faded = *slowly became dimmer (and possibly eventually disappeared)*
pattered = *made a soft light sound as it landed*
dripped = *fell in small drops of liquid*
flickering = *weak, unsteady (normally used to describe light)*
tear = *to move quickly, possibly both noisily and violently*

**2**

| Movements | Sounds | Lights |
|-----------|--------|--------|
| slipped   | splash | winked |
| shift     | hiss   | faded  |
| dripped   | pattered | flickering |
| tear      |        |        |

**4**   1 pattered   2 to slip   3 to flicker / flickering   4 hiss   5 tore   6 winked   7 splash   8 to shift   9 to drip / dripping   10 faded

## Listening: multiple-choice  p.68

1C (*you've been on and on about nothing else*)   2C (*it's not that bad;* listen to her tone of voice)   3A (*you were so tired you didn't even feel up to going out for a pizza*)   4D (*I had exams every morning;* Jenny says *I'm only a nurse,* implying that Susan is / will be more important)   5C (listen to the tone of her voice)   6A (*they don't have a problem with it ... I'm a grown woman after all*)

**Tapescript**

**Susan:** *I can't believe it! You're really set on going again this weekend, aren't you?*

**Jenny:** *Yes! You don't know what you're missing, Susan. Instead of just sitting there moaning and groaning about how dangerous it is, you ought to come with me ... give it a try ... you'd probably love it.*

**S:** *Yeah, right! Anyway, that's not the point. Ever since you joined that hang-gliding club you've been on and on about nothing else ... you're obsessed with it ... apart from that ... well, to be honest, I think you're mad! Do you know how dangerous it is? Have you ever thought, have any idea how many fatal accidents there've been in the past year or so? I don't know ... it must be at least six ... maybe more.*

**J:** *Come on, Susan. It's not that bad ... it really isn't as dangerous as you make it out to be. Provided you take it step by step ... that you have someone who's qualified to take you through all the things you need to do ... you know, how to fix the harness properly ... how to position your body ... what movements to make ... how to work the controls, and all that ... I can't see what all the fuss is about. It's certainly no more dangerous than ... say ... fencing. And that's something you're always going on about, isn't it?*

**S:** *I'm not always going on about it!*

**J:** *Yes you are. And it doesn't seem to do you much good either, does it? When you dropped in last week after that fencing match of yours ... it must have been at least 9 o'clock by the time you finally showed your face ... and us lot hanging around waiting for you for over an hour... then you were so tired you didn't even feel up to going out for a pizza. Don't you remember? You just slumped in front of the telly ... grunted at me once or twice ... then went off home again. If that's what fencing does for you, give me hang-gliding any day!*

**S:** *Hold on, that's not fair, Jenny ... I'm not like that usually. Last week was a really gruelling week for me, you know that ... I had exams every morning ... Physiology, Anatomy, Pathology ... I can't remember what else ... and then it was down to the maternity ward in the afternoons ... nights spent working into the small hours swatting up for the next ordeal. Of course I was worn out ... you'd be too if you'd had all that!*

**J:** *I've done all that! I know what it's like. Of course, I'm only a nurse ... but I'm sure it can't be that much different. Anyway, it'll all seem worthwhile when you qualify, won't it? The thing is, you've got to get used to working long hours on a ward, Susan ... fencing or no fencing ... don't run away with the idea that life gets any easier ... because from what I can see it doesn't. So! How about coming hang-gliding with me this weekend? It won't tire you out, you know ... it's ... um ... invigorating. You might land up in hospital ... but at least you'd be good company in the evening!*

**S:** *Go on then... rub it in. I was only thinking about how lethal it is, you know. I mean ... you're a bit impetuous now and then, aren't you? Have you really thought it through? What would happen if the air currents suddenly changed ... or, or disappeared ... or something ... I don't know how it works!*

*It's no laughing matter, Jenny. What would your parents say if they knew what you were up to?*

J: *Actually, Susan, they know exactly what I'm doing ... and they don't have a problem with it ... I'm a grown woman after all ... You know, Susan, hang-gliding's something I get a lot out of. You can't even begin to appreciate what it's like up there – nothing between you and the ground, hundreds of feet below ... the hiss of the wind as you fly through the air ... it must be what an eagle feels like ... you just want to go on and on and on ...*

S: *That's it! I've had enough of this! Let's change the subject. Are you going to Jason's party? ... it's ...*

## Vocabulary: phrasal verbs and expressions: *bring* p.68

**1** 1 ... **should have been brought up** at the meeting
2 ... of **bringing off** such a difficult dive in the competition tomorrow are slim   3 ... **brings in** over half of what ...
4 ... lady **brought her round** by ...   5 ... **has brought about** a change in the habits huge numbers of ...   6 ... **can be brought round to** our way of ...

**2** 1 ... if / that she'll **be brought to her senses** by ...
2 ... failure in the championships **brought home** (to him) the importance of ...   3 ... will be **brought into disrepute** by the ...   4 ... what he did **I couldn't bring myself to** talk to him ...   5 ... **brought the house down** ...

## Vocabulary: dependent prepositions and prepositional phrases p.69

1 from   2 with   3 with / by   4 on   5 to   6 for   7 in
8 in   9 of   10 of   11 with   12 upon / on   13 on   14 on
15 towards   16 in   17 in   18 of   19 for   20 with

## Writing: discursive composition (1) p.69

**1** key words = team sports; best way; characters

**2** 3 The writer has used *method B* from the box in Unit 1, p.15 – using examples to illustrate the points made.

**3** 1a)  2b)  3a)  4a)  5b)  6a)  7a)  8b)  9b)  10b)
11a)  12a)  13b)  14a)  15b)  16b)  17a)  18a)

**4** 1a)  2b)  3a)  4b)  5c)  6b)  7b)  8c)  9a)  10c)

# UNIT 9

## Vocabulary review: multiple-choice p.72

1A (*fixed phrase*)  2A(*colloc.*)  3C (*colloc.*)  4B  5C (*colloc.*)
6A  7A (= *improve*; *recover is used more generally for the whole body and / or mind; treat and cure = transitive verbs which need an object*)  8D (*colloc.*)  9C (*groaning / whimpering = expressing pain, usually without words; yelling = shouting very noisily*)  10B (*glare / glance = actions, rather than facial expressions; scowl = very negative, angry expression*)

## Vocabulary: verb + noun collocation p.72

1 slap   2 gestures   3 decision   4 try   5 glance
6 recollection   7 recovery   8 gulp   9 offer   10 effect
11 smile   12 think   13 cry   14 intention

## Grammar: verb patterns (*-ing* and infinitive) p.73

**1** 1 The builders **hope to have finished** the renovations by / before ...   2 The police **omitted to mention** whether or not the ...   3 Although we **tried sending** a message, there ...
4 I **don't remember finding** this book.   5 The school rules **must not be / are not to be ignored**.   6 I **object to** having to work overtime   7 She **insisted on my** leaving immediately.   8 I (absolutely) **refuse to** lend you any more money!

**2** 1 He appears **to be having difficulty** finding someone ...   2 I'm looking forward to the completion of ...
3 I regret **not paying more / having paid so little** attention to ...   4 I've arranged **for** the tickets **to be sent** to us (by the travel agent ) ...   5 I'm starting **to have** (a few) money problems.   6 Robert confessed **to forgetting** to turn on ...
7 She avoided **having** to repeat the course by taking ...
8 He denied **being given / receiving** ...   9 I am not **used to having** to work this hard.   10 The film was considered (by the censors) **not to be suitable / to be unsuitable** for ...

## Use of English: comprehension and summary p.74

**2**

1 Games are invented by parents and teachers in a disorganised fashion.
2 They can teach and stimulate the mind.
3 the type of game the child chooses to play, the way the game is approached, the importance attached by the child to the game
4 The child would try to avoid taking part, or would spoil the fun of other children playing the game.
5 Children may feel proud, or have little confidence in themselves, and worry about looking stupid if they make mistakes.
6 that it is hidden or undesirable
7 the need to dominate others
8 They can express themselves more creatively and independently.
9 tendency or inclination
10 because play is the childhood equivalent of a job, and develops the child in important ways

**3** 2 *Points required*

1 adults must not interrupt games and should respect their seriousness
2 games develop children in important ways – sociability and co-operation
3 things that go wrong: avoiding / ruining games = worries about performance / over-dominance = competitiveness
4 opportunities for creativity
5 playing suggests future career

**4** *Sample answer*

Games are vital in the development of children's abilities, and adults should not trivialise them, or interrupt children when playing. From games, adults can learn about children's sociability, and whether they can act co-operatively. Attempts to disrupt or avoid games show that the child is proud or insecure, while a tendency to dominate games suggests over-competitiveness. Creative games can reveal children's talents, and which jobs they may excel at in the future. (*72 words*)

## Vocabulary: dependent prepositions and prepositional phrases p.75

1 of  2 on  3 in  4 at  5 with  6 on  7 at / on  8 at  9 in  10 in  11 of  12 out  13 to / from  14 on  15 in  16 after  17 about / around  18 under  19 to  20 In

## Grammar: emphasis (2) (cleft sentences) p.76

**1**  1 1A, 2B  2 1A, 2B  3 1B, 2A  4 1A, 2B  5 1B, 2A  6 1B, 2A

**Tapescript**

**1**

**1**

1 A *What I'd like to know is ...*
  B *What I'd like to know is ...*
2 A *Actually, he didn't help me ...*
  B *Actually, he didn't help me ...*
3 A *What I can't understand ...* (no emphatic stress)
  B *What I can't understand ...*
4 A *It was a comedy we saw last night ...* (no emphatic stress)
  B *It was a comedy we saw last night ...*
5 A *What's happening now ...*
  B *What's happening now ...*
6 A *The first time I knew something was wrong ...*
  B *The first time I knew something was wrong ...*

**2**

1 A *What I'd like to know is not important, so it seems.*
  B *What I'd like to know is how on earth did they do it?*
2 A *Actually, he didn't help me, she did.*
  B *Actually, he didn't help me to fix the car.*
3 A *What I can't understand is this problem on page 66.*
  B *What I can't understand is why he didn't ask her to marry him.*
4 A *It was a comedy we saw last night at the cinema.*
  B *It was a comedy we saw last night, not a thriller.*
5 A *What's happening now is that more people are breaking the law.*
  B *What's happening now doesn't concern you at all.*
6 A *The first time I knew something was wrong I suddenly broke out in a cold sweat.*
  B *The first time I knew something was wrong was when he didn't come to work on time.*

**2**  1B  2A  3B  4A  5B  6A

**Tapescript**

**2**

**1**

1 *No, I'm sure he couldn't have turned up late.*
2 *Really? I couldn't believe how **rude** he was.*
3 *Yes, I can't believe just how **hard** he studies.*
4 *Well, why didn't he **do** it then?*
5 *Are you sure? I thought **Saturday** night was a problem for her.*
6 *So it's **only** been tried out on **animals** in the past?*

**2**

1 *– I think it was Peter who waltzed in over an hour late for the meeting. – No, I'm sure he couldn't have turned up late.*
2 *– It was his dishonesty which amazed me more than anything else. – Really? I couldn't believe how rude he was.*
3 *– He always seems to have his head buried in a book. – Yes, I can't believe just how hard he studies.*
4 *– What he really wanted to do was go abroad to study. – Well, why didn't he do it then?*
5 *– I think it's tomorrow night that Anna can't come to the party. – Are you sure? I thought Saturday night was a problem for her.*
6 *– What's new is that this test is being done on a human subject. – So it's only been tried out on animals in the past?*

**3**  1 What is really interesting / really interests me is that ...  2 What I really like / enjoy is going ...  3 All he ever does is (to) complain about the weather.  4 What I remember most is my father playing ...  5 The only thing I can remember is the doctor giving ... *This structure is very useful for adding impact to descriptions and narrative compositions.*

**4**  1 **It must've been** her twin sister **(that) you saw** ...  2 What **I can't understand is why** you didn't telephone me ...  3 **It's his arrogant attitude that** I find ...  4 **All you think about is** going out to parties  5 **What baffles me is** his lack ...  6 **It's not so much** your finishing the job **that concerns me as** the state of your health.  7 **What they have decided to do is** of no interest to me.  8 What **they will ask you to do is** (to) attend an interview.  9 The person **you should complain to** is the manager.  10 **The first time** I realised something was wrong **was when** ...

## Listening: sentence completion p.77

1 biological reason  2 awarded money or penalties  3 working properly  4 random events  5 more optimistic  6 won't happen  7 remember events  8 a reputation for  9 an attraction  10 intuition  11 life's experience  12 risky

**Tapescript**

**Interviewer:** *For thousands of years philosophers and ordinary people have pondered the question of luck and good fortune. Why is it, for example, that some people seem to have 'all the luck' as the saying goes? What is it about these people that makes them different from others? In the studio with us tonight is a psychologist who has made luck and intuition the subject of serious scientific research. I'd like to welcome to our programme Dr Sandra Beckett, from the University of Manchester.*
**Sandra Beckett:** *Good evening.*

*I:* Dr Beckett ... perhaps you'd like to tell us a bit about what exactly it means to be lucky or unlucky, and what you've discovered in the course of your research at Manchester ....

*SB:* Yes, of course. Before I talk about my own research, though, I'd like to briefly mention a study which was carried out in America recently ... at the Iowa College of Medicine ... which seems to suggest that good or bad luck might be something biological ... Whether or not this is actually true, of course, is open to question ... but the study itself was very interesting. Um ... scientists at the University of Iowa had isolated a type of mildly brain-damaged person who ... er ... despite good intelligence and memory ... had a tendency to 'foul up'. In the study ... um ... they set up an experiment whereby two groups of patients were given cards ... some of which awarded money and others penalties. Now, what they found was that the group with brain defects took longer to assess the difference between the cards ... and, in fact ... even after finding out the difference, still chose the penalty card.

*I:* In other words ... ?

*SB:* In other words ... unlike the control group ... they acquired no 'hunch', as it were, that the cards were duff.

*I:* I see. And what conclusions did they draw from that?

*SB:* Well, they concluded that the mildly brain-damaged probably made bad decisions due to the presence of damage in the part of the brain which is believed to store data about past rewards and punishments. Um ... whatever allows other people access to the 'intuition' or 'gut feeling' was missing or not working properly.

*I:* That's interesting ... Now, you mentioned your own research, Dr Beckett. What kinds of conclusions have you reached about what makes lucky people different from others?

*SB:* Well ... first of all ... let me say that it is true that some people do seem to be exceptionally lucky ... and their luck is not just manifest in health and wealth, but ... um ... even more random events seem to go in their favour. Just why this is so is still a bit of a mystery ... but there do seem to be a number of factors involved. Um ... one important factor is that lucky people are optimistic... For example, a person like this will fall down the stairs ... break a leg ... and say afterwards 'How lucky I was not to break my neck!' We found in our research that unlucky people were pessimistic in comparison, you know ... luck seems to be a self-fulfilling prophesy. People who believe that good things won't happen find that, sure enough, bad things happen instead...

*I:* And this outlook on life is also reflected in other areas, I imagine?

*SB:* Yes ... there's a great difference in the way lucky and unlucky people remember events, for example. People who are lucky remember good times ... while unlucky people tend to focus on personal failures.

*I:* Mmm. And what about the impression people give to others? That's important I think. Some people do seem to acquire a reputation for bad or good luck, don't they?

*SB:* Yes, that's true. I've even come across people who have such a reputation for being jinxed that their friends won't catch the same aeroplane as them! Behaviour in the end really is mediated by those around you ... if people expect you to knock a wine glass over, you will. Um ... generally speaking .... if you put out that you are competent ... then people will treat you likewise ... um ... even in small children ...

we've been studying the body language of children recently in Manchester ... even in small children this reciprocal process seems to start as early as six months old. Whether we like it or not, some people do create an underlying attraction that brings good things to them.

*I:* Yes, that's very true. What then is luck, would you say?

*SB:* Well, that's the big question, isn't it? It's difficult to put your finger on it. Um ... the lucky often put their good fortune down to intuition – which is not something mysterious or magical but based on learning and expertise. While decisions may not seem rational and we don't know why they feel good or bad, they often turn out to be based on life's experience.....

*I:* Which would be very important in something like business, of course.

*SB:* Yes. In the business community, they take luck and intuition very seriously. I often hear senior businessmen say of someone 'he's got good intuition' ... they mean, of course, that someone is good at making risky decisions ... and that person is almost certainly seen as being 'lucky'. But intuitive ideas have to be tested with hard graft, knowledge and understanding. It goes without saying that the best gut decisions are made by people who are highly experienced.

*I:* Mmm. What would you say then of somebody who ...

## Writing: narrative composition (2)  p.78

**2**  1b)  2d)  3a)  4c)

**4**

2  Casting her mind back to when she was a child, she (vaguely) remembered how she had often seen the old woman outside the church, railing against the injustice of life.

3  How stupid she had been to believe her! She had obviously been drunk! How (on earth) could she have known that something was wrong?

This is an improved version of the composition, including the flashbacks from Exercise 4 (in *italics*) and some more sophisticated vocabulary (in **bold** – make a note of any words which you consider to be useful).

Standing alone on the platform, Ruth began to feel her spirits sinking. It was already 4 o'clock. If the train didn't arrive in the next ten minutes, she would be late for her job interview – and that would be a disaster. *Sadly she remembered how much her mother had encouraged her that morning, how she had looked on admiringly, reassuring her and making suggestions as to what she should wear and what she should say.* Her mother really was the only person who understood what this job meant to her.

Her thoughts were suddenly interrupted by someone's hand tapping gently on her shoulder. She **spun** round and looked into the **wrinkled** face of an old lady who was **peering** at her through **spectacles which were dirty and cracked**. There was something familiar about her. *Casting her mind back to when she was a child, she vaguely remembered how she had often seen the woman outside the church, railing against the injustice of life.* She didn't seem to have changed much in appearance. 'I'm sorry to frighten you, my dear,' she **murmured**. 'but you must go home immediately. Something is wrong.' **Staring in astonishment** at the old lady, Ruth **jumped up** and rushed out of the station.

**159**

Five minutes later she was standing at the front door. As she **fumbled** for the key in her handbag, she began to feel rather angry with herself for listening to the woman. *How stupid she had been to believe her! She had obviously been drunk! How on earth could she have known that something was wrong?* **No sooner had she** opened the door, though, **than** she noticed the **sickly** smell of gas in the house. She ran **frantically** to the kitchen to find her mother unconscious on the floor and the door of the oven open.

She had obviously had one of her 'dizzy spells'. Fortunately, though, she was still alive. **Firmly grabbing** her under the arms, she **dragged** her out into the garden and brought her round. As she did so, she thought about the day's events. How grateful she felt that she had listened to the old woman. (*357 words*)

## U N I T *10*

## Vocabulary review: multiple-choice p.80

1A   2B (*fixed phrase*)   3D   4A (*colloc.*)   5C   6D (*fixed phrase*)   7B   8A   9A (*fixed phrase = a total ban, without exceptions*)   10B (= *someone with no worries about the morals of his actions. The other three options all relate to appearance or attractiveness*)

## Grammar: determiners and pronouns p.80

**1**   1 ... no business of ...   2 ... matter what ...   3 ... right to be / feel ...   4 ... both of ... (neither *before the gap indicates that* all *would be incorrect*)   5 ... contacted by anyone ... (*notice the singular verb form* has, *indicating that* people *would be incorrect*)   6 ... need to make ...   7 ... neither (of them) ... (*because there are two,* none *would be incorrect*)   8 ... none of which ...

## Grammar: adjectives p.81

**1**   1C   2C   3D   4B   5A   6C

**2**   1 **Almost nobody** turned up ...   2 I know you are **capable of** producing good .....   3 I am **proud to be meeting / will be proud to meet** ...   4 His **sole intention in** joining the project is to ...   5 It will be **virtually impossible to** find somebody to ...   6 I am **baffled by your unwillingness to** give ....   7 In the some countries the sale of tobacco is **restricted to** people over the ...   8 Harry's homework wasn't **quite** perfect.

## Reading: non-fiction p.82

**1**   a newspaper or magazine (*it's a current news item*)

**2**   1B (*the revival in green woodworking*)   2C (*the chairman ... emphasised that nobody should see the cutting-down of ancient trees as an act of destruction or vandalism*)   3D (*His words were to the point, but he rather gave away his own lack of practical skills ...*)   4B (*hand tools will be the order of the day*)   5A (*they will also need to be fairly impervious to scrutiny ... visitors to the arboretum ... will doubtless flock*

*around*)   6A (*... a striking blend of ancient and modern ... the most striking innovation ... since the arboretum was founded in 1829*)

## Use of English: cloze p.83

1 consulting (+ *on*)   2 ways / methods / means   3 on (*colloc.*)   4 draw   5 involved (+ *in*)   6 hit (*fixed phrase*)   7 had (*notice the past participle* implanted *which follows*)   8 able   9 his (+ *every*)   10 positioned / installed / located   11 it (*the system*)   12 left (*you need to consider the meaning of the whole sentence*)   13 appeal (+ *to*)   14 impact / effect (*colloc.*)   15 cheap   16 Research (+ *into; don't forget to use a capital letter*)   17 on   18 worn (*reduced relative clause*)   19 position / location / whereabouts (*this is rephrased in the next sentence*)   20 using (*participle clause*)

## Vocabulary: adverb + adjective collocation p.84

**1**   1 deadly dull   2 wildly exaggerated   3 widely available   4 highly skilled   5 deeply moved   6 closely guarded   7 entirely convinced   8 strictly forbidden

**2**   1 deadly dull   2 closely guarded   3 deeply moved   4 widely available   5 strictly forbidden   6 highly skilled   7 wildly exaggerated   8 entirely convinced

## Vocabulary: phrasal verbs and expressions: *work* p.84

**1**   1 work out why   2 work out how   3 working out between   4 work up any   5 worked up over   6 works out at

**2**   1 short   2 cut (*this expression tends to be used in this 'prediction' context, with the modal* will)   3 rule (= *protest by doing work extremely slowly, stating that you have to obey all of the rules exactly*)   4 bone   5 frenzy (= *get upset, or hysterical*)   6 courage

## Grammar: the future p.85

**1**

1   1b) (= *it's already arranged*)   2b) (= *do you want to ... ? - you've kept me waiting ... , sarcastic tone*)   3a) (= *what the timetable says, as opposed to when trains actually run*)   4b) (= *he's about to do it*)   5a) (= *we can see what is about to happen*)   6b) (= *I've already planned this*)   7a) (= *I'm planning to do this anyway, so it's easy for me to do you a favour*)   8b) (= *a threat about the future*)

2   *Sample answers*

1 I'll / I might play tennis with Roger tomorrow ...   2 Will you marry me ...   3 The train will be delayed by over an hour ...   4 He will have resigned ...   5 That tree will / may have fallen down ...   6 I'll / I could wear a red pullover ...   7 I'll go to the supermarket later ...   8 You may have to work overtime next week ...

**2**   1 It won't **be long before he gets** promoted.   2 He is **unlikely / not likely to** win ...   3 His refusal to work overtime **is bound to** create problems ... 4 Scientists are on **the verge / point of** discovering ... 5 My licence **is due to be renewed / for renewal** ... 6 The house **is expected to / will probably have been sold** ...

## Writing: report (2) p.86

**1** 1 extract 1 comes from a report 2 a), b), c) and e) are all unlikely in a report

**2** 2 The most appropriate conclusion is A. Conclusion C would be appropriate for a discursive composition.

# UNIT *11*

## Vocabulary review: multiple-choice p.88

1A (*colloc.*) 2A 3B (influence / effect + *had*) 4D 5B 6B (*colloc.*) 7B (*fixed phrase*) 8D (*colloc.*) 9A (*fixed phrase*) 10C (*fixed phrase*)

## Grammar: reflexive verbs p.88

**1** 1 Anne **prides herself on** her ... 2 **Help yourself** to a drink ... 3 You shouldn't **blame yourself for** what happened. 4 She wants to **distance herself from** the scandal caused ... 5 ... **lends itself to** being made into a film. 6 He has **dedicated himself to** raising ... 7 He **resigned himself to** spending ... 8 You don't need to **commit yourself** now about whether ... 9 Did the children **behave themselves** ...? 10 She **couldn't trust herself not to** eat the ...

**2** 1 should / must pull yourself (*this expression sounds rather critical, so might cause offence if you say it directly to s.b.*) 2 wear yourself 3 couldn't concentrate 4 assert yourself 5 I make 6 suits me down 7 couldn't help 8 (from) my

## Use of English: comprehension and summary p.89

**1**

1 egotism
2 that they are generally agreed on something which is not true
3 The ease of communication between people when they speak has led researchers to under-estimate how complex language is / imagine that people can communicate with computers as easily.
4 Language is passed on from parent to child in the genes, so it does not have to be taught or copied.
5 This view has been shown to be untrue.
6 that these would all be understood by a human being, but not by a computer
7 lack of shared experience
8 to stop computers from trying to process every word the operator says, even if it doesn't make sense
9 because computers will never be able to respond to speech like people can, to develop a sense of humour, or

any of the abilities we recognise as conversation skills
10 Business management has become less hierarchical and authoritarian.
11 They don't care about being polite when giving instructions.
12 Instructions have to be given in a very direct and precise way which is not very natural to most people.

**3** *Sample answer*

Modern life doesn't prepare most people for giving orders, and they might be unable to do this clearly. Many would feel strange talking to a machine, and workplaces would also become very noisy. Additionally, people and computers do not share the sorts of life experiences which make language comprehensible, and an enjoyable way of communicating, between people. Consequently, computers are not natural interpreters of human speech, and there would probably be numerous confusions and mistakes in their attempts to carry out commands. (*82 words*)

## Use of English: guided sentence transformations p.92

**2**

1 to be, dramatic decrease, in sales, the company might ...
2 has recently been, under, attack
3 no circumstances, are you, to alter the settings ...
4 refusal, to obey ..., could result in, instant dismissal

**3**

1 He's having his **hair cut** tomorrow. (haircut = *a noun*, hair cut = *a noun + a past participle. The structure being tested is* to have s.t. done)
2 **Had I not** stayed up so late ... (Had not *can't be contracted to* hadn't *here, because the inversion is to add emphasis, and not* is stressed)
3 It was at the age **of** eight ...
4 I wish you wouldn't leave your socks around **so** untidily! (so = *as untidily as you do. It replaces* really *in the original sentence. So is especially common in transformations featuring conditionals or wishes.*)
5 All of the jewellery **seemed** to have ... (look *isn't followed by an infin.*)
6 ... of his **being** allowed to ... (*this transformation needs a passive verb form*)

**4**

1 People who **do not** have a knowledge of nuclear physics will be **unable** to comprehend his research. / People who have a knowledge of nuclear physics **are the only ones** who will be able to understand his research / will find his research comprehensible. (*Either you could use a double negative to answer this transformation, or you could use an emphatic expression. Both alternatives are equally correct.*)
2 **What beats me is** why ... (*this is a cleft sentence with a fixed phrase = what really surprises or confuses me*)
3 There may be **some / occasional unpredictability** in his behaviour. (*this transformation focuses on your ability to change the forms of words and to supply the correct dep. prep.*)
4 **Did it ever occur to you** that he ...? (*fixed phrase*)
5 She was **under no obligation** to participate ... (*here you*

have to recognise the noun to go with the dep. prep. under, and supply the correct verb form to follow the noun)

6 No other building (in the city) is **nearly as** tall **as this one**. (The key phrase in the original sentence is by far. Look for adverbs like really, nearly, too, very, seldom, etc in the original sentences of transformation exercises, as these must be transformed. Failing to do this is one of the commonest reasons for losing marks on this type of exercise.)

7 **Were it not for** a small defect in the timing device this machine would be accurate. (inverted conditional expression)

8 **At no time was** the outcome of the mission in doubt. (inverted adverbial expression)

9 This book **lends itself to adaptation / being adapted**. (reflexive verb form + dep. prep. + ger. / noun)

10 **Unless** we **run out of** fuel, we'll ... (this tests a phrasal verb with the opposite meaning to continue, as if in the original sentence is changed to unless in the transformation)

11 There **was such a** violent **public reaction** / reaction **from** the public **to** the announcement of the news that several ... (this tests so / such, and supplying the correct form of words, + dep. preps.)

12 **Had it not been for** your **contribution**, I wouldn't have **been able to** ... (inverted conditional expression)

13 There is **little likelihood of his being picked** for the team. (This tests the colloc. little + likelihood, and the structure which follows it: of + noun / -ing form.)

14 There **has been a** large / huge / dramatic **increase / rise in** crime this year / since last year / in the last year. (You have to supply the noun rise or increase + the dep.prep. in, and a suitable adj. to show that crime is **much** higher.)

## Writing: discursive composition (2) p.93

**1**

**1** 2 = too blunt and direct

**2** 1 It is likely that / There is every likelihood that this trend will continue
2 have to a large extent been ignored / have largely been ignored / appear / seem to have been ignored
3 People tend to dismiss / are apt to dismiss / there is a tendency for people to dismiss
4 It is rather sad
5 do not seem to / appear to worry

**2**

**1** two = explain how, what could be done

**2** 2, 4 (only in the briefest terms at this stage) and 6 (try to 'echo' the composition title in both your introduction and your conclusion if you can)

**3** 2 (the first two sentences outline the situation today), 4 (mobile telephones and the Internet) and 6 ('people have perhaps become more isolated from their immediate surroundings')

**3** 1a)  2c)  3b)  4a)  5b)  6b)

**4** Conclusion A is more balanced, echoes the composition title and ends on a constructive point for

action. Conclusion B, on the other hand, is rather extreme in its views, and contains the distracting new detail about the health risks of mobile phones.

**5** Outline B has been used to plan this composition.

# UNIT *12*

## Reading: non-fiction  p.96

**2** The extended metaphor is of war. The words and phrases which illustrate this are: standing to arms, encampments, scavenging medieval army, attacks everywhere most beautiful, onslaught of the barbarians, so violent are its assaults.

**3** 1D (this is not said directly, but implied by the descriptions of mess, wine and ugliness)   2C (it reduces ... to the level of commercial gimmicks)   3A (the very word 'tourist' has become a kind of shorthand for all things unlovely)   4B (... the tourist version of travel)   5A (happy advantages for local people – concerts, plays ...)   6B (... tells them the truth about one another)

## Vocabulary review: multiple-choice  p.97

1A (= get stronger)   2B   3A(colloc., except +for, bar + no prep.)   4C   5D (determined / resolved + infin., serious + about)   6D (fixed phrase)   7B (colloc.)   8A (adhere + to, obey + no prep, observe + customs and traditions, not individual decisions)   9A   10D (= created especially)

## Grammar: indirect speech  p.98

**1**

1 ... **blamed her for their missing / the fact that** they (had) missed the train. (their is necessary, to include Sandra's mother in missing the train)

2 She **advised me not to** say anything about it to the manager. (Don't forget that the not in a negative infin. has to come before the to – ~~to not say ...~~)

3 She **enquired of** John **whether** he would have finished the paper work by the time they came back. (This is rather more formal in tone than asked.)

4 Our mother **threatened to** take away / **not to** give back our pocket money if we didn't behave ourselves. (~~threatened us to ...~~)

5 She **promised never to tell** anyone about the money we had given her. (not + ever = never)

6 He **denied having stolen / that he had stolen** the money.

7 She **urged us / me / them not to** pay any attention to / **to ignore** ...

8 He **complimented us on** the (excellent) job / work **we had done / on doing** an excellent job.

**2** 1 me of stealing   2 her against   3 the blame on
4 would / might have taken   5 (that) they should keep / they kept   6 to put us

## Grammar: impersonal passive constructions p.99

1 He **is alleged to have had** no knowledge / **not to have known** ...
2 He is thought **to be arriving** ...
3 The police **are reported to have already arrested** ...
4 It **was believed that** she had been using a false passport ...
5 It is thought **that she was not** involved / It is **not** thought that she **was** involved ...
6 He **was said not to have been** aware of ... (*Be careful!* He was not said to have been aware of ... *has a slightly different meaning.*)

## Listening: multiple-choice p.99

1D (*I found the air growing thinner and breathing even more difficult*)   2A (*Our first night in tents, erected for us by our porters, had been cold – though nothing like the night we had spent at Chivay, earlier in the holiday,*)   3C (*straggled onwards at whatever pace we found tolerable*)   4B ( *... but I refused, afraid to sit down until I knew I had no farther to climb.*)
5B (*listen to her tone of voice*)   6B (*the group was large enough to dilute the irritations that emerge on any organised tour but small enough to maintain the sense of adventure*)

### Tapescript

*There was a moment, as I scrambled along the Inca Trail, when I really thought I might die. The so-called Dead Woman's Pass – at 14,000 feet – lay ahead. Nothing could have been more aptly named!*

*Clambering upwards, with a wall of mountain before my eyes, I found the air growing thinner and breathing even more difficult. Even the porters looked over-stretched. Conrad, who was another member of our party, had fallen into step alongside me and we calculated every movement forward. Ten or fifteen steps and then a pause. Ten, fifteen steps ... then another pause.*

*At first, the climb had not been too tough. The worst of altitude sickness was past – our party had already spent a fortnight acclimatizing as we travelled around Peru in a giant truck ... and the first day of our 24-mile walk had been a moderate affair, to get us into the swing. Our first night in tents, erected for us by our porters, had been cold – though nothing like the night we had spent at Chivay, earlier in the holiday, where the water froze in our water bottles and the tents were stiff with ice by morning. At Chivay, even a sleeping bag designed for temperatures down to minus ten seemed to offer no more protection than a sheet ... and then the truck refused to start the next morning!*

*Anyway ... here ... on the Inca trail ... life seemed a lot less demanding at first. But after our easy introduction, the second day of the journey was much, much tougher. We set off all together, but we soon became separated by the steepness of the path, travelling up through the woods, mountain pastures and on to Dead Woman's Pass. Mark and Liz, our truck-driving tour leaders, leapt on ahead, with Monica and Abigail close behind them, but, finding it tough. And the rest of us straggled onwards at whatever pace we found tolerable.*

*Reaching the top, I staggered to the edge. Mark and Liz beckoned me to join the first arrivals, who were already sitting waiting, but I refused, afraid to sit down until I knew I had no farther to climb. The sight was quite something ... miles and*

*miles of steep mountains and rainforest. Absolutely stunning! A land from another time. Conrad and I posed for photographs, feeling a very real sense of achievement, and, eventually, all of the members of the group safely reunited, we descended to where the porters had prepared lunch.*

*Our journey then continued up and down ... up and down ... this time on stone steps – some of them knee-high – where the Inca messengers once ran from the city of Cuzco ... and by the fourth morning, we were nearly at Machu Picchu.*

*Rising in pitch darkness at 4am, we dressed and set out by torchlight. At dawn we had reached the Sun Gate and the city lay below us. It was enormous, quite unbelievable! Nothing could have prepared me for what I saw or felt at that moment! Everywhere there were the ruins of palaces and temples ... some of them dating from the fifteenth and sixteenth centuries. It was simply too much to take in, in one go!*

*What is interesting, I think, about Machu Picchu is that for more than three centuries only the local Peruvians had known about it, and it was not until 1911 that an American archaeologist, Hiram Bingham, who was looking for the lost city of the Incas, first revealed Machu Picchu to the rest of the world. I can't even begin to think what he must have felt when he first saw the city: a sense, probably, of having discovered another world.*

*Getting back to our little expedition, I would have to say that the walk to Machu Picchu made all of us feel like real explorers. Everyone in the group got on well together and the group was large enough to dilute the irritations that emerge on any organised tour but small enough to maintain the sense of adventure. Walking the Inca trail is something none of us will ever forget. It was the kind of experience which ...*

## Use of English: guided gapped sentences p.100

**1**   not be allowed / permitted to   2 Earth couldn't
3 to have read / finished / received   4 had made
5 to have set

**2**   1 in his ability   2 the risk of being   3 having paid no / not having paid any / the fact that she (had) paid no / having paid little / not having paid much / the fact that she (had) paid little   4 though he was   5 time you made

**3**   1 whatever / no matter what he says (*notice the comma which follows*)   2 it not been for the (*help* here is a noun, *and* had *at the start of the sentence suggests an inversion*)   3 account must / should you (*the opening of the sentence suggests an inversion*)   4 must / should bear in (*fixed phrase*)   5 not able to come / couldn't come (*fixed phrase*)   6 if he's been working (*notice* as *before the gap and* hard, *which collocates with* work)   7 is no reason (whatsoever *indicates that a negative expression is required*)   8 wouldn't have been in (*the first part of the sentence indicates that a conditional structure is necessary*)   9 have caused (you) so (*cause collocates with embarrassment, the time reference indicates that the infin. needs to be perfect, and* much *directly after the gap suggests* so)   10 blame for (*fixed phrase*)   11 better not tell (tell *collocates with secret;* had better not = *strong advice or warning.* **Always be careful with contracted forms in gapped sentence exercises:** 'd *could be* had *or* would, 's *could be* is *or* has.)   12 not / n't have gone (*fixed phrase, very commonly used with* needn't)

## Vocabulary: prepositions and prepositional phrases p.101

1 What attitude **do you have towards** people who .....
2 She'll be **in good / safe hands**   3 This building is **in urgent need** of renovation.   4 Dr Jenkins is **out of touch with** recent ...   5 I'm **not averse to** a bit of hard work ... (*this expression is always used in the negative*)
6 Her homework hasn't been **up to scratch** recently. (*This expression also normally appears only in the negative.*)
7 **In the long run** there'll be ...   8 The escaped prisoner is still **at large**.

## Grammar review: future forms with modal verbs p.101

1 Cars **might / may / could be made of** plastic in the future.
2 **You should have finished** that report by tomorrow.
3 You **should've been given** the test results ...   4 You **shouldn't get involved in** this.   5 People **might / may / could be living** in colonies on the moon ...   6 You **might get / be bitten** by a snake in that long grass, so be very careful ...   7 Your friend **should already have arrived** at the station by the time you get there.   8 The meeting may **not have finished** by the time / when you arrive.

## Writing: descriptive composition (3) (places) p.102

**2**

**1**   Introduction 1 is more appropriate. Introduction 2 is more complex, and certainly well written, but would be much more appropriate for a discursive essay.

**2**   No, the composition fails to answer the second part of the task: *Explain why it affected you so much.* It is also rather too short for Proficiency.

**3**   very cold = *bitterly cold*
had no lights on = *shrouded in darkness*
the streets = *the narrow cobbled streets*
looking at = *gazing up in awe*
to be in = *to grace*
the old buildings ... = *there was an air of mystery about ...*
a layer of = *a thick blanket of*
softening = *muffling*
I will never forget ... = *New Year's Eve was particularly memorable*

**3**   1b)   2a)   3e)   4f)   5c)

**4**   *Complete improved composition*
Cracow. The ancient capital of Poland. Just the name of the place is enough to bring back a flood of happy memories. It was around Christmas time, a few years back, when I first visited this city with a group of friends.

We arrived in Cracow at around midnight. I remember it was bitterly cold and there was a lot of snow about. Our hotel was shrouded in darkness when we arrived, but fortunately the receptionist was on duty. What amazed us was how friendly and hospitable she was, even though it was late and she was obviously tired.

Our first few days in Cracow were spent looking around, exploring the narrow cobbled streets and Castle, and gazing up in awe at the statues and monuments which seemed to grace every public square we came across. There was an air of mystery about the old buildings lining the streets, and throughout our stay in the city, we were frequently overwhelmed by the sense that we had somehow walked back into a magical kingdom belonging to another age.

The snow continued to fall constantly, reminding me of scenes from novels I had read by Tolstoy and other Russian and Polish writers. Eveywhere was covered in a thick blanket of snow, which had the effect of muffling the sounds of cars and passing trams. It also made us feel like travellers in some mysterious, silent land, far away from the noise and bustle of modern city life.

New Year's Eve was particularly memorable. An enormous crowd had gathered in the main square of the city, and most people were dancing. The fact that everyone seemed so happy and well-behaved – and intent on enjoying themselves – made an enormous impression on us.

Our week in Cracow was something I shall never forget. I have been back there several times since, and each time I am still struck by the sheer beauty of the city and the friendliness and openness of the inhabitants. Cracow is one of those places which reminds us of the splendour that has unfortunately been lost or destroyed in so many of our cities today. (*350 words*)

## UNIT *13*

## Vocabulary review: multiple-choice p.104

1B   2C (*colloc.*)   3C (*prep. phrase*)   4A (*the other options are all ways of speaking*)   5D (*colloc.*)   6A   7D (= *created a thin coating over the surface*)   8B   9D   10A

## Grammar: continuous aspect p.104

**1**   1 1a), 2b)   2 1b), 2a) and c)   3 1b), 2a)   4 1a), 2b)
5 1b), 2a) and c)   6 2a) and b)

**2**   1 They **have been negotiating** a settlement for over ...
2 The minister's policies **have been attacked** (by journalists) several times ...   3 The fact that **he was being sarcastic** was ...   4 Politicians **have already begun** talks to bring ...
5 By the time he was eighteen **he had left** home to go ...
6 They **have been trying to sell** that house for ...

**3**   1 help / stop thinking   2 hasn't been keeping your
3 he's making a / some kind of   4 thought it   5 must've been having   6 morning doing the   7 has run   8 has been telling

## Use of English: comprehension and summary p.106

**2**

1   that they are sacrificed in huge numbers, like soldiers going into battle
2   emotional casualty rate

3  Just as the First World War generals didn't question the point of all the killing, so educationists do not question the point of exams.

4  They are very unwilling to study.

5  They may not be very good at their jobs, or not well-suited to them.

6  by encouraging children to believe that they have to be successful at school and university, in order to get a good job in later life

7  As the top managers in industry, they are in a good position to say whether good exam grades are an important factor in later success.

8  the fact that researchers with the highest grades are ultimately less successful than those who obtained lower results

9  The highest marks do not indicate originality or the ability to think, but rather the desire to please examiners.

10  Their greatest achievement (their top-grade university mark) comes too early in their career.

11  the exam system, which regards the highest possible mark as the ultimate goal

12  *Sample answer*

Although school and university exams do not necessarily indicate intelligence or talent, they still cause many people to feel like failures. In addition, many retail companies nowadays do not find them helpful, and use their own tests for applicants instead. In business and industry, exam results do not determine later success, and even in scientific research a good degree does not mean that someone can think originally or be self-motivated. In fact, their degree may already be their greatest achievement, resulting in a loss of competitiveness and adaptability. (*84 words*)

## Vocabulary: phrasal verbs and expressions: *stand* p.107

**1**  1 stand by him, whatever  2 REM stand for in this  3 stand for such (*this expression is normally used with* won't, *indicating that something is unacceptable*)  4 make the sign stand out  5 had stood up for him when they started making  6 you unfairly until you stand up to  7 stands out among / as the best of  8 standing in for Robin while

**2**  1 Abrams will **stand trial** ...  2 Their marriage has **stood the test of time**.  3 How do our sales **stand in relation to** those of other firms?  4 He **stands little chance of** winning ...  5 If you really want to leave, **I'm not going to stand in your way**.  6 **It stands to reason that** hard work and determination lead to success.

## Vocabulary: verb + noun collocation p.108

1 take  2 made  3 handled  4 jump  5 set  6 seized  7 get / achieve  8 achieve  9 set  10 made

## Vocabulary: dependent prepositions and prepositional phrases p.108

1 on  2 under  3 to  4 into  5 in  6 for

## Listening: three-way choice  p.108

1B (*the most common mistake is lack of preparation / Mmm, yes.* – listen to Rita's intonation – *Another thing they could do is look at the company's market ...*)  2R (*Most candidates need to display more confidence in themselves and their skills / there's too much over-confidence about these days, I'd say*)  3A (*'I'll walk in and give them a short spiel about myself and that will convince them'. That really is not enough –*)  4B (*Candidates should go into the interview with their minds fixed on the four or five key strengths that they want to get across... / and make sure they can back up those claims* – finishing someone else's sentence is a common way of signalling agreement)
5A (*I think it's best to be honest with the employer / which could cost you the job, I think. It's probably best to steer clear of such areas if you can*)  6B (*Instead, say, of listing all the duties you had in your previous job, I'd mention things like ... um ... 'I increased turnover by x per cent' or 'I completed this project ahead of schedule'... / there's certainly a lot to be said for being as specific as possible.*)  7A (*most employers will have a few tricky questions*)  8B (*resist the urge to babble /* Rita finishes Angela's sentence here, signalling agreement)  9A (*it's probably not a very good idea to say 'in your job!' / Would anyone ever say that?* – listen to Rita's intonation)  10B (*So many people forget they are still being interviewed / ... imagining how you would behave with a client ...*)

### Tapescript

**Presenter:** *Thank you Dave for that report, which I'm sure our listeners found very interesting. We're going to move on now to a related topic ... job interviews. How can you make sure that that all important job interview you go for doesn't turn into your worst nightmare? Giving us their views on the matter tonight are Angela Simpson, of the Alpha Recruitment Agency, and Rita Gilbert, who works for Drake Ream Tollin, an agency which specialises in finding jobs for people who have been made redundant.*

**Angela Simpson/Rita Gilbert:** *Hello.*

 **P:** *Without further ado then ... Angela ... what is your advice to our listeners about what they should do in an interview ... and – perhaps more importantly – what they should not do?*

**AS:** *Well, the most common mistake is lack of preparation. Recruitment companies are always reporting that most candidates still don't make enough effort to find out about their prospective employer and the business they're in. And they don't think enough about what they're going to say when the interview takes place. It is a pitfall that even those going for senior jobs fall into. You see, I think that candidates really need to sit down and study the organisation's annual report and accounts and maybe look at any relevant web sites as well.*

**RG:** *Mmm, yes. Another thing they could do is look at the company's market ... you know, determine whether it is expanding, consolidating or declining, and the company's likely direction and aims for the future.*

 **AS:** *Yes, that would be good as well.*

**RG:** *I'm not too sure, though, that lack of preparation is the most common mistake. I would say it's probably lack of confidence. Most candidates need to display more confidence in themselves and their skills in the interview situation ... um ... they need to be a lot more sure of themselves ... impress the employer that they're up to the job ...*

AS: *Yes, well, there's too much <u>over</u>-confidence about these days, I'd say … especially if people are being headhunted. There's a sense of … well, you know … 'I've been headhunted so they must want me. I'll walk in and give them a short spiel about myself and that will convince them'. Well, that really isn't enough – invariably they will be up against five or six candidates as well-qualified as themselves … some of whom will have done their preparation.*

RG: *Well, confidence or lack of confidence aside … you mention the importance of preparation, Angela … and … well, the other side of the coin is knowing what the employer is looking for and matching it to your own skills and experience. Candidates should go into the interview with their minds fixed on the four or five key strengths that they want to get across …*

AS: *… and make sure they can back up those claims.*

RG: *If you say you are good at managing people, for instance, you should be able to cite an example of a job or a team project in which you have managed people well. Um …*

AS: *But, what about areas you might not know very much about … or know that you are weak in? You see, I think it's best to be honest with the employer. Say that you're willing to learn … or that your knowledge of something is fairly limited …*

RG: *… which could cost you the job, I think. It's probably best to steer clear of such areas if you can … you know …. focus more on your strengths … your achievements. I'd also not focus too much on things which are run of the mill. Instead, say, of listing all the duties you had in your previous job, I'd mention things like … um … 'I increased turnover by x per cent' or 'I completed this project ahead of schedule'…*

AS: *Mmm … well, there's certainly a lot to be said for being as specific as possible. I'm sure you've found as well, Rita, that most employers will have a few tricky questions up their sleeve which the interviewee should have prepared for. You know, the obvious ones, of course … like … um, let's think, … 'Tell me about yourself' … or … 'Why are you leaving your present job?' You see, it's very important, I think, to resist the urge to babble when answering questions like these. Um … I think your answers should be two-minute resumés …*

RG: *… emphasizing the parts which are relevant to the job you are applying for …*

AS: *Yes, of course – well, that goes without saying, doesn't it? It's important, as well, not to be overbearing … you know if the interviewer says 'Where do you see yourself in five years' time?' it's probably not a very good idea to say 'In your job'!*

RG: *Would anyone ever say that, do you think?*

AS: *I'm sure they would! Particularly if they have an inflated ego! It's important not to forget that in most cases the interviewer is looking for someone to fill a vacancy, so relieving the organisation of a problem – they don't want someone who is intent on shooting through the ranks, because then it won't be long before they have to fill the vacancy all over again.*

P: *Do you agree, Rita?*

RG: *You do have to be very careful what you say, of course … and how you behave … even if your prospective boss takes you out after the interview for something to eat. So many people forget that they are still being interviewed!*

AS: *Yes, quite. You have to remember that your boss is going to be looking at you and imagining how you would behave with a client, or colleagues. You have to show that you can socialise and lighten up a bit. Ask intelligent questions, dress smartly … even if the company professes to be informal. It really is amazing that a surprising number of candidates still …*

## Vocabulary: dependent prepositions and prepositional phrases p.109

1 to   2 of   3 for   4 between   5 as   6 between   7 from
8 to   9 for   10 on   11 about   12 of   13 to   14 on
15 with   16 at   17 beyond   18 to   19 in   20 in

## Writing: magazine article p.109

**1**

**1** Statements 3, 4 and 6 could be interpreted as slightly sceptical. All of the statements are neutral or slightly formal, with statements 3 and 6 being the most formal in tone.

**2** 1c)   2f)   3d)   4b)   5a)   6e)

**2** 1 be seen to be believed   2 thing that strikes you is 3 more like a warehouse than a place for wining and dining 4 as the eye can see   5 is now making / turning a handsome profit

**4** 1a)   2b)   3c)   4a)   5b)   6a)

**5** A is the more appropriate conclusion, as the tone is more personal and light-hearted, and so fits the rest of the article better.

## UNIT 14

## Vocabulary: multiple-choice revision p.112

1A (*colloc.*)   2A (= *gradually worn away*)   3D (= *against*)
4B (*fixed phrase*)   5B (= *ignoring the rules*)   6A (*colloc.*)
7D (*fixed phrase*)   8C (*fixed phrase*)   9A (*fixed phrase*)
10B   11C (*colloc.*)   12D (*colloc.*)   13D   14A (*colloc.*)   15D

## Vocabulary: phrasal verb revision p.113

1A (= *obey the rules of*)   2B (= *ran away with*)   3C (= *doing, normally used when we expect it's something bad or unexpected*)   4B (= *caused*)   5D (= *tolerate s.t. irritating*)
6D (= *shocked or surprised*)   7C (= *gave the impression of being*)   8A (= *creating bills, without really noticing or caring, normally used to express disapproval*)   9A (= *suggesting, without directly saying*)   10D (= *done s.t. wrong without being caught*)   11B (= *be received or accepted, normally used in the negative*)   12D (= *get over-excited about*)   13B (= *suggested or proposed, normally in a formal context like a meeting*)
14A (= *thought of or invented*)   15A (= *write in the details on an official document, this verb is also used for the last testament which somebody writes before they die*)

# Use of English: cloze p.114

1 deal (*colloc.*)  2 vary (+*from*)  3 reason  4 whom (*some of* before the blank *indicates that a pronoun is required, the commas indicate that this is a relative clause*)  5 seethe / react / respond (+ *with,* you need to look at the whole sentence)  6 up  7 deemed / thought / considered (*is* before *the blank, and the infin. which follow it, both indicate that a passive verb form is required*)  8 What (*don't forget the capital letter*)  9 however (*notice the commas around the blank*)  10 preventing / stopping (+ object +*from* + *-ing* form)  11 way / light  12 unable (+ *infin.*)  13 around  14 ideas (*colloc.*)  15 until  16 all (*colloc.*)  17 anyone / anybody (hardly *cannot be followed by* nobody, nowhere, *etc.*)  18 so (*notice an* after *the adj.* comfortable)  19 compared / likened (+ *to*)  20 another (*colloc.*)

# Use of English: sentence transformations p.115

1 Mark's father **congratulated him on having finally been accepted** on the course. (Well done *indicates that the reporting verb* congratulate, + *dep. prep.* on + *-ing form, are required*)
2 She is alleged **to have been receiving** ... (*impersonal passive form + perfect continuous infinitive, the verb* giving *has been changed for clarity –* to have been being given ...)
3 Had **it not been for** the football match on TV, he **wouldn't have stayed** at home. (*The position of* had *suggests an inversion, while the meaning of the original sentence indicates a third conditional.*)
4 The government **came in for** (a lot of) **criticism over** its plans ... (*you need to supply the phrasal verb, the correct noun form* criticism + *dep. prep.* over)
5 Nobody who **has not seen** his paintings is in **any** position ... (*this double negative could be avoided by saying* 'Nobody who **is ignorant of** his paintings is in any position ...')
6 It was **with the purpose / aim of** acquainti**ng** people with the facts that this meeting **was called**.
7 I wish they **would / were prepared** to talk about ... (*here,* would *is used with the meaning of volition – they* won't, *or are unwilling to, talk about the plans*)
8 **Ever since** his riding accident, **he has been unable to** write ... (since + *perfect tense*)
9 **No matter how much** you shout at me, I won't ...
10 I want to **distance myself from** all the rumours ...

# Use of English: gapped sentences p.115

1 must have been (to have invested *indicates that a past form is needed*)  2 neither of whom (*the two commas suggest a non-defining relative clause,* neither *is required because there are two of them*)  3 is by no (*fixed phrase*)  4 are still reading / will still be reading / still won't have finished (still *is necessary in all alternatives, to emphasise that something will have continued for a very long time*)  5 however much (*notice the comma before the gap, and the word order of the object and verb which follow*)  6 anyone listens (hardly + *anyone,* listens

+ *to*)  7 attention has been (*perfect tense +* so far, attention + *paid*)  8 to have made up (*fixed phrase,* seem + *infin., in this case a perfect infin.*)  9 animals were in (*prep. phrase*)  10 not to have taken (*impersonal passive construction + negative perfect infinitive, phrasal verb*)  11 no obligation (under + obligation, whatsoever + no)  12 it not for (would have *indicates a conditional form, the position of* were *suggests an inversion*)

# Use of English: key word transformations p.116

1 **I'm getting used to** stay**ing** / hav**ing** to stay on ... (*the original sentence suggests that this is still changing for me, so* I am used ... / I've got used ... *are not such good answers*)
2 She seems **intent on** mak**ing** you stay in ...
3 The new regulations **take effect from** June ... (**on** June 1st *fails to express the fact that they will only* **begin to** apply *on this day*)
4 Making sacrifices in your personal life **is part and parcel of** being ...
5 There seems (to be) **little likelihood that they'll make him** resign. / **of their making him** resign. / **of his having to** resign. (little *is a colloc. with the noun* likelihood, *which can be followed by* that + *clause, or of* + *-ing form*)
6 Charles **is bound to have bought** them a lovely present for their wedding. (bound + *perfect infin.*)
7 She has **set her heart on** (winn**ing**) the first prize. (*fixed phrase*)
8 Although I assured him **to the contrary**, ... (*prep. phrase, normally used with the verb* assure)
9 She made (very) **little effort to** ... (*colloc.* + *fixed phrase*)
10 Our experiments cannot continue because of the serious problems we have **come up against** ... (*phrasal verb*)
11 It's difficult to **keep a straight face** when ... (*fixed phrase*)
12 There's **no question of** our agree**ing** to... (*Be very careful with this structure! Compare:*
there's no question **of** our agreeing = *it is impossible for us ever to agree*
there's no question **that** we'll agree = *of course we'll agree, and it would be foolish to doubt this*)

# Use of English: summary writing and editing p.117

The first draft of the summary is **much** (50–60 words) too long.

*Sample answer*

Buying books from an Internet bookshop is often cheaper than buying them from a conventional bookshop. It is additionally possible to find almost any book in print and to order it quickly and easily. As well as providing information about books by the same author or on a related subject, many Internet bookshops encourage readers to send in reviews of books they would recommend to others. Finally, books ordered over the Internet are usually sent by airmail, which means they arrive in less than a week. (*86 words*)

# PRACTICE EXAM

## Paper 1: Reading comprehension p.120

### SECTION A
### Vocabulary multiple choice questions p120
*One mark per question (total = 25)*

1B   2C (= *to make her feel better,* brighten + *her mood,* alleviate + *her suffering*)   3A (= *had a disagreement, this is a three-word inseparable phrasal verb*)   4C (*colloc., painfully* + aware *is also used*)   5D (*fixed phrase = it should be taken seriously/not rejected*)   6C (= *at a similar level of achievement*)   7D (*colloc.*)   8D   9B (= *cut into very thin, long pieces, by pushing against a grater,* sliced = *cut with a knife into pieces, like bread,* mashed = *squashed to a soft consistency, like cooked potato,* minced = *pushed through a machine into small pieces, like meat*)   10B (plead + *with* + object + infin., insist / suggest (+ *that*) + *clause*)   11D (= *this enabled her to do it*)   12C (= *discouraged me from*)   13D (= *unskilled work with low pay*)   14C (virtually *can only be used with an adjective that has a fixed meaning, like* perfect, *or* complete, *which has the wrong meaning for this context*)   15D   16D (*colloc.*)   17B (*in* + danger / peril)   18C (= *pushing out into the environment*)   19B (= *a limited or fixed period of work or effort*)   20A (= *made a facial expression quickly*)   21A (= *happen*)   22C (*colloc.*)   23C (*colloc.*)   24D (= *made the people leave*)   25A (= *she said she had, but we have no proof that this is true*)

### SECTION B
*Two marks per question (total = 30)*

### First passage p.122

26D (... *it is fortunate that these feelings exist in so many wealthy nations, who are able to afford and support 'saving' operations*)   27C (*For the majority, conservation was initially thought of as only relevant to creatures ... now it is recognised that conservation must also be applied to the environment* – B is only true for **many** people, not everyone)   28B (*man's interests ... have clashed with, and taken precedence over, the needs of wild animals* – A, C and D are often, but **not always**, true)   29A (*If those people's welfare, let alone their survival is at stake, then obviously these must take priority* – B, C and D are true in many cases, but **not always**)   30D (*these ... of course, have it in their power to do the most damage, as well as the most good*)

### Second passage p.124

31D (*these seers, obsessed by the mystery of nature*   32A (*he hunted, fished, sowed, reaped, danced and performed ceremonies at the times the heavens dictated* – D is wrong because the heavens did not tell **how** religious ceremonies should be performed, only **when**)   33C (*The farmer ... who made his living tilling the soil which the river covered with rich silt during its annual overflow ... his home, equipment and cattle had to be temporarily removed* – A and D are both true, but they only **partially** answer the question)   34A (*these holy people ... sometimes exploited this knowledge to retain dominance over the uninformed masses* – C is also true, but is not the **principal** benefit, only a **means** of securing and maintaining power)   35B (*it was as natural for the ancient priests to work out a formula ... based on the motions of the planets and star*

constellations as it is for the modern scientist to study and master nature with his techniques* – A and C are true **today**, but were not **in ancient times**, D was **one** use of astrology, but the text does not suggest it was the **primary** one)

### Third passage p.126

36A (**he started with a joke, and spoke with** *careful informality* – C is wrong because he didn't **continue** to make jokes, while D is too extreme: he didn't **intend deliberately** to patronise the staff)   37C (*'Ready?' he asked with an over-elaborate smile. 'Right, then we'll start again.'*)   38B (*... old habits were too strong ... her faithful bark* – she is compared with a dog, to emphasise her loyalty and sense of duty)   39B (*the confident salesman lost in the dream world of the grandiose schemes he was putting before them*)   40B (this is not explicitly stated in the text, but is implied by the uncomfortable air of this meeting, the tension of the staff and the way in which Hobday feels the need to 'sell' himself and his ideas to them.) *You can see that the third passage in Paper 1,* **the literary text,** *focuses on the skills of* **interpretation and inference** *rather more than passages one and two. Although this passage is normally a little shorter than the other two, make sure you give it* **at least equal time.**

### Paper 1 total marks = 55 marks
*(convert this to a mark out of 40)*

## Paper 2: Composition p.128

### *A maximum of 20 marks per composition (total = 40)*

The marks are based on the following criteria:

- how well the **task is fulfilled** (*Are all of the parts answered, in a composition of an appropriate length?*)
- how appropriate the **style and register** of the composition are for the purpose outlined in the task (*Is the register consistent throughout? How would the target reader react upon reading this composition?*)
- the range and accuracy of **structures and vocabulary** used in the composition (*Is it a complex, natural and well-expressed piece of writing? Is the spelling accurate?*)
- the **organisation** of the composition. (*Have clear, logical paragraphs been used? Is there an underlying, well-planned structure, e.g. emphatic organisation of details in paragraphs / chronological order of storytelling / good use of flashbacks in a narrative, etc.? Does the composition look like a letter / report / article?*)

When writing your composition, **don't waste time worrying** about:

- **individual errors** – in general, you are rewarded for attempting more adventurous language
- **your opinion being assessed** – the examiner is not interested in what you say as much as how you say it
- **the exact number of words in your composition** – don't bother to count them! Instead, get used to writing to the specified length while you are preparing for the exam, so you can recognise just by looking at the size of your work. Remember that writing too much can also lose you marks.

The table opposite gives a very general outline of the standard expected to attain certain ranges of marks.

| range | general features |
|-------|-----------------|
| 16–20 | • task fully completed, without any omissions or irrelevance, within the specified length<br>• substantial portion of the composition showing a wide range of sophisticated and appropriate vocabulary and structures, and appropriate register for the task<br>• well organised details, with a range of connecting words and phrases, to make a coherent, logical piece of writing<br>• no basic errors and no really inappropriate vocabulary; few spelling mistakes |
| 11–15 | • task well-answered, with little or no irrelevance, within the specified length<br>• some of the composition showing sophisticated use of vocabulary and structures, including some errors, resulting from attempts to use high-level language; generally appropriate register, with only a few inconsistencies<br>• coherently organised details, with appropriate linking<br>• few, if any, basic errors or spelling mistakes |
| 8–10 | • **task answered adequately, but with some irrelevance or slight omission, close to the specified length**<br>• **competent, but possibly unadventurous, use of vocabulary, structures and textual organisation.**<br>• **some inappropriate style and register, though still broadly suitable to the task**<br>• **some basic errors, but very few which actually impede understanding** |
| 5–7 | • task not answered adequately, with substantial irrelevance, repetition or omission; composition length significantly too long to indicate concise expression, or too short to fulfil task<br>• vocabulary and structure too basic for this level, and large number of register inconsistencies<br>• poor organisation of details or linking of paragraphs<br>• a number of basic errors which impede understanding |
| 0–4 | • task not really attempted, or highly irrelevant answer provided; composition much too short<br>• inadequate range of vocabulary and structure, and too many errors, for meaning to be communicated successfully<br>• little evidence of planning or clear organisation of ideas, and very little demonstration of sensitivity to register or style |

The section 8–10, marked in **bold** above, illustrates the general level required to **pass** the Proficiency exam.

The following compositions in answer to the questions on Paper 2 are provided to help you to get a more accurate idea of the standard required to obtain certain marks. Remember that you should only write **two** compositions!

---

**Question 1**

I'm not so keen on going out to eat. It's so much a part of who I am, that I sometimes forget, how this aversion to the restaurants first came about. In fact, thinking back to when I was a child – I'm sure that I liked nothing more than visiting cafes etc, but since this one terrible incident there is no time when I fancy going to a restaurant again.

I suppose it all took place when I was thirteen or fourteen, the kind of age where you easily are embarassed, and just don't want to be the noticed one in the crowd. It was a week before my birthday I suppose, and my mother was to treat me by inviting my closest friends to dinner with me at the schnitzelkeller Restaurant. I'd been looking forward to it for weeks, and was both thrilled and a little nervous when the night of our party finally arrived.

It was a traditional place, with a powerful sense of years gone by. There was a huge barn with dark wooden beams overhead and in the flickering candlelight you could barely make out the face of the person, sitting next to you, let alone the food on your plate. Gentle music and wonderful smells drifted, from somewhere in the darkness, and we all chatted excitedly about the coming summer holidays. It all seemed so romantic and grown-up and I found myself quite carried away with the occasion.

After a mouthwatering first course, the main plates arrived, and everyone ate with relish. The flavours of the food were marvellous, and I began to feel that perhaps being a chef was what I really should be wanting for my career. Then suddenly something happened to shatter my illusion ... The girl next to me lifted a forkful of food from her plate, and let out an ear-piercing scream, hurled the food to the floor, and ran from the restaurant, still screeching as she went.

Naturaly, we were all extremely taken aback with this – until we looked to her smashed plate on the floor, and saw, to our horror, the long tail of a rat coming from the plate! Disgusted, I vomited instantly in front of my friends, a degrading experience I can never forget having had. Never again would I feel at ease in the restaurants. (391 words)

---

The topic of this composition is very unpleasant, perhaps even offensive, but not to a degree that would stop an examiner from assessing it. There is a good range of appropriate vocabulary (e.g. *flickering candlelight, drifted, mouthwatering, shatter my illusion, hurled, screeching, taken aback, degrading*). Some sophisticated language has been used (e.g. *I sometimes forget how this ... came about, thinking back to when I was a child, I'm sure that I liked nothing more than ...,* you could barely make out ..., screeching as she went), but there are equally some noticeable errors (e.g. since this terrible incident there is no time ...) A number of spelling mistakes (aversion, fourteen, embarrassed, music, naturally) and problems with word order and punctuation, especially the use of commas, stand out to create an unfortunate impression. The composition is also 40 words too long, and **an examiner can decide to mark only that portion within the 350 word limit**. Although this composition suffers occasionally inconsistent register, it fulfils the task well, with a nicely planned and excellently connected description, which deals with part two of the question (how the writer felt) very effectively, and would achieve a good pass mark.

*Mark = 13*

---

### Question 2

Without any doubt, crime is one of the biggest problems facing society today. Hardly a day goes by without we hear of another bank robbing, or murder of somebody. Many people became tired of waiting for the police to do something about, and even are vigilante groups springing up in many big cities. For all this, no-one knows really why is crime rising so much, and everyone wants to blame someone in particular for it. The question is, is it the parents who are to blame for, or schools, or indeed politicians and society in general for creating such a devastating problem?

It is certainly true that there is a grave decline in the values of the family in the recent years. This must be the direct result that so many women nowadays are going to work, outside the house, and so children grow up with guardians or estrangers paid to look for them by the hour. This can be dangerous, as we saw with all the recent legal cases involving babies that had died.

Many fathers too seem to have stopped to take responsibility of the discipline of the young people. Too many children are spoilt by parents who don't see them enough as are overworked, and then try to make up for by buying the child many toys and they never learn the meaning of the word 'no'.

I would assert, however, that such dramatic rise of crimes like car theft and shop lifting (the vast majority of them are perpetrated by juveniles) as we have seen lately cannot be only due to the decline in parenting. The schools are equally now in decline, without strong rules or any true moral sense. Furthermore, children cannot be expected to gain any idea of equilibrium in their lives if they cannot find role models for to aspire to, between their teachers, and heroes like popstars and filmstars. The police are even corrupt in many places.

In conclusion, perhaps the principal part of the blame for all this problems with juvenile crime is with the parents, who are too occupied with bribing their children or idolise them. It is not that they are unwilling to teach right and wrong, but that they maybe forget to, because they are too busy. (379 words)

---

This composition suffers from a number of relatively basic grammatical errors (e.g. people became tired, for the police to do something about ..., as are overworked) and problems with vocabulary choice (e.g. guardians and strangers, equilibrium, occupied). Although much appropriate language is used (e.g. without any doubt, hardly a day goes by without .., grave decline in ..., the direct result of ..., cannot only be due to ...), overall, there is a failure to maintain a consistent register, with a number of words and phrases which are too informal (e.g. for all this, the question is ...). The organisation is mostly competent, with a few irrelevant or distracting points (e.g. vigilantes, legal cases, corrupt police) and some repetition (spoiling/bribing children, overworked/busy parents, moral sense/equilibrium) which, if removed, should create a composition of a better length.

*Mark = 10*

---

### Question 3

Sonia picked up the telephone and listened without speaking. She knew exactly what she had to do when she put it down and ran out of the flat and put her keys in her hand bag. She sweated profusely and wondered herself how could this have happened.

When she had reached Peter's flat, she could seen why he was so unhappy and panic on the phone. Everything was in disarray, with furniture turned over around the floors, all the windows had smashed, and also the vendals painted all over the walls. It looked horrendous - as a war was happened in the flat. 'Tell me the true!' she demanded. 'How has this happened?' She sat down and looked at Peter, who upsetly looked through the window.

Three cups of tea and two hours later, she had known the whole sorry tale ... Peter was become an addict gambler, run up the debts above £30,000, and now was there a gang of thugs after him to repay back all the money. His TV, sterio, everything worth was gone from the flat. Sonya gasped, as she thought about his situation.

Suddenly was a bang at the door! Peter and sonia looked in horror at each other, when a dark figure bursted in shouting and holding a big gun at them. They knew that they were done for at once. Then with a crash tripped the man loudly on a turned over chair. He shouted then didn't move again - he was knocked off cold. Peter and Sonia ran from the flat and hadn't stopped running before they reached the police station. (269 words)

---

Poor language control impedes understanding (e.g. why he was so unhappy and panic on the phone, also the vendals painted all over the walls). The task is not adequately fulfilled: the given sentence has been changed, and the composition, 80 words too short, fails to make real sense of the situation outlined in the task, or to satisfactorily conclude the action. The language used is rather unadventurous and repetitive, and fails to explore or extend the topic in a convincing way, while a number of distracting details add nothing to the progression of the story (e.g. put her keys ..., sweated profusely ..., the vendals painted ...).

*Mark = 5*

## Question 4

Andreas Iannolou
14 Frances King Street
Thessaloniki
Greece
tel: 30 31 241056

10th October

The Director
Happy Flyer Airline
108 Glasgow Avenue
London N23 9YH

Dear Sir/Madam,

I am writing to you to express my deep disappointment with the flight I recently had the misfortune to take with your airline. Having been attracted by your high profile advertising campaign, which promised the cheapest fares to be available in Europe, I wasn't expecting the height of luxury. However, I do feel that the catalog of disasters I experienced was intolerable.

It was only on arriving at Huntstead Airport that I discovered that our plane was to be delayed for over three hours. It later became clear that this was because of a long-term problem. Surely then, it would have been possible to inform passengers in advance? As it was, we found ourselves having to wait in an over-crowded area with inadequate seating, and no effort being made to provide us with refreshments of any kind.

When we did finally board the plane, I was disgusted, but by this point not surprised, to find that my seat was covered in discarded orange skin! Then, during the flight, the special diet meal I had ordered failed to materialise, and I had to make do on bar snacks. The flight assistants did not seem at all apologetic for this terrible state of affairs; indeed, at one point one of them shouted at me!

After a long, deeply uncomfortable flight, we all arrived feeling crumpled at Athens, only to discover that our luggage had been mislaid. To add insult to injury, one of your staff there implied this was my fault, by suggesting that I must have labelled my cases wrongly.

I feel I must complain in the strongest terms about the poor organisation I experienced from the hands of your airline, and the unhelpful personnel you employ. Never again will I be seduced into believing that the cheapest deal has to be a bargain! I have no intention ever to fly with you again, and would additionally expect a substantial refund for the poor service I experienced. Unless I hear from you in the coming week, I shall have no option but to publish details of my experience in the local press and national consumer magazines.

I look forward to your prompt reply.

Yours faithfully,

Andreas Iannolou

Andreas Iannolou

(365 words)

There is a lot of sophisticated language, which is very appropriate to the task of complaining (e.g. *I had the misfortune to take ..., catalogue of disasters, no effort being made to provide us with ..., failed to materialise, terrible state of affairs,* *to add insult to injury, never again will I, complain in the strongest terms*), and the details of the complaint are excellently organised and connected. There are few errors of vocabulary and only one of spelling, and there is vocabulary suitable to the topic (e.g. *the height of luxury, board the plane*) and a consistently formal tone throughout. The task has been fully and effectively completed. The only area which could be significantly improved is in the avoidance of 'lifting' words from the title (e.g. *unhelpful personnel, mislaid luggage*).

***Mark = 17***

# Paper 3: Use of English p.129

## SECTION A

### 1 Cloze p.129

***One mark per question (total = 20)***

1 especially (*read the whole sentence to see that this last part adds emphasis*)   2 few (*read the whole paragraph to find the word required*)   3 enjoyed (enjoy + *luxury; by directly after the blank suggests a passive construction*)   4 country (*contrasts with the discussion of city life in the previous sentence*)   5 With (= *after this happened; don't forget the capital letter*)   6 which (*read the whole sentence to see that this part of it is a relative clause*)   7 odour / smell   8 longer (= *not any more*)   9 outside   10 mention (*fixed phrase*)   11 whether (*notice* or not, *which follows the blank*)   12 hardly (+ anyone; *you have to read the whole sentence to find the meaning*)   13 window (*colloc.; notice the comparison with* balconies)   14 enough (large + *enough*)   15 against (*colloc.*)   16 mistrust (*colloc.; rejection also has the dep. prep.* of, *but doesn't fit the meaning of the sentence as well*)   17 on (*phrasal verb*)   18 effect (*prep. phrase*)   19 either (either + *or; two choices are offered, indicating that* either, *opposite of* neither, *is required*)   20 purposes (*fixed phrase*)

### 2 Sentence transformations p.130

***One mark per question, or item marked (*) (total = 12)***

(a) He shouldn't have been (*) so savagely criticised for (*) his efforts to find a solution. = **2 marks**   (b) There has been a huge / dramatic increase in the number of road accidents in recent months. = **1 mark**   (c) If she hadn't received so much (*) support from social workers, she wouldn't be leading (*) (such) a normal life now. = **2 marks**   (d) Not until (*) the correct documents are / have been received (*) will a work permit be issued. = **2 marks**   (e) Didn't it occur to you that he was only pretending? = **1 mark**   (f) The work was to have been completed (*) (by the end of) last week. = **1 mark**   (g) It won't be long (*) before they find out (*) what she's been doing. = **2 marks**   (h) Ice-cream can now be bought all / throughout the summer in / from most newsagents. = **1 mark**

### 3 Gapped sentences p.130

***One mark per question (total = 6)***

(a) better give her a (*hadn't you* + better + *bare infin.*; give + *call = colloc.*)   (b) Earth couldn't you have (*why on Earth is a fixed phrase; the past participle* waited *indicates that you can't use the auxiliary* didn't *here to make your question*)

**171**

(c) will/should have been taken (*time prep.* by *indicates that a perfect tense is required;* taken + *steps* = *colloc.*) (d) to have been set (*impersonal passive construction* + *infin., in this case a perfect passive infin.;* set + *free* = *colloc.*) (e) whatever you (= *avoid this at all costs; you need to consider the sentence as a whole to find the meaning required*) (f) myself to having (*this reflexive verb is followed by the preposition* to + -*ing form; notice the infin. which directly follows the gap, indicating that* having to *is required for the sentence to be grammatically correct*)

## 4 Key word transformations   p.131

***One mark per question, or item marked (\*) (total = 12)***

(a) We must avoid adverse publicity **at all costs.** = 1 mark (*fixed phrase*) (b) I **don't** worry **nearly as much** about trivial matters these days **as** I used to. = 1 mark (c) I've **never set eyes on her** before. = 1 mark (*fixed phrase, usually very surprised or defensive in tone*) (d) Since my arrival, **you have done nothing but criticise me.** / **You've done nothing but criticise me** since I arrived. = 1 mark (e) His **chances of** be**ing** (*) picked for the Olympic swimming team **are** (rather / very / a bit) **slim** / **poor** (*). = 2 marks (*colloc.*) (f) If you go there without a map, you **run the risk** (*) **of** get**ting** (*) lost. = 2 marks (*fixed phrase*) (g) I know I can **bring Dave round to** (*) **my way of thinking on** (*) this matter. = 2 marks (*phrasal verb* + *fixed phrase*) (h) He **bears little** / **hardly** (*) **any resemblance to** (*) his brother. = 2 marks (*colloc.*)

## SECTION B

### Comprehension and summary   p.132

### Comprehension questions   p.133

***One mark per question or item marked (\*) (total = 16)***

(a) It is likely to generate / be greeted with fuss, noise or controversy. = **1 mark**
(b) Somebody else solves the problem you are working on / they announce or publish their findings first. = **1 mark**
(c) disconsolately shuffle = **1 mark**
(d) uncharted territory = **1 mark**
(e) The scientist may not be allowed to continue / funding may be withdrawn (*) if the scientist does not publish results or findings from his / her current work (*). = **2 marks**
(f) as infinitely / extremely varied and complicated = **1 mark**
(g) as obscure / not worthwhile / unrelated to matters of human importance = **1 mark**
(h) that studying something apparently / which seems to be unrelated (*) could eventually result in finding medical cures for serious diseases (*) = **2 marks**
(i) that it is seen as abstract and remote / not concerned with real life and normal people / nobody could feel passionate about it = **1 mark**
(j) (any **two** answers) You can encounter / run into financial problems (*), it can cause problems with your personal relationships (*), you are always thinking and worrying about it (*). = **2 marks**
(k) to look for another job / retrain for a job (*) which is more conventional / better paid / easier / safer (*) = **2 marks**
(l) buzz = **1 mark**

### Summary   p.134

***One mark per point marked (\*) (up to a maximum of 4)***

(m) *Sample answer*
Scientific research is challenging because it involves wrestling with a large number of complicated natural phenomena every day (*). You are under constant pressure to publish your findings, to assure the funding of future projects (*). Research is additionally a very focused, personal activity, occupying all your thoughts, time and energy (*). Knowing that you have discovered something unique, and previously unknown (*), is extremely exciting, as is the knowledge that the study of something obscure and apparently unimportant could eventually bring tremendous benefits to mankind (*). (*82 words*)

***Up to 8 marks for:***

- **organising** the points to make a logical and coherent argument
- **linking** the sentences together appropriately
- evidence of **using your own words**, rather than 'lifting' vocabulary from the text
- writing with a **concise style**, within or close to the **required length** (no more than 5 words over the limit).

***= 12 marks total for summary***

***Total for marks Section B = 12 + 16 = 28***

***Paper 3 total marks = 20 (cloze) + 12 (sentence transformations) + 6 (gapped sentences) + 12 (key word transformations) + 28 (comprehension and summary) = 78 total***
(*convert this to a mark out of 40*)

The exact marks for Paper 3 vary with each individual exam, but this Practice exam paper represents the weighting of importance normally given to each individual task.

## Paper 4: Listening comprehension   p.135

***One mark for each question (total = 25)***
(*convert this to a mark out of 20*)

### PART ONE   p.135

1C (*it's more a programme about food and the relationship that people have with it … describing what the food means to them*) 2A (*we could well see developments in so-called 'scratch and sniff' radio*) 3D (*you're not helped at all by the fact there are so few words to describe smells and tastes*) 4C (*some cultures have adapted climates to meet their needs. Take Iceland …*) 5A (*whilst he included them for the flavour and not necessarily for their properties … Traditional reasons are important, D, but not the* **only** *reasons spices are used.*)

### Tapescript

***Presenter:*** *Television programmes about food – and ways of preparing and cooking it – have been riding a wave of popularity in recent years. Not surprisingly, the same is also true for programmes designed for radio. Many of our listeners will already have sampled the delights – at least in their imaginations – served up by the recent series 'Just a Taste' and will agree that listening to people from different countries talking about cooking and eating … and sharing their recipes … can be a fascinating, as well as a* *mouthwatering, experience! Anne Winslop asked Katherine Hodgson – the presenter of 'Just a Taste' – to explain what she felt lay at the heart of the series' success.*

**Katherine Hodgson**: *Oh, food as a very meaningful part our lives, I'd say. Um … although 'Just a Taste' does feature people cooking, eating and telling us about their favourite recipes, of course, I don't really like to call it a cookery programme as such … it's, it's more a programme about food and the relationship that people have with it. The people featured are not necessarily professional chefs … they're simply lovers of food who prepare traditional, everyday dishes whilst describing what the food means to them … or what special memories it might have for them.*

**Anne Winslop**: *Mmm, right. How difficult was the series to make, Katherine? On the face of it, television would seem to be a much easier medium for a programme about food, wouldn't it? How does such a programme translate to radio?*

**KH**: *Well, in a blind situation listeners rely almost entirely upon their sense of hearing. There are so many sounds in the kitchen which are very evocative … there are the wonderful sounds of chopping and boiling, for example, which do conjure up a picture of somebody's kitchen surprisingly well. Smells, of course, are another matter … um … I think that in the not too distant future we could well see developments in so-called 'scratch and sniff' radio …but until that day arrives, listeners I'm afraid will just have to do with their imagination, when it comes to the smell of the food being described. Describing food, of course, is not as easy as it might seem and there can be problems. When you first taste a dish all you can say is 'mmm' and then you have to try and put that into words … what it looks like, what it tastes like, the texture and feel of it, so that people have some idea of the processes the dish goes through and what sort of taste you should be aiming for … and you're not helped at all by the fact there are so few words to describe smells and tastes.*

**AW**: *What things, Katherine, did you find particularly surprising or interesting while you were making the series?*

**KH**: *Oh, the influence of geography and culture on food, I think. Oh, yes … and the way they interact. For example, if you live in a very barren climate you'd think that you'd be less likely to have recipes based around fresh salad vegetables. However, rather than be dictated to by the weather, some cultures have adapted climates to meet their needs. Take Iceland … it's called the land of ice and fire and it really is. There are huge volcanic, black plains. Now, how can people have anything else to eat but fish? But then you see, they have great greenhouses where they grow all sorts of vegetables and fruits, which are heated by the natural thermal hot springs. Food can also be literally infused by the culture that it is made in … for example … when we did South Indian foods in the first series, the man cooking the food explained how the different spices that he used have different health benefits. He explained the benefits of asafoetida and turmeric, and whilst he included them for the flavour and not necessarily for their properties, traditional medicine and beliefs are so part of the Indian culture, so part of his life, that it has filtered through into his everyday food.*

**AW**: *And for many cultures food is also heavily entwined with notions about hospitality, isn't it?*

**KH**: *Yes. One of the nicest things about making this series is that we have experienced some amazing hospitality. We haven't been able to leave a house without having a feast. But the best thing about the series is that we get to eat all of the food and nobody has ever asked us to do the washing up.*

## PART TWO p.136

Relevant parts of the tapescript below have been marked in **bold** to help you to locate the answers in the text.

6 (open) heart surgery   7 by helicopter   8 a perilous situation / an emergency   9 on the spot   10 a heavy pack   11 not tall enough   12 one or two nights   13 (to) switch   14 professional company   15 stays late at the   16 so tired / worn out   17 sports medicine

### Tapescript

**Interviewer**: *When Doctor Heather Clark performed **open heart surgery** on a man on the floor of a busy East End pub recently, she certainly hit the headlines. Not only did she bring the glamour of an American hospital drama to London's streets, but her patient was also one of only a handful in the world to survive such a procedure outside the pristine conditions of the operating theatre. Heather is a member of the Royal London Hospital's helicopter emergency service – or Hems for short – so it's fitting that we met high above the city in a room perched on the hospital's roof, next to the helipad. I asked her just how stressful it was, knowing that at any second she could be whisked away **by helicopter** to such a **perilous situation**.*

**Heather Clark**: *Actually my heart's in my mouth and my whole body floods with an adrenaline rush when I get that emergency call and head for the helicopter, you know. It's certainly a buzz. When you get in, you never know what you're going to find – it could be a major incident with lots of casualties, or a road accident, or anything. But I do fortunately have an incredibly low boredom threshold. With this job, the day's always varied, you never know what you could be doing. It's also the only area of medicine where you really save people **on the spot**, as it were … where you really know right away whether you've been able to make a difference.*

**I**: *Mmm … well I have to ask, Heather … where on Earth do you find the oomph, the… er, strength to deal with such a demanding job? And you're only – what is it? – 5ft 1? How do you do it?*

**HC**: *Well … I know I'm small, but I'm in pretty good shape. You have to be in this job … we often have to run quite a way from the helicopter to the patient, carrying **a pack weighing 15 kilos** or so. Then there's all the kit in my suit, which is another 8 kilos at least. I stay fit because I dance any spare minute I can. As a teenager growing up in Bristol I desperately wanted to be a dancer. I had a place to train with the Royal Ballet as a teenager, but I **just never grew tall enough** to be a ballerina, and my parents drew the line at my idea of giving up my scholarship at school. I knew my own mind, but they won through in the end, so I stayed on at the sixth form and did my A-levels. But I still dance **one or two nights** a week, which keeps me in good shape.*

**I**: *Don't you get tired though, Heather? Most of the doctors*

*I know are so worn out ... you know, by the demands of the job ... that all they can manage at the end of the day is to stagger home and put their feet up in front of the telly.*

**HC:** *Dancing, actually, is a fantastic way to relax, and believe me, in this job, you really need to **switch off**. I dance for a **professional company** and we rehearse at all hours, often till one or two in the morning. When I finish work here, I head straight off to rehearsals. In fact, I'm going to be in a BBC programme... a programme about jive dancing, some time soon. It's true, though, I do get very tired, but I just love dancing and cramming lots into my life. But I have loads of energy. I'm really not too bothered about relaxation.*

**I:** *And social life?*

**HC:** *Having any kind of social life at all while you do this job is nigh on impossible. I just never know where I'm going to be and I often end up **staying late** at the hospital ... to talk to my colleagues, you know; we all debrief each other, if you like. But I suppose I'm used to it. As a junior doctor, I regularly did a 100-hour week. At one point, I was even admitted to the hospital I was working at when I wound up with a kidney infection, **I was just so worn out**. There's no way any government should be increasing the hours young doctors work, as they always seem to be suggesting – it's dangerous – you just can't function.*

**I:** *No, I can imagine. Mmm ... What about plans for the future? I can see you set your sights high ... um, what do you see yourself doing in, say, ten years' time?*

**HC:** *Well, I'm going to do an MSc in **sports medicine** which should link my interests in dancing and medicine together – killing two birds with one stone, really. But I'll have to find the funding myself, of course. Ultimately I would love to be the Royal Ballet's on-site doctor.*

**I:** *Really? Now, what I'm sure many of us would like to know is ...*

## PART THREE  p.137

18A (*it could just be that more crimes are reported / it's probably the other way around ...*)  19B (*we don't really consider them to be crimes anymore / we've come to accept a lot of things that people didn't accept in the past*)  20J (*crime nowadays tends to increase along with wealth / I've always found that argument a bit too glib*)  21A (*Are we to believe that when people were much poorer ... that the incentives to steal were lower than they are today?*)  22J (*they're more lenient these days / they're slightly tougher on the most serious crimes today*)  23B (*offenders today serve a much smaller portion of their sentence / I suppose I'd have to go along with that*)  24B (*nothing is going to happen to the culprits... get off very lightly or scot free, even – Andy finishes Joe's sentence, signalling agreement*)  25A (*the police don't seem to be able to catch criminals the way they used to / Do you think so?*)

### Tapescript

**Andy:** *I wonder really if crime has not actually risen at all in recent years. It could just be that more crimes are reported to the police than in the past ... Don't you think, Joe?*

**Joe:** *Oh, I've heard that one too. But I think ... it's probably the other way around. And, for minor offences especially, I think it's true that nowadays a large number of crimes actually go unreported because we don't really consider them to be crimes anymore. You know – a short scuffle in a pub ... um*

*... a garden trampled by kids ... No – I think that we have to accept the fact that crime really has increased over the past thirty or forty years.*

**A:** *Mmm ... it's true, of course, that we've come to accept a lot of things nowadays that people didn't accept in the past, isn't it? There are many people, I think, who can remember a time when – in some neighbourhoods – when houses could safely be left unlocked ... and bicycles could be left just propped up on a wall. I remember my parents talking about the shock they felt when someone they knew experienced a crime ... or even vandalism ... um ...*

**J:** *Uh huh ... people have become much more hardened to crime, haven't they Andy? The rot began to set in 20 or 30 years ago, I think. Who knows what went wrong? Maybe crime tends to increase along with wealth, I don't know ... People now have videos and colour televisions and what have you, all worth stealing, whereas they didn't before ...*

**A:** *Yeah. Frankly, I'd say I've always found that argument a bit ... too, er ... glib, if you know what I mean. What, for example, is the link between rising living standards and rising violent crime, would you say, Joe? Even when it comes to theft, er, the logic ... I don't know ... the logic seems a bit dubious to me. Are we to believe that when people were much poorer, or more in need of the bare necessities, that the incentives to steal were lower than they are today? And people today can receive all sorts of government help if they really need it, can't they? Are colour televisions, for example, easier to steal now than pound notes were 40 years ago?*

**J:** *Yeah ... anyway. The courts have a lot to answer for, I think. They're more lenient these days ... I read in the paper the other day that if you were found guilty before a judge in 1954, you ran more than a two-out-of-three chance of a prison sentence for an offence that was serious. For murder, you'd ... you'd hope you were insane! Of the 25 people found guilty of murder in 1954, apparently, 21 were sentenced to hang.*

**A:** *Well ... they may be slightly more forgiving for the less serious crimes ... I don't know ... but I would say that that – in fact – they're slightly tougher on the most serious crimes today.*

**J:** *Oh, come on Andy, ... offenders today serve a much smaller portion of their sentence than they used to, don't they?*

**A:** *Well, mmm ... I suppose I'd have to go along with that ... even a murderer is likely to be released after only twelve or fifteen years.*

**J:** *And the police often say that there's no point in making arrests because nothing is going to happen to the culprits anyway. It's true, isn't it, that criminals often get off very lightly or ...*

**A:** *... or scot free, even. Yes, that's true ... for every category of crime, I think, the odds that you'll be found guilty if you commit a crime have fallen by some two thirds or more, I think I read that somewhere. And you mentioned the criminals that the police do manage to catch, didn't you? Isn't that one of the problems today? That the police ... the police don't seem to be able to catch criminals the way they used to?*

**J:** *Do you think so? I think it's more likely that they feel disheartened, fed up ... you know ... I mean, I think they're pretty hot on ... when it comes to catching criminals, I'd say they were fairly good ... but I'm sure they're always thinking, you know, well, 'what's the point?'. I know a policeman, for instance, who ...*

## Paper 5: Interview  p.138

*5 marks for each of 6 categories (total = 30)*
*(convert this to a mark out of 40)*

The interview is about fifteen minutes long. Normally there are two examiners, one who talks, and the other who doesn't take part in the conversation, but assesses the student. Occasionally, the interview takes place with two or three candidates together, and the time for each task is therefore extended.

The marking categories for the interview are:

- **interactive communication** – maintaining a natural conversation, turn-taking, listening and understanding, speaking with appropriate register for the situation
- **fluency** – speaking at a reasonable speed and with a natural 'flow'
- **range and appropriacy of vocabulary** – responding with sophisticated and precise vocabulary for the situation
- **range and accuracy of grammatical structures** – demonstrating that you are able to use a wide range of structures to express your ideas precisely and fully
- **pronunciation of individual sounds** – you are not expected to sound exactly like a native speaker, but to be very easy to understand
- **pronunciation of sentences** – this includes being able to produce stress and intonation which makes your meaning clear.

The table below gives a very general view of the standard you are expected to reach to obtain each mark.

| mark | general features |
|------|------------------|
| 5 | at or near native-speaker level in all areas |
| 4 | communicating appropriately and fluently in all except perhaps very specialist areas; using a wide range of sophisticated vocabulary and structures successfully, with only minor lapses; few pronunciation problems, none of which impede understanding |
| 3 | **adequate communication with little hesitation, except in more abstract areas; using a reasonably sophisticated, though occasionally limited, range of vocabulary and structures; competent pronunciation which shouldn't impede understanding** |
| 2 | significant problems with hesitation and the communication of ideas, possibly when discussing everyday topics, and certainly in more abstract areas; adequate, often basic vocabulary and structures, with a number of basic errors; noticeable pronunciation problems, some of which impede understanding |
| 1 | excessive hesitation and poor interaction, even in everyday contexts; inadequate range of vocabulary and structures, used with a number of basic errors which impede communication; poor pronunciation a serious obstacle to understanding |
| 0 | inadequate performance in all areas, preventing any form of natural or successful communication |

Section 3, marked in **bold** in the table, illustrates the general level required to **pass** the Proficiency exam.

### PART ONE: PHOTOGRAPHS  p.138

Useful vocabulary: supermarket **checkouts**
ordering **over** the phone / **by** credit card   mail order
traditional **shop-front**   produce / products **on** display
self-service   barcode **scanners   stock control**

### PART TWO: PASSAGES  p.139

1. This is a piece of spoken language – the punctuation is informal, and the register is relaxed and personal (e.g. *buzz /* repetition of *maybe*, suggesting that the expression of ideas is spontaneous */ I must be the ideal consumer / takes my fancy / I've just got to*).

2. This is from an academic textbook – the perspective is historical, and the register is rather formal, with quite long and complex, carefully connected sentences (e.g. *created the preconditions for / in its modern sense / from that period / directed at frequenters / and significantly, ...*).

3. This is the text of a 'product recall' advertisement – the language is very impersonal and formal, with quite long, complex sentences. There are a number of passive constructions, and language both with a marketing or selling aim, and which has a 'legal' tone (e.g. *... which, while not dangerous to the user, may affect ... / is requested to examine / may not meet the high standards you rightly expect ... / should be returned immediately / contact our freephone Cosy Customer 24-hour Helpline*).

### PART THREE: COMMUNICATION ACTIVITIES  p.140

There are no fixed answers for this section, as it is based on your own ideas. The examiner will be assessing you on your ability to communicate interactively, connect your ideas logically, and fulfil the task adequately within about five minutes.

## Practice Exam marking

*Papers 1, 2, 3,* and *5 have a total of 40 marks each*
*Paper 4 (Listening comprehension) has a total of 20 marks*
*This creates a total mark for all five papers of 180 marks*

*You need to achieve around 60% (= 108 marks out of 180) to gain a pass in the Proficiency exam at grade C.*

Pearson Education Limited
Edinburgh Gate
Harlow
Essex CM20 2JE
England
and Associated Companies throughout the world.

www.longman-elt.com

Set in 10/12.75 Gill Sans and 10/12.75 Admark

Printed in Spain by Graficas Estella

First published 2000
Third Impression 2001

ISBN 0 582 32575 7

The author would like to thank Kate Mellersh for her hard work,
encouragement and advice during the writing of this book.

The publishing team wish to express their appreciation to Frances
Cook for invaluable editorial support, and to Lisa Girling and
Georgia Zographou for guidance and suggestions on the
development of this project.

Text Designed by Neil Adams